Mary Shepherd's *An Essay upon the Relation of Cause and Effect*

OXFORD NEW HISTORIES OF PHILOSOPHY

Series Editors
Christia Mercer, Melvin Rogers, and Eileen O'Neill (1953–2017)

*

Advisory Board
Lawrie Balfour, Jacqueline Broad, Marguerite Deslauriers, Karen Detlefsen, Bachir Diagne, Don Garrett, Robert Gooding-Williams, Andrew Janiak, Marcy Lascano, Lisa Shapiro, Tommie Shelby

*

Oxford New Histories of Philosophy provides essential resources for those aiming to diversify the content of their philosophy courses, revisit traditional narratives about the history of philosophy, or better understand the richness of philosophy's past. Examining previously neglected or understudied philosophical figures, movements, and traditions, the series includes both innovative new scholarship and new primary sources.

*

Published in the Series

Mexican Philosophy in the 20th Century: Essential Readings
Edited by Carlos Alberto Sánchez and Robert Eli Sanchez Jr.

Sophie de Grouchy's Letters on Sympathy: *A Critical Engagement with Adam Smith's* The Theory of Moral Sentiments
Edited by Sandrine Bergès and Eric Schliesser. Translated by Sandrine Bergès

Margaret Cavendish: Essential Writings
Edited by David Cunning

Women Philosophers of Seventeenth-Century England: Selected Correspondence
Edited by Jacqueline Broad

The Correspondence of Catharine Macaulay
Edited by Karen Green

Mary Shepherd's Essays on the Perception of an External Universe
Edited by Antonia LoLordo

Women Philosophers of Eighteenth-Century England: Selected Correspondence
Edited by Jacqueline Broad

Frances Power Cobbe: Essential Writings of a Nineteenth-Century Feminist Philosopher
Edited by Alison Stone

Korean Women Philosophers and the Ideal of a Female Sage: Essential Writings of Im Yungjidang and Gang Jeongildang
Edited and Translated by Philip J. Ivanhoe and Hwa Yeong Wang

Louise Dupin's Work on Women: *Selections*
Edited and Translated by Angela Hunter and Rebecca Wilkin

Edith Landmann-Kalischer: Essays on Art, Aesthetics, and Value
Edited by Samantha Matherne. Translated by Daniel O. Dahlstrom

Mary Ann Shadd Cary: Essential Writings of a Nineteenth-Century Black Radical Feminist
Edited by Nneka D. Dennie

Slavery and Race: Philosophical Debates in the Eighteenth-Century
Julia Jorati

Maria W. Stewart: Essential Writings of a Nineteenth-Century Black Abolitionist
Edited by Douglas A. Jones Jr.

Slavery and Race: Philosophical Debates in the Sixteenth and Seventeenth Centuries
Julia Jorati

Mary Shepherd's An Essay upon the Relation of Cause and Effect
Edited by Don Garrett

Mary Shepherd's
An Essay upon the Relation of Cause and Effect

Edited by
DON GARRETT

OXFORD
UNIVERSITY PRESS

Oxford University Press is a department of the University of Oxford. It furthers
the University's objective of excellence in research, scholarship, and education
by publishing worldwide. Oxford is a registered trade mark of Oxford University
Press in the UK and certain other countries.

Published in the United States of America by Oxford University Press
198 Madison Avenue, New York, NY 10016, United States of America.

© Oxford University Press 2024

All rights reserved. No part of this publication may be reproduced, stored in
a retrieval system, or transmitted, in any form or by any means, without the
prior permission in writing of Oxford University Press, or as expressly permitted
by law, by license, or under terms agreed with the appropriate reproduction
rights organization. Inquiries concerning reproduction outside the scope of the
above should be sent to the Rights Department, Oxford University Press, at the
address above.

You must not circulate this work in any other form
and you must impose this same condition on any acquirer.

Library of Congress Cataloging-in-Publication Data
Names: Shepherd, Mary, Lady, 1777–1847, author. | Garrett, Don, editor. |
Shepherd, Mary, Lady, 1777–1847. Correspondence.
Title: Mary Shepherd's An essay upon the relation of cause and effect /
[edited by] Don Garrett.
Other titles: Essay upon the relation of cause and effect, controverting
the doctrine of Mr. Hume, concerning the nature of that relation; with
observations upon the opinions of Dr. Brown and Mr. Lawrence, connected
with the same subject | Essay upon the relation of cause and effect
Description: New York, NY : Oxford University Press, [2024] |
Series: Oxford new histories of philosophy | Originally published in 1824 under
title: Essay upon the relation of cause and effect, controverting the
doctrine of Mr. Hume, concerning the nature of that relation; with
observations upon the opinions of Dr. Brown and Mr. Lawrence, connected
with the same subject. | Includes bibliographical references and index.
Identifiers: LCCN 2024013890 (print) | LCCN 2024013891 (ebook) |
ISBN 9780197649626 (HB) | ISBN 9780197649633 (PB) | ISBN 9780197649657 (epub)
Subjects: LCSH: Shepherd, Mary, Lady, 1777–1847. | Causation. |
Science—Philosophy. | Hume, David, 1711–1776.
Classification: LCC B1609.S543 E88 2024 (print) | LCC B1609.S543 (ebook)
| DDC 122—dc23/eng/20240531
LC record available at https://lccn.loc.gov/2024013890
LC ebook record available at https://lccn.loc.gov/2024013891

DOI: 10.1093/oso/9780197649626.001.0001

Contents

Series Editors' Foreword	ix
Acknowledgments	xi
Short Titles and Forms of Citation	xiii
Notes on the Text	xv
Editor's Introduction	1

AN ESSAY UPON THE RELATION OF CAUSE AND EFFECT

Advertisement to the Reader	32
Preface	33
Introductory Chapter	36
Chapter the Second	43
Chapter the Third	73
Chapter the Fourth: Observations on Dr. Brown's Essay on the Doctrine of Mr. Hume	88
Chapter the Fifth: Observations on Mr. Lawrence's Lectures	95
Chapter the Sixth	106
Errata	115
Appendix I: Two Essays of 1828	117
Observations by Lady Mary Shepherd on the 'First Lines of the Human Mind'	118
On the Causes of Single and Erect Vision	120
Appendix II: Letters	129
Letters to Charles Babbage (Letters 1–8)	130
Letters to William Whewell (Letters 9–11)	142
Letter to Robert Blakey (Letter 12)	148
References	149
Index	155

Series Editors' Foreword

Oxford New Histories of Philosophy (ONHP) speaks to a new climate in philosophy.

There is a growing awareness that philosophy's past is richer and more diverse than previously understood. It has become clear that canonical figures are best studied in a broad context. More exciting still is the recognition that our philosophical heritage contains long-forgotten innovative ideas, movements, and thinkers. Sometimes these thinkers warrant serious study in their own right; sometimes their importance resides in the conversations they helped reframe or problems they devised; often their philosophical proposals force us to rethink long-held assumptions about a period or genre; and frequently they cast well-known philosophical discussions in a fresh light.

There is also a mounting sense among philosophers that our discipline benefits from a diversity of perspectives and a commitment to inclusiveness. In a time when questions about justice, inequality, dignity, education, discrimination, and climate (to name a few) are especially vivid, it is appropriate to mine historical texts for insights that can shift conversations and reframe solutions. Given that philosophy's very long history contains astute discussions of a vast array of topics, the time is right to cast a broad historical net.

Lastly, there is increasing interest among philosophy instructors in speaking to the diversity and concerns of their students. Although historical discussions and texts can serve as a powerful means of doing so, finding the necessary time and tools to excavate long-buried historical materials is challenging.

Oxford New Histories of Philosophy is designed to address all these needs. It contains new editions and translations of significant historical texts. These primary materials make available, often for the first time, ideas and works by women, people of colour, and movements in philosophy's past that were groundbreaking in their day but left out of traditional accounts. Informative introductions help instructors and students navigate the new material. Alongside its primary texts, ONHP also publishes monographs and collections of essays that offer philosophically subtle analyses of understudied topics, movements, and figures. In combining primary materials and astute philosophical analyses, ONHP makes it easier for philosophers, historians, and instructors to include in their courses and research exciting new materials drawn from philosophy's past.

ONHP's range is wide, both historically and culturally. The series includes, for example, the writings of African American philosophers, twentieth-century Mexican philosophers, early modern and late medieval women, Islamic and Jewish authors, and non-western thinkers. It excavates and analyses problems and ideas that were prominent in their day but forgotten by later historians. And it serves as a significant aid to philosophers in teaching and researching this material.

As we expand the range of philosophical voices, it is important to acknowledge one voice responsible for this series. Eileen O'Neill was a series editor until her death, December 1, 2017. She was instrumental in motivating and conceptualizing ONHP. Her brilliant scholarship, advocacy, and generosity made all the difference to the efforts that this series is meant to represent. She will be deeply missed, as a scholar and a friend.

We are proud to contribute to philosophy's present and to a richer understanding of its past.

Christia Mercer and Melvin Rogers
Series Editors

Acknowledgments

I am grateful to many people for making this volume possible.

Christia Mercer first suggested Shepherd as a subject for research to me. She and Melvin Rogers encouraged me to edit this volume for the Oxford New Histories of Philosophy series. Antonia LoLordo provided an excellent model to follow with her 2020 edition of *Essays on the Perception of an External Universe*, and she generously provided important corrections and comments on the final draft of this volume. Ariel Melamedoff and Carl Christian Abrahamsen checked the accuracy of the text and the annotations of *An Essay upon the Relation of Cause and Effect*. Tito Magri helped me to decipher the meaning of a puzzling reference. Throughout the process, Peter Ohlin's encouragement and support were essential.

My understanding of Shepherd has benefited from the work of many scholars, including Margaret Atherton, Martha Bolton, Deborah Boyle, Maité Cruz, David Landy, Antonia LoLordo, Ariel Melamedoff, and Samuel Rickless. Chloe Armstrong, Ruth Boeker, Daniel Collette, M. Folescu, Kristopher Phillips, and Curtis Sommerlatte all made many very valuable contributions as members of a 2018 summer seminar on Shepherd that was generously sponsored by the *Journal of the History of Philosophy*. I also benefited from a meeting with the 2022 Harvard University graduate seminar on Shepherd led by Alison Simmons and Jeffrey McDonough. Everyone working on Shepherd's philosophy owes a special debt of gratitude to the pioneering work of Jennifer McRobert, Margaret Atherton, and Eileen O'Neill in rediscovering her philosophy.

A fellowship of the New York University Global Research Institute provided essential support for research in London and Cambridge.

Finally, I thank my wife, Frances, who makes everything that I value most in life possible.

Short Titles and Forms of Citation

This volume employs the following abbreviations for the works of Mary Shepherd:

EPEU: Mary Shepherd, *Essays on the Perception of an External Universe*. Citations are by page number of the Oxford New Histories of Philosophy edition (Shepherd 2020), followed (after a slash) by page number of the original 1827 edition. (Original page numbers are included in the margins of Shepherd 2020.)

ERCE: Mary Shepherd, *An Essay upon the Relation of Cause and Effect*. Citations are by page number of this volume, followed (after a slash) by page number of the original 1824 edition. (Original page numbers are included in the margins of this volume.)

This volume also employs the following short titles. In each case, Shepherd employs her own short title for the work as well. Although she does not provide full bibliographical information for the works she cites, it is often possible to determine through internal evidence which edition she is using, as indicated below:

Enquiry: David Hume, *An Enquiry concerning Human Understanding*. This work was first published in 1748 as *Philosophical Essays concerning Human Understanding* and was later included in all editions of Hume's *Essays and Treatises on Several Subjects*, which was first published in 1753–54. Editorial citations are by section and paragraph number as found in Hume 2000. Shepherd cites this work from *Essays and Treatises on Several Subjects* as "Essays" using volume, part, section, and page number of Hume 1800.

Essay: John Locke, *An Essay Concerning Human Understanding*. This work was first published in 1689. Editorial citations are by book, chapter, and section number as found in Locke 1975 and other sources. Shepherd cites it as "Essay," also using book, chapter, and section number. Because she does not use page numbers, it is not possible to determine definitively which edition she is using.

Inquiry: Thomas Reid, *An Inquiry into the Human Mind on the Principles of Common Sense*. This work was first published in 1764. Editorial citations are by chapter number, section number, and page number of Reid 1997. Shepherd cites it as "Inquiry," using chapter number, section number, and (once) page number of Reid 1764.

Lectures: William Lawrence, *Lectures on Physiology, Zoology, and the Natural History of Man, delivered at the Royal College of Surgeons by W. Lawrence, F.R.S.* This work was first published in 1819. Editorial citations are by lecture number and page number of Lawrence 1819. Shepherd cites it as "Physiological Lectures" using page number of Lawrence 1819.

Lines: John Fearn, *First Lines of the Human Mind*. This work was first published in 1820. Citations are by chapter number, section number, and page number of Fearn 1820. Shepherd refers to it as "*Lines of the Human Mind.*"

Logic: Isaac Watts, *Logic: or, the Right Use of Reason, in the Inquiry After Truth, with a Variety of Rules to Guard Against Error, in the Affairs of Religion and Human Life, as Well as in the Sciences*. This work was first published (using the spelling *Logick*) in 1726 and went through many editions. Citations are by page number of Watts 1809. Shepherd cites it as "W. Logic."

Observations: Thomas Brown, *Observations on the Nature and Tendency of the Doctrine of Mr. Hume concerning the Relation of Cause and Effect*, second edition, enlarged. This edition was published in 1806. Editorial citations are by page number of Brown 1806. Shepherd refers to it (in a chapter title) as "Dr. Brown's Essay on the Doctrine of Mr. Hume" and includes quotations from it, but she does not provide specific page references.

Optics: David Brewster, *Optics*. This work was originally published in 1827 or 1828 as a pamphlet in a biweekly series, *The Library of Useful Knowledge*, produced by the Society for the Diffusion of Useful Knowledge. It was subsequently published (as Treatise IX) in Brewster 1829. Editorial citations are by chapter, part, and page number of Brewster 1829. Shepherd cites it as "Optics" from the pamphlet version by part number (within Chapter XVII) only.

Treatise: David Hume, *A Treatise of Human Nature*. This work was first published in 1739–40. Editorial citations are by book, part, section, and paragraph number as found in Hume 2007. Shepherd cites this work as "Treatise on Human Nature," using book, part, section, and page number of Hume 1817.

Notes on the Text

An Essay upon the Relation of Cause and Effect

Only a single edition of *An Essay upon the Relation of Cause and Effect* was published in Shepherd's lifetime. I have compared the proof text (from the collection of the University of California Southern Regional Library Facility) with the copies at the British Library, the Cambridge University Library, the University of Edinburgh Library, and the National Library of Scotland, and I have found no differences among them. In order to keep the text as close as possible to Shepherd's intentions, I have not, except as described below, altered the spelling, punctuation, italicization, or capitalization (including the use of SMALL CAPS) of the original edition of 1824. This includes the retention of a few variant or now-obsolete spellings such as 'developement', 'dependant', 'holley', 'coalesence', and 'shew'. The page numbers of the original edition are given in the margins. In editorial material, I refer to *An Essay upon the Relation of Cause and Effect* by the abbreviation ERCE.

The original edition included a list of nine "ERRATA." I have incorporated the indicated corrections into the text and reproduced the list at the end. I have also made editorial corrections of obvious typographical errors, mostly involving punctuation; these are listed following the "Errata."

The original edition marked Shepherd's own footnotes not with numbers but with symbols such as the asterisk (*) or dagger (†). For simplicity, I have employed a single system for numbered footnotes that includes both Shepherd's (to which editorial commentary or further citation is often added) and my own. In all footnotes, any material within square brackets is mine, while all material outside square brackets is Shepherd's. My references to the Bible are to the King James version, which is the translation she would have known.

Shepherd often puts quotation marks around a term or short phrase to indicate its significance to an author under discussion, but she also puts quotation marks around longer passages freely and not always to the same purpose. In some such cases, she is merely formulating or summarizing a position or response in her own words, but often she is paraphrasing an author under discussion in a way that draws particular phrases or sentences from several different portions of the author's text. In the majority of cases, she is quoting from a single passage, either with or without a page citation, but even these quotations are rarely entirely exact. She typically changes punctuation and italicization, and she often adds, omits, or changes words or phrases. I have tried to provide specific citations where possible, and to indicate in a general way the degree of closeness of the material in quotation marks to the passage or passages from which it is derived. In the small number of cases in which Shepherd's alterations might substantially affect the sense, I have tried to note that as well.

The original edition of *ERCE* regularly italicized semicolons and colons that concluded italicized material; I have followed Shepherd 2020 in not italicizing these, although such italicization is retained in Appendix I. It also employed a convention according to which any line that continues an existing quotation begins with additional quotation marks; this convention is confusing to modern readers and has been dropped. I do, however, follow the original edition in not indenting quotations, no matter how lengthy.

Appendix I: Two Essays of 1828

For both essays, I have numbered the footnotes (again inserting all editorial material in brackets) and provided the page numbers of the original in the margins while retaining all original spelling and punctuation. I have again dropped the convention, employed in "Observations by Lady Mary Shepherd on the 'First Lines of the Human Mind,'" according to which any line that continues an existing quotation begins with additional quotation marks.

"On the Causes of Single and Erect Vision" was originally published in *The Philosophical Magazine, or the Annals of Chemistry, Mathematics, Astronomy, Natural History, and General Science* and then reprinted (in two parts) in *The Kaleidoscope: or, Literary and Scientific Mirror*. This later version makes minor changes in punctuation. As I have indicated in an editorial note, it also changes one erroneous citation, although the result is itself still erroneous. The version of the article (with page numbering) presented in this volume is that of *The Philosophical Magazine*.

Appendix II: Letters

I have personally transcribed Shepherd's letters to Charles Babbage (Letters 1–8) from the originals held as part of the Babbage collection in the British Library and her letters to William Whewell (Letters 9–11) from the originals held in the Trinity College Library at Cambridge University. In both instances, I have endeavored to retain Shepherd's spelling (including 'beleive" and 'beleif', which some others writers of the period also used in epistolary contexts); her use of abbreviations (using superscripts in italics for underlined superscripts); her original capitalization (although this is quite often ambiguous, especially with the letters 'b', 'c', 'e', 'm', 'n', and 'p'); and the general form of her indentation. I have also endeavored to retain her distinctive original punctuation, although the marks are sometimes ambiguous. Notably, she makes liberal use of dashes of varying lengths and distances from the surrounding materials, sometimes in place of periods; because I did not discern any distinctions intended by the variations, I have transcribed them uniformly as em dashes with a space on either side. Where Shepherd underlines any word, either wholly or in part, I have put the word in italics (with two exceptions where underlining only a prefix was clearly intended). Where she underlines a word or phrase twice, I have added underlining to the italics.

The original of Shepherd's letter to Robert Blakey (Letter 12) is lost. I have reproduced his transcription of it from Blakey 1879: 160–62.

For all of the letters, the footnotes are exclusively editorial and are therefore presented in brackets.

Editor's Introduction

Mary Shepherd (1777–1847) became a well-known philosopher in Britain during the first half of the nineteenth century. She published two books: *An Essay upon the Relation of Cause and Effect* in 1824 and *Essays on the Perception of an External Universe* in 1827. Her intellectual circle included such prominent thinkers as the mathematician and computer pioneer Charles Babbage; the polymath historian and philosopher of science William Whewell; the geologist Charles Lyell; the political economists David Ricardo and Robert Malthus; the scientist and mathematician Mary Somerville; the philosopher and archbishop of Dublin Richard Whately; and the author, wit, and founder of the *Edinburgh Review* Sydney Smith.[1] Her daughter later recalled that Whewell made one of her two books "a text book at Cambridge," where he was for many years Master of Trinity College, and she reported hearing both Whewell and Lyell describe her as "an unanswerable logician, in whose argument it was impossible to find loophole or flaw."[2] Of the nearly four dozen articles in Robert Blakey's 1848 four-volume *History of the Philosophy of Mind* that are devoted to "metaphysical writers of Great Britain from 1800 to the present day," only three were longer than the one devoted to Shepherd,[3] and Blakey describes her work as "justly entitled to high praise" for the "great acuteness and subtilty displayed in them, and an intimate knowledge of all the leading and profound controversies in modern metaphysics" (Blakey 1848: IV.60). Although she offered trenchant and detailed rebuttals of the arguments and conclusions of many important predecessors—including George Berkeley, David Hume, Thomas Reid, Dugald Stewart, Thomas Brown, and William Lawrence—she was no merely negative thinker. On the contrary, her critiques were always in the service of her own distinctive and

---

[1] Shepherd's friends and acquaintances also included James Mill and the writers Elizabeth Barrett Browning, Samuel Taylor Coleridge, and Mary Shelley.
[2] Brandreth 1886: 29. Much of our knowledge about Shepherd's life comes from this family memoir of her eldest daughter, Mary Elizabeth Shepherd Brandreth.
[3] The three longer articles were devoted to Dugald Stewart, Thomas Brown, and William Whewell. The article on James Mill was slightly shorter.

highly original doctrines in epistemology, metaphysics, the philosophy of science, and the philosophy of mind.

Nevertheless, by the latter decades of the nineteenth century Shepherd—like many other prominent women philosophers before her—had been almost entirely forgotten, and it was only in the last decade of the twentieth century that her work began to attract the attention of historians of philosophy.[4] In the twenty-first century, there has been a welcome groundswell of interest in her ideas: the study of her writings is increasingly being incorporated into courses in the history of modern philosophy, academic journals now regularly publish articles on various aspects of her philosophy, and books surveying her work are beginning to appear.[5] Accordingly, there has been an ever-growing need for an edition of her entire body of writings that is complete, corrected, annotated, and widely available.[6] The two volumes devoted to Shepherd in the Oxford New Histories of Philosophy series together aim to meet that need.

The present volume contains Shepherd's 1824 first book, which bears the full title *An Essay upon the Relation of Cause and Effect, controverting the Doctrine of Mr. Hume, concerning the Nature of that Relation; with Observations upon the Opinions of Dr. Brown and Mr. Lawrence, connected with the same subject*. (This is now often abbreviated as *ERCE*.) The other volume devoted to Shepherd in the series, entitled *Mary Shepherd's Essays on the Perception of an External Universe* and edited by Antonia LoLordo, appeared in 2020. It contains Shepherd's 1827 second book, which bears the full title *Essays on the Perception of an External Universe and Other Subjects Connected with the Doctrine of Causation*. (This is now often abbreviated as *EPEU*.) A book published anonymously in 1819 in Edinburgh has sometimes been attributed to Shepherd, but Deborah Boyle has now shown convincingly that the book was in fact the work of an Edinburgh architectural engineer and author, James Milne.[7]

---

[4] Of particular importance was the pioneering work of Eileen O'Neill (1997); Margaret Atherton (1994, 1996); and Jennifer McRobert (2000, 2002/2014).

[5] Examples include LoLordo 2022 and Boyle 2023.

[6] Digitized scans of Shepherd's two books are available online, and facsimiles of good quality are contained in Shepherd 2000, which is, however, now difficult to obtain. Shepherd 2004 is a lightly edited and corrected version of her 1824 first book contained in a valuable ten-volume set of early responses to Hume. Shepherd 2018 contains very useful selections from her writings, helpfully annotated and arranged topically.

[7] See Boyle 2020. The full title of the 1819 book—which was included by McRobert without definitive attribution in Shepherd 2000—is *Enquiry Respecting the Relation of Cause and Effect; in which the Theories of Professors Brown, and Mr Hume, are Examined; with a Statement of Such Observations as are Calculated to Shew the Inconsistency of these Theories; and from which a New Theory is Deduced, More Consonant to Facts and Experience. Also a New Theory of the Earth, Deduced*

In the years immediately following the publication of her two books, three additional essays written by Shepherd appeared in print. In 1828, she published an article "On the Causes of Single and Erect Vision." In the same year, "Observations by Lady Mary Shepherd on the 'First Lines of the Human Mind'"—a critique of John Fearn's book *First Lines of the Human Mind* that Fearn had solicited from her—was published by his arrangement without her approval. These two essays by Shepherd are included in Appendix I to this volume. She subsequently responded to Fearn and elaborated further on her views in 1832 with the publication of "Lady Mary Shepherd's Metaphysics." That essay is included in Antonia LoLordo's edition of *Mary Shepherd's Essays on the Perception of an External Universe.*

Shepherd did not publish again after 1832, but twelve letters written by her—the earliest likely from 1824 and the latest from 1843—are currently known: eight to Charles Babbage, three to William Whewell, and one to Robert Blakey. Only the last of these has appeared in print (Blakey 1879: 160–61), while those to Whewell have not been publicly available outside Trinity College, Cambridge in any form.[8] All twelve letters are included as Appendix

---

from *Geological Observations*. Attribution of the book to Shepherd was no doubt encouraged by the fact that, like *ERCE*, it criticizes the views of both Thomas Brown and David Hume on causation. By way of supplementing Boyle's ample and powerful evidence, however, three additional points may be noted. First, Shepherd's daughter lists only *ERCE* and *EPEU* as her mother's books (Brandreth 1886: 29)—even though she was herself ten years old in 1819 and so would likely have been aware of any book published by her mother at that time. Second, the preface to the 1819 work compares an author defending his own theory against objections to a "veteran engineer" trying to fortify a city he has already built (pp. v–vi)—and Milne was himself a veteran engineer of bridges and public works. Finally, the 1819 work cites Brown exclusively from the *Inquiry into the Relation of Cause and Effect* (Brown 1818); indeed, its author describes the publication of that book as the primary impetus for writing. Yet in striking contrast, Shepherd's one chapter devoted to Brown in *ERCE*, published five years later, does not engage with or mention Brown's 1818 book at all; instead, it quotes from and engages exclusively with his much-earlier *Observations on the Nature and Tendency of the Doctrine of Mr. Hume, concerning the Relation of Cause and Effect* (Brown 1806). (For details, see the descriptions of Brown's writings and the contents of *ERCE* later in this introduction.) The fact that Milne and Shepherd each criticize the views of both Hume and Brown on causation merely shows how controversial and widely discussed those views were in early nineteenth-century Britain, especially by writers with ties to Edinburgh.

It should be noted that the 1819 book also includes a "theory of the earth, deduced from geological observations," and several of Shepherd's later letters (specifically Letters 4, 10, and 11) express interest in geology and the history of the earth. However, the letters show no signs of the rather fanciful specific theory—positing collisions of the earth first with a comet and then with the moon—presented in that book. This topic, too, was a subject of great public attention in the early 1800s (following discoveries of fossilized remains in distinct strata that called into question the Biblical account of Creation), and interest in it is not surprising for either an engineer involved in excavation (as Milne was) or a friend of the geologist Charles Lyell (as Shepherd was).

[8] Provisional transcriptions of the eight letters to Babbage, still containing a significant proportion of inaccuracies, are included in a set of notes and drafts uploaded to an online archive (McRobert 2005).

II in the present volume. After her death, Whewell urged that her unpublished writings, if there were any, be brought to light (Brandreth 1886: 119), but none were. Thus, all of Shepherd's known extant writings are now available as part of Oxford New Histories of Philosophy in time for the bicentenary of the publication of *An Essay upon the Relation of Cause and Effect*.

Shepherd's Life

Mary Shepherd was born Mary Primrose on December 31, 1777, at Barnbougle Castle on the Dalmeny estate, located on the Firth of Forth outside Edinburgh. She was the second of six children of Neil Primrose, who held the title of Third Earl of Rosebery (hence her courtesy title "Lady"), and Mary Vincent Primrose. The young Mary and her two sisters were educated at home by a tutor who reportedly taught them Latin, mathematics, history, geography, and "a vast deal of thinking upon the elements of Truth as to things in general" (Brandreth 1886: 26). She soon developed a passion for metaphysics and philosophy, and between the ages of seventeen and twenty-seven, she composed "many M.S. books full of metaphysical disquisitions, exposing errors in the reasoning of Hume's atheistical treatises, and the unitarian doctrines of the then new philosopher, Priestley" (Brandreth 1886: 28–29).

Further spurring Shepherd's interest in rebutting Hume's metaphysics was the so-called Leslie Affair of 1805. John Leslie had been provisionally appointed to fill a vacancy as Professor of Mathematics at the University of Edinburgh, but ecclesiastical opposition soon mounted. Much of the opposition was political in origin, as many of the ministers of Edinburgh aimed to distribute professorial chairs among themselves and had one of their own as a preferred candidate. In their effort to block Leslie's final appointment, the ministers focused especially on an endnote in his book, *An Experimental Enquiry into the Nature and Propagation of Heat*, published in the previous year. Elaborating on his remark that "science has experienced much obstruction from mysterious notions long entertained concerning causation" (Leslie 1804: 136), the lengthy endnote began:

> Mr. Hume is the first, as far as I know, who has treated of causation in a truly philosophical manner. His *Essay on Necessary Connexion*[9] seems a

---

[9] Leslie's reference is to *An Enquiry concerning Human Understanding* (Hume 2000) Section 7, entitled "Of the Idea of Necessary Connexion."

model of clear and accurate reasoning. But it was only wanted to dispel the cloud of mystery which had so long darkened that important subject. The unsophisticated sentiments of mankind are in perfect unison with the deductions of logic, and imply nothing more at bottom, in the relation of cause and effect, than a *constant and invariable sequence*. (Leslie 1804: 521–22n16)

The ministers argued that Hume's view of causation undermined any argument for a divine First Cause and that Leslie's endorsement of it was therefore tantamount to encouraging atheism. They further argued that their historic right of advisement (*avisamentum*) on university appointments constituted a right of veto. As they well knew, Hume's own candidacy for Edinburgh's Chair of Ethics and Pneumatic[10] Philosophy (which subsequently became the Chair of Moral Philosophy) had come to naught sixty years earlier chiefly through the opposition of the ministers of Edinburgh that was based largely on accusations of encouraging atheism.

Fearing future ecclesiastical interference in university appointments, many prominent University of Edinburgh professors rallied to Leslie's defense, including the philosopher Dugald Stewart and the mathematician and geologist John Playfair; another notable public defender was the philosopher and poet Thomas Brown. Although the case was taken both to civil court and to the General Assembly of the Church of Scotland, Leslie and his allies ultimately prevailed. By that time, however, much ink had been spilled and the controversy had captured a remarkable degree of attention from the public at large. One of the long-term consequences of the Leslie Affair was to produce a renewed public interest in Hume's philosophy, and especially his views about causation. Indeed, Shepherd recalled decades afterward that in the Edinburgh of those days "every ambitious student piqued himself on maintaining there was no such thing as Cause and Effect" (Blakey 1879: 161; Letter 12 in this volume).

The Primrose family regularly spent portions of the year in London during Shepherd's youth. In 1808, she married Henry John Shepherd, an aspiring London barrister—and later also an occasional legal author, playwright, and poet—six years her junior who was the son of the eminent jurist Samuel Shepherd. (Thorne 1886 reports that the couple eloped.) After

---

[10] 'Pneumatic' in this context meant "spiritual or mental."

her husband served a term in Parliament from 1818 to 1820, he studied for a Master's degree at Cambridge, which he took in 1823. At Cambridge, they would likely have come into contact with William Whewell, who was then a mathematical lecturer and assistant tutor in his mid-twenties. Her husband's own interests were more literary and political than philosophical, but he appreciated the importance of her two books and helped to arrange for their publication. When in London, they hosted a well-known intellectual and literary salon, in which "her humour seems to have been as well-known as her logical powers, and occasional causticity" (Brandreth: 1886: 4, 41–42).

All of Shepherd's publications appeared between 1824 and 1832, and they are described in sections that follow. The letters that remain demonstrate her continued engagement with philosophical issues at least through 1840—although an 1838 letter to Whewell (Letter 10) mentions having "left Town very ill" and gone to Brighton for her health, while she writes in a letter to Babbage, perhaps in the following year, of a recent "serious affliction" that "indisposes me, to receiving the same pleasure, I had used to do in general society" (Letter 7). Her letter to Blakey in 1843—at the age of sixty-five, less than four years before her death—cites diminished energy from "weakness and indisposition" as preventing her from engaging in a fuller philosophical discussion. Although she reports to Blakey that *An Essay upon the Relation of Cause and Effect* has gone "entirely out of print," she encourages herself "to hope for the future success and prevalence of my own notions" (Letter 12). Mary Shepherd died in London on January 7, 1847.

An Essay upon the Relation of Cause and Effect (1824)

An Essay upon the Relation of Cause and Effect, controverting the Doctrine of Mr. Hume, concerning the Nature of that Relation; with Observations upon the Opinions of Dr. Brown and Mr. Lawrence, connected with the same subject was published in 1824 in London for T. Hookham, bearing no indication of its author's name. In addition to an "Advertisement to the Reader" and a "Preface," it contains six chapters in all: three addressing the "doctrine" of David Hume, one addressing the "opinions" of Thomas Brown, and two addressing the "opinions" of William Lawrence. The contents are by no means merely critical, however; as she later states, "The ideas there advanced are the foundation of all sound philosophy" (Letter 12).

Controverting the Doctrine of Mr. Hume (Chapters 1–3)

David Hume (1711–1776) was one of the most important and most famous philosophers of the eighteenth century, writing on topics in epistemology, metaphysics, mind, ethics, politics, economics, and religion; he also wrote a multi-volume *History of England*. Shepherd targets his epistemological and metaphysical views about causation as they are expressed in Book 1, Part 3 of *A Treatise of Human Nature* (first published in 1739) and in Sections 4, 5, and 7 of *An Enquiry concerning Human Understanding* (first published in 1748). In both works, he argues that causal inference depends on an experienced "constant conjunction" of objects or events of one kind being followed by objects or events of a second; the resulting mental transition to a belief concerning a similar conjunction in an observed case is mediated not by the faculty of *reason* but by the *imagination*, through the operation of "custom or habit." By 'imagination', he means the faculty of having image-like ideas through operations other than memory or reasoning (*Treatise* 1.3.9.19.n22); by 'custom or habit', he means the feature of the mind by which "the repetition of any particular act or operation produces a propensity to renew the same act or operation, without being impelled by any reasoning or process of the understanding" (*Enquiry* 5.5). We think we perceive a "necessary connexion" between causes and effects themselves, he argues, only because we project onto them an inner feeling of mental "determination" that occurs when we make that involuntary transition, and we then regard "power" as "that very circumstance in the cause, by which it is enabled to produce its effect" with this necessary connection between them (*Enquiry* 7.17). In consequence, he offers two definitions of 'cause'—one in terms of temporal priority and constant conjunction, and one in terms of temporal priority and mental transition (*Enquiry* 7.29). Hume sought to draw many important consequences from this understanding of causation. A self-described "sceptic," he was often interpreted, especially by those influenced by Thomas Reid, as denying all prospects for justified belief resulting from causal inference and as denying the reality of genuine causal relations.

The reason Shepherd gives in her Preface for writing against Hume's doctrines on causation is that they "lead directly to a scepticism of an atheistical tendency, whose dangerous nature can require no comment, nor any apology for its refutation" (*ERCE* 34/4). Hume was not her contemporary—he died in the year before she was born—but she defends the continued relevance of his views by observing:

> It is not many years since Mr. Hume's notions were the occasion of much dispute, on the very ground on which I have undertaken it; a dispute which

nearly lost the mathematical chair in one of our universities to the present possessor of it, on account of his favouring this doctrine. (*ERCE* 34/5)

Her reference is clearly to the 1805 Leslie Affair, although by 1824 Leslie was in fact no longer the "present possessor" of the Chair of Mathematics, having resigned it in 1819 to take up the Chair of Natural Philosophy, which was better suited to his primary interests.[11]

Hume's *Treatise*, like Shepherd's *ERCE*, was originally published anonymously. It is now regarded as one of the great masterpieces of philosophy, but the only edition published in his lifetime did not sell out before his death, and he remarked near the end of his life that it "fell dead-born from the press"[12]—even though it did serve as the basis for denying him the Chair of Moral Philosophy at the University of Edinburgh just a few years after its publication. *An Enquiry concerning Human Understanding* fared better and, unlike the *Treatise*, was subsequently included in his collected *Essays and Treatises on Several Subjects*, which went through many editions in his lifetime. In an "Advertisement" first added to Volume II of that collection (the volume that included the *Enquiry*) in 1776, Hume asked that critics not base their objections on the *Treatise*.[13]

Shepherd's "introductory" first chapter aims to set out Hume's position concerning "the necessary connexion of cause and effect" by using extensive (if often inexact) quotations—first as he presents it in the *Treatise* and then as he presents it in the *Enquiry*. Hume's key "material proposition," as she sees it,

---

[11] It is possible that Shepherd, residing in England, had not become aware of this particular academic development by 1824. That would be rather surprising, however, since she retained significant connections to Edinburgh's intellectual society through friends and family—including her father-in-law, Samuel Shepherd, who served there as Lord Chief Baron of the Court of Exchequer of Scotland from 1819 to 1830. Furthermore, her friend Charles Babbage was considered as a candidate to replace Leslie as Professor of Mathematics in 1819 (despite the relative disadvantage of his not being Scottish). It is quite possible—especially given her use of the phrase 'not many years since'—that Shepherd wrote this portion of the Preface in or before 1819 and did not revise it.
[12] "My Own Life," in Hume 1987: xxxiv.
[13] The Advertisement reads more fully:

> Most of the principles, and reasonings, contained in this volume, were published in a work in three volumes, called *A Treatise of Human Nature*: a work which the Author had projected before he left College, and which he wrote and published not long after. But not finding it successful, he was sensible of his error in going to the press too early, and he cast the whole anew in the following pieces, where some negligences in his former reasoning and more in the expression, are, he hopes, corrected. Yet several writers, who have honoured the Author's Philosophy with answers, have taken care to direct all their batteries against that juvenile work, which the Author never acknowledged, and have affected to triumph in any advantages, which, they imagined, they had obtained over it.... Henceforth, the Author desires, that the following Pieces may alone be regarded as containing his philosophical sentiments and principles. (Hume 1777, vol. II)

is that "Nature may be conceived to alter her course, without a contradiction" (*ERCE* 34/3 and 39/18). As she describes his reasoning, he bases this material proposition on the claim that "our observation of the action of a Cause, affords no grounds for the conclusions of reason respecting it" (because we have neither a priori nor a posteriori knowledge of the "secrets of Nature"), and he then uses it to support the further claim that "it must be '*custom*' only which forces 'the imagination' to *fancy* there is a 'necessary connexion' between Cause and Effect" (*ERCE* 39–40/18–19). She justifies directing her critical attention to the *Treatise* as well as to the *Enquiry*—contrary to Hume's explicit request—on the grounds that his fundamental doctrines on causation are the same in both works and involve a dangerous thesis that, while implied in the *Enquiry*, is explicitly stated and defended by argument only in the *Treatise*. This is his negative thesis that "[i]t is neither intuitively nor demonstrably certain" that "whatever begins to exist must have a cause of existence" (*Treatise* 1.3.2.1–3). Shepherd often paraphrases this thesis in more positive and metaphysical language as "beings can begin their existences of themselves." Hume must remain committed to this thesis in the *Enquiry*, she avers, because it is demanded by his continuing to hold that we merely "fancy" a causal necessary connection in the imagination and do not perceive the existence of one by reason. It is of the highest importance to refute Hume's negative thesis, she states, because it leads directly to the dangerous irreligious consequence that there is no "necessity of a great first Cause, and 'productive principle' of all things" (*ERCE* 40/19).[14]

Accordingly, the crucial second chapter of *ERCE* begins by seeking to demonstrate, against Hume, that

> *Reason*, not *fancy* [i.e., imagination] and '*custom*' leads us to the knowledge, That every thing which begins to exist must have a Cause. (*ERCE* 43/27)

---

[14] For Hume's defense against the accusation that his negative thesis leads to atheism, see his *A Letter from a Gentleman to his Friend in Edinburgh* §§26–30 (Hume 2007: 426–28), written in defense of his candidacy for the professorship at Edinburgh. There he states that he had never denied the "*Principle, that whatever begins to exist must have a Cause.*" Instead, he asserts, he denied only that the certainty of this principle is the result of immediate intuition or demonstration, while fully granting that it has "moral certainty"—that is, the high degree of certainty that results from experience. The 'must' of this principle is thus not, in his view, a "metaphysical" necessity, which would make its denial contradictory and inconceivable (*Treatise* 1.3.14.25), but only a causal necessity—that is, something that follows from the actual (but metaphysically contingent) laws of nature. Shepherd does not explicitly discuss this defense, but she also does not allow his distinction—for her, all genuine causal necessities must also be at bottom metaphysical necessities, even if we are not in a position to know them a priori.

The proposed item of knowledge itself is now often called Shepherd's "Causal Principle" in the secondary literature:

Causal Principle—Every thing which begins to exist must have a Cause.

Shepherd describes *reason* as the faculty of "drawing out to observation the relations of things as they are included in their juxtaposition to each another" (*EPEU* 32/3),[15] and in her view no source for the Causal Principle other than reason could justify our acceptance of it as true. She acknowledges that there is some initial plausibility to Hume's *Treatise* argument for his negative thesis, which appeals to the imaginable separation of causes and effects, but she diagnoses this plausibility as the result of a merely partial consideration of the objects, together with the unwarranted assumption that effects always succeed their causes in time. She offers—and quickly recapitulates—an argument for the Causal Principle that depend on the premise that a beginning of existence must be an "action" or "quality" of something in existence (*ERCE* 46–47/34–36), and she concludes the first section of the chapter by warning that "unless this step [of granting the Causal Principle] is allowed, I can make no further progress in this argument."

In the second section of the chapter, Shepherd turns to Hume's account of the origin of the idea of necessary connection, with the aim of establishing that it is likewise

Reason, and not *Custom*, which guides our minds in forming the notions of necessary connexion, of belief and of expectation. (*ERCE* 49/42)

The notions of a "necessary connexion" and a "productive principle," she states, arise when the mind experiences a new quality coming into existence and so reasons, from the Causal Principle, that the difference between that quality's previous non-existence and its present existence must be due to the action of one or more surrounding objects. This same kind of reasoning, she continues, "forces the mind to perceive" the truth of a second crucial principle, now often called her "Causal Likeness Principle":

---

[15] See Landy 2023 for one treatment. For his part, Hume characterizes reason as the faculty of demonstrative and probable inference (*Treatise* 1.3.9.19.n22), but he, too, holds that it is always a "discovery of ... relations" (*Treatise* 1.3.2.2).

Causal Likeness Principle—Similar causes must necessarily produce *similar effects.*

She argues that this principle follows directly from the Causal Principle, on the grounds that any difference between effects in the absence of any difference in their causes would *itself* be an effect without a cause.[16]

Shepherd's account of the source of our idea of necessary connection sets the stage, in turn, for an outline of her own positive and original theory of causation,[17] which she calls "the really philosophical method of viewing this subject." This theory begins from her distinctive conception of "objects" as "masses of qualities" or powers. She distinguishes two ways of considering objects:

> Objects in relation to us, are nothing but masses of certain qualities, affecting certain of our senses; and which, when independent of our senses, are *unknown* powers or qualities in nature. (*ERCE* 51/46)

This way of putting things naturally suggests to modern readers Immanuel Kant's distinction between *things as they appear to us* and *things as they are in themselves*, and indeed both would agree that we cannot know the intrinsic nature of things as they are in themselves. Crucially, however, Shepherd holds that we *can* know a great deal about the *relations* of things as they are in themselves—including many of their causal relations and extending to the reality of space and time independent of our cognition of them.[18]

---

[16] Shepherd's argument thus treats "differences" between two objects as themselves things subject to the Causal Principle. As she interprets this extension of scope, it demands that all causes be fully deterministic. Hume, too, accepts the deterministic principle that "the same cause always produces the same effect" (*Treatise* 1.3.8.13 and 1.3.15.6; *Enquiry* 8.13)—although Shepherd does not explicitly acknowledge this—but he regards it as something shown by experience, rather than as a demonstrative consequence of the Causal Principle (which he also accepts on the basis of experience, but does not regard as demonstrable).

[17] Important pioneering articles on Shepherd's theory of causation include Bolton 2011, Paoletti 2011, and Fantl 2016.

[18] Shepherd continues to elaborate and deploy this distinction throughout *EPEU*, where she mentions Kant in a brief footnote that mischaracterizes (at least terminologically) his view of space and time (*EPEU* 55n10/59n). Kant's philosophy was not well understood in Britain at the time when Shepherd was writing *ERCE*—and his three *Critiques* had not been translated into English—but there was certainly some early interest in his philosophy. One especially notable early and engaged reader of Kant was her acquaintance Samuel Taylor Coleridge. For more discussion of Shepherd and Kant, see Antonia LoLordo's "Introduction" in Shepherd 2020; for discussion of the early British reception of Kant, see Guyer 2015.

Given this conception of objects, causation can now be understood as the production of new qualities through the "union" or "conjunction" of two or more such objects (*ERCE* 53/50). Although the objects that come into union must have existed previously—and may therefore be considered individually as partial contributing causes—the *whole cause* begins to exist only when the union actually occurs, and the existence of this whole cause is synchronous with, rather than antecedent to, the existence of the new effects. Even the process of nourishment, which may seem to be an obvious case of asynchronous causation, is, she argues, really just a series of many individually synchronous causal relations (*ERCE* 53/50–52). The resulting qualities may then be "exhibited," in Shepherd's terminology, by producing sensations in the mind, either directly through junction with sense organs and the mind, or by acting on other objects that do so.

On the basis of this outline, Shepherd proceeds in the third section of the chapter to provide her own positive definition of 'cause':

> A Cause, therefore, is such action of an object, as shall enable it, in conjunction with another, to form a new nature, capable of exhibiting qualities varying from those of either of the objects unconjoined. (*ERCE* 58/63)

She also offers corresponding definitions of 'effect', 'necessary connexion', and 'power'. After contrasting her definition of 'cause' with those that Hume provides in the *Enquiry*, she raises several objections to them and concludes that his definitions are inadequate.

In the fourth and final section of the second chapter, Shepherd seeks to refute Hume's original "material proposition" by establishing the contrary principle:

> Nature cannot without a contradiction be imagined to alter her course. (*ERCE* 67/85; see also 43/27–28)

Hume had maintained that whatever "secret powers" bodies might have could be conceived to change without contradiction, so that (for example) an object falling from the sky might resemble snow in all other respects and yet have "the taste of salt or the feeling of fire" (*Enquiry* 4.18). Shepherd's argument to the contrary appeals to the necessity of the Causal Likeness Principle. According to this principle, objects that are exactly similar must *necessarily* have exactly the same effects, while any objects that do *not* have all of the same effects cannot have been entirely similar; in neither case, however, will nature have "changed its course" with respect to the powers of things—all of which are essential to their identity. Indeed, she remarks, not even God could bring it about that nature should change its course by violating the Causal Likeness Principle, although the Deity could produce a miracle by introducing a *new* quality into the circumstances that would result in a new difference between two *previously* similar sets of contributing causes (*ERCE* 62/72).

Shepherd completely agrees with Hume that only experience can show us which particular effects will result from the unions of which objects, but she argues that our inductive reasoning about those causes is fundamentally the same in form as mathematical reasoning: we perceive something to be true in one case and then infer that it must be the same in all other cases of the same kind unless there is something *else* present in those other cases to *make* or *produce* a difference (*ERCE* 63 64/77–79, 69–70/91–93; see also Letter 2). She concludes the section by addressing a theological worry about her combinatorial view of causation: Although causation requires a union of two or more contributing causes, God can still be the sole ultimate and sufficient cause of everything, she holds, because there is a multiplicity of divine attributes within God that can be combined (*ERCE* 71/96).

Although Shepherd holds that Hume's fundamental doctrines about causation are the same in the *Treatise* and the *Enquiry*, she remarks that the latter work makes (in *Enquiry* 4) "the *addition* of an application of them to the affairs of ordinary life; as affording a ground of scepticism concerning the powers of the understanding having any part to perform in the regulation of her expectations" (*ERCE* 36/9). The third and last of the chapters of *ERCE* devoted to Hume therefore seeks to complete her rejection of *custom* in favor of *reason* by showing that

> *Custom and Habit* alone are not our guides; but chiefly reason, for the regulation of our expectations in ordinary life. (*ERCE* 43/28)

In order to do so, she states, it is necessary to explain in general why "the operation of the apparent qualities of an object upon the senses, lead[s] the mind to expect the action of its untried qualities, when placed in fit circumstances for their operation" (*ERCE* 73/99). That is, to take one of Hume's examples, "Why should bread, on account of its formerly nourishing the body, be expected to nourish it again?" This is a further and more directly practical task, for simply from the fact that two objects are observed to have *many* of their qualities in common, it does not follow from the Causal Likeness Principle that they must have *all* of the same effects.

Shepherd's solution to this practical problem is that we regulate our expectations by combining *two* cognitive elements: one a matter of demonstration, and one a matter of high probability. First, we can demonstrate from the Causal Likeness Principle that *if* two apparently similar objects were produced entirely by the union of exactly similar contributing causes, *then* those objects *are* exactly similar and hence will have exactly similar effects. Second, by investigating the *observable* similarities of those contributing causes, and the observable similarities of *their* contributing causes, and so on, we can render it highly *probable* that the objects were *in fact* produced by exactly similar causes and so *will* have exactly similar effects. Admittedly, it still remains *possible for all we can demonstrate* that two objects *apparently* alike in causal histories and sensible qualities will nevertheless differ in some respect and so have different effects. She reads Locke as having raised this problem in his *Essay Concerning Human Understanding*, and she proposes that Hume was misled by Locke's concern into questioning (as Locke did not) whether things might "change their secret powers." She maintains, however, that Locke exaggerated the practical scope of the problem. For we find that nature possesses a "regularity in fact" (*ERCE* 80/118) that goes well beyond the mere necessity that nature not alter its course. This "regularity" consists in the fact that the objects we find existing in nature are of a manageably small number of kinds (whose members resemble one another exactly) and which are sufficiently different in their effects from those of other kinds that we can generally sort their members accurately, without undue later surprises, by means of sufficiently careful sensory observation and experimentation. The existence of *this* kind of regularity, Shepherd argues, is a further *effect* which itself requires a *cause*—namely, a providential God. After providing a set of principles for reasoning about kinds, she concludes the chapter by summarizing the gist of Hume's line of argument as she understands it and diagnosing no fewer than seven "illogical sophistries" in it.

Observations upon the Opinions of Dr. Brown (Chapter 4)

Thomas Brown (1778–1820) was a philosopher and poet who had also studied medicine and law. His first book was a critical engagement with

Erasmus Darwin (grandfather of Charles Darwin) on the laws of animal life (Brown 1798). In 1805, he interjected himself into the Leslie Affair by publishing a forty-five-page pamphlet, described in its preface as "the work of a few days." This work, entitled *Observations on the Nature and Tendency of the Doctrine of Mr. Hume, concerning the Relation of Cause and Effect* (Brown 1805), is structured around five propositions of Hume's, which it distinguishes and assesses in turn, agreeing with the first three and rejecting the last two. In Brown's view, the mind always has an *instinctive* belief, derived neither from reason nor from custom, in the uniformity of nature; it is therefore always ready to attribute a causal relation upon the *first* observation of a succession, without the need for stimulation by more instances in constant conjunction—although this initial attribution is very often erroneous and may well be withdrawn in the light of subsequent experience. The idea of causal power, he holds, derives from the application of this belief. But although Hume's own account of the psychological origin of the idea of causal power in constant conjunction is thus mistaken, Brown argues, Hume rightly affirms the *irresistibility* of the application of that idea; furthermore, he argues, such an acknowledgement is itself entirely sufficient to avoid the dangerous denial of the need for a First Cause of the universe.

In the following year, Brown published a 220-page "Second Edition, enlarged" of the *Observations* (Brown 1806). That work develops his own views of causation further and, in the process, provides his own definition of 'cause':

> A *cause* may be defined *the object or event which immediately precedes any change, and which existing again in similar circumstances will be always immediately followed by a similar change*. (*Observations* 45–46)

This definition is very similar to Hume's first definition, which likewise appeals to temporal priority and constant conjunction. Brown also defends Hume against Thomas Reid's skeptical interpretation of him as denying the existence of causal power altogether. Like its predecessor of the previous year, the 1806 *Observations* distinguishes and assesses the five propositions in turn, and it defends Hume's account of causation against the charge of encouraging the denial of a First Cause.

In 1808–9, Brown substituted at the University of Edinburgh as deputy lecturer for his former teacher Dugald Stewart, who had become ill, and in 1810 he became joint holder with Stewart of the Chair of Moral Philosophy. His lectures were reportedly very popular with students. In 1818, he published his 561-page *Inquiry into the Relation of Cause and Effect* (Brown 1818). Its title page describes the book as a "third edition" of the *Observations*, but its preface describes it as "so much enlarged and altered, as to constitute almost a New Work" (Brown 1818: v). Only in the lengthy Part IV of the book does he take up the discussion of Hume in detail, and that discussion, while thorough, no longer sets out the list of five propositions explicitly.

In her Preface to *ERCE*, Shepherd justifies extending her critical attention beyond Hume by noting that Leslie's opinion

> as far as it related to any countenance it might afford to the principles of atheism, was defended from the insinuation, by a learned treatise, from the then Professor of Moral Philosophy in the same university. This treatise, whilst it controverts Mr. Hume's opinions in some respects, denies that atheistical inferences may be deduced from them. (*ERCE* 35/5–6)

Although Brown had not yet joined Stewart as Professor of Moral Philosophy at Edinburgh at the time of the Leslie Affair, her reference is obviously to Brown, not to Stewart, who is not mentioned anywhere in *ERCE* (although she discusses him in other writings). For while Stewart had published his own 127-page defense of Leslie, it was not a "learned treatise" but rather a practical intervention that Stewart himself called (in language like Brown's of that year) "the hasty production of a few days" (Stewart 1805: 5), and its content is not well summarized by Shepherd's further description. That further description does match Brown's 1805 *Observations*, but at forty-five pages, that "work of a few days" was much too short to be considered a "learned treatise." A comparison of passages shows the more comprehensive 1806 second edition to be the exclusive source of her quotations from Brown in Chapter 4, and it is clearly this work to which she refers. She does not even mention Brown's 1818 *Inquiry* in that chapter, although Chapter 5 addresses Lawrence's appeal to it.

Shepherd has three main aims in Chapter 4. First, she disputes Brown's Humean definition of 'cause' in terms of temporal succession. Second, she discusses and assesses Brown's five Humean propositions in order:

(1) The relation of Cause and Effect cannot be discovered *à priori*.
(2) Even after experience, the relation of Cause and Effect cannot be discovered by reason.

(3) The relation of Cause and Effect is an object of *belief* alone.
(4) The relation of Cause and Effect is believed to exist between objects only after their "*customary*" conjunction is known to us.
(5) When two objects have been frequently observed in succession, the mind passes readily from one to the other, the transition in the mind itself being the impression from which the idea of the necessary connexion of the objects as Cause and Effect is derived.

Shepherd argues that the first proposition, which Brown accepts, is ambiguous; for while any particular causal relation can indeed be discovered only by experience, the Causal Principle itself, and so the necessity of the connection of causes and effects, can be known by reason. On the basis of her account of the role of reason in causal inference, she also rejects the second and third propositions, which Brown accepts from Hume. In contrast, she praises Brown's arguments against the fourth and fifth propositions, concerning the purported need for constant conjunction in making causal judgments and the source of the idea of necessary connection, respectively. Finally, she argues against Brown that Hume's account of the origin of the idea of power in the operation of custom rather than reason cannot avoid atheistic implications. Indeed, she holds, Brown's own conception of the idea of power, as the consequence of an unavoidable instinctive belief whose truth cannot be established by reason, is fundamentally no better than Hume's in this respect.

Observations upon the Opinions of Dr. Lawrence
(Chapters 5–6)

Sir William Lawrence (1783–1867) was a distinguished surgeon and anatomist. Elected to the Royal Society in 1813, he became a professor of anatomy and surgery at the Royal College of Surgeons in 1815, where he soon became involved in a famous public dispute about the nature of life. In his first series of lectures, published as *An Introduction to Comparative Anatomy and Physiology* (Lawrence 1816), he praised French science and repeatedly declared that the vital functions of an organism result entirely from its "organization"—that is, from the specific structure of its parts. This directly contradicted the view of his colleague and former mentor, John Abernethy, who (following his own mentor, John Hunter), held that life requires the presence of a separate vital substance or principle. In his own lectures to the College in 1817, Abernethy did not mention Lawrence by name, but he strongly criticized the "modern sceptics" who embrace French materialism. The issue was particularly fraught, in part for political reasons connected to the perceived dangers of the French Revolution, but primarily for moral and theological reasons. Abernethy regarded *mind* as an entirely immaterial substance, distinct from but on analogy with the principle of life, and one whose existence therefore promised the prospect of personal immortality. The dispute influenced, among others, Lawrence's patient and friend Mary Shelley, who published her famous novel, *Frankenstein*, directly concerned with the nature of life, in 1818.[19]

Lawrence responded directly to Abernethy in his lectures of 1817–18, published in 1819 as *Lectures on Physiology, Zoology, and the Natural History of Man* (Lawrence 1819). In addition to defending his view of life, he directly addresses mind, declaring that "there is no thought without a brain" (*Lectures* II: 61). More generally, he asserts that a proper inductive logic will protect the physical sciences "from the incursions of extra-physical or metaphysical chimeras, and from the intrusion of immaterial agencies" (*Lectures* III: 77–78). In a later division of the book, he also expresses skepticism about the Biblical account of creation and the origin of humanity (*Lectures* 247–49). Because of the book's alleged blasphemy, the British government refused to protect Lawrence's copyright (with the consequence that there were several unauthorized editions). He was ultimately obliged to retract his views in order to rescue his career, and his subsequent writings were much more cautious. In 1857, he was appointed sergeant-surgeon to Queen Victoria, and in 1867 he was made a baronet.

Shepherd's stated reason for extending her critical attention to a third author concerns not the danger of denying a First Cause, as with Hume and Brown, but rather the danger of denying the immateriality (and hence presumably also the immortality) of the soul:

> Also a modern and living author, of great celebrity, Mr. Lawrence, in his late Lectures, has adopted Mr. Hume's and Dr. Brown's notions of the relation of cause and effect, as containing a proof of the materiality of the soul;—a doctrine of sufficient importance to justify a further investigation of the argument on which it is supposed to be well founded. (*ERCE* 35/6)

---

[19] It seems likely that Mary Shelley (then twenty-one years old) had not yet met Mary Shepherd.

In an ironic echo of the Leslie Affair, the connection to Brown, and so implicitly to Hume as well, was made in a lengthy footnote. Lawrence's lectures as originally presented explained the causal "necessary connexion" between a particular "structure of muscular fibers" and "irritability" (that is, capacity for contraction) and that between a particular "structure of nervous fibres" and "sensibility" (that is, capacity for inducing sensation) as consisting entirely in their universal concomitance—just like that between "gold" and its properties of being "yellow, ductile, and soluble in nitro-muriatic acid"—without any need to bring in additional vital or immaterial entities. In the published version, he adds a footnote beginning:

> Since I delivered these Lectures, I have become acquainted with Dr. BROWN's *Inquiry into the Relation of Cause and Effect*, third edition, 8vo. Edinburgh, 1818; a most instructive work, calculated to dispel much of the obscurity and confusion, by which both physical and metaphysical discussions have been perplexed and retarded, and to interest strongly all those who derive pleasure from perspicuous language and close reasoning. As it is extremely important to possess clear notions of causation, of the relations expressed by the words *cause, effect, property, quality, power*, I subjoin an extract, in which these matters are more satisfactorily explained than in any other book I have met with. (Lawrence 1819: 78n–81n)

Lawrence then quotes a lengthy passage from Brown's 1818 *Inquiry* that includes his Humean definition of 'cause'.[20]

In Chapter 5 of *ERCE*, Shepherd responds to Lawrence by distinguishing between two possible meanings of the term 'necessary connexion'. Because "an object is a combined mass of qualities, determined to the senses from unknown causes in nature, to which an arbitrary name is affixed," there is a verbal necessary connection between a named kind of substance and the various properties that we include as part of the meaning or definition of that name. This is the kind of necessity that applies to the relation between gold and ductility. The second is that between an object and the effects that its union with another object must necessarily produce on any occasion of

---

[20] *Inquiry* 15–21. Following the quotation of this passage, Lawrence concludes the footnote by taking his former-teacher-turned-critic John Abernethy to task for not providing, in Abernethy 1817, any alternative definition of 'cause'.

their union. This is the kind of necessary connection that applies to irritability and "living muscular fibres," or to sensibility and "living nervous fibres" (*ERCE* 95-96/152-55). But, she argues, Lawrence fails to recognize that *life* and *mind*, respectively, must be added to the physical structure of parts in order to produce these respective effects.

Shepherd traces Lawrence's alleged errors to his acceptance of two elements of the passage he quotes from Brown. The first is Brown's definition of 'cause', which she has already rejected in Chapter 4. The second is Brown's claim that "the words *property* and *quality* admit of exactly the same definition, expressing only a certain relation of invariable antecedence and consequence in changes that take place on the presence of the substance to which they are ascribed" (*ERCE* 98/159-60). In both cases, she argues, the fundamental error lies in thinking that a necessary connection can be found in a relation of temporal antecedence and consequence between distinct objects. In contrast, she approves a third quoted statement of Brown's—"the properties of a substance are only the substance itself in relation to various changes which take place, when it exists in peculiar circumstances"—that seems to accord with her own view of objects and qualities, but she regards that proposition as incompatible with conceiving of causation as a relation of temporal sequence (*ERCE* 98-99/160-62).

In Chapter 6, Shepherd distinguishes and criticizes in detail what she takes to be six different and mutually incompatible definitions of 'life' offered by Lawrence. She then provides her own positive view of *life*, as a quality originating from God and mixing with matter to produce a living thing, much as a spark must be added to combustible materials in order to produce a fire. Next, she offers eight propositions in recapitulation of "what I have advanced" about the relation of cause and effect (*ERCE* 110-11/187-89) and adds a criticism of Lawrence for ignoring what may be other causally necessary conditions (*ERCE* 111-12/189-92). She concludes by describing the fundamental principles of *ERCE* as the "true foundations of scientific research, practical knowledge, and belief in a creating and presiding Deity" (*ERCE* 113/193-94).

Composition and Use

Shepherd's "Advertisement to the Reader" remarks that *ERCE* sets down the "suggestions which at different times have occurred to me upon the theory of the relation of Cause and Effect, adopted by Mr. Hume, Dr. Brown, and Mr.

Lawrence" (*ERCE* 32/v). It seems plausible that its various elements were not only conceived but drafted at different times. By her daughter's account, she was already writing "disquisitions" against Hume in the period 1794–1804, even before the Leslie Affair, so it possible that some of that material may have found its way into the later *ERCE*.[21] The fact that the chapter on Brown relies entirely on his 1806 *Observations* without reference to the greatly expanded and revised *Inquiry* suggests that it may have been substantially drafted prior to 1818. Much of the Preface itself may have been drafted in or prior to 1818 as well (see footnote 11). In contrast, the two chapters in response to Lawrence (as well as the single-sentence paragraph about him in the Preface [*ERCE* 35/6]) must have been written after the first publication of his *Lectures* in 1819.[22]

If, as later reported, William Whewell did indeed make one of Shepherd's books a text at Cambridge at some point in his academic career, there are several good reasons, based on his interests and views, to think that it was *ERCE*. Whewell was an impressive polymath, but his predominant philosophical interest throughout his career was in the methodology, character, and content of science and scientific reasoning. (Indeed, he coined the term 'scientist'.) Furthermore, several aspects of his views on those topics correspond directly to elements of *ERCE*. His earliest philosophical publication, "On the Nature of the Truth of the Laws of Motion" (Whewell 1834), argues that even causal laws that must be discovered empirically are nevertheless necessary truths. He explicitly criticizes the views of both Hume and Brown on the nature of the idea of causation (Whewell 1840b: 163–69). His essay entitled "Discussion of the Question: Are Cause and Effect Successive or Simultaneous" defends the thesis that effects are synchronous with their causes (Whewell 1842) and even discusses at some length the apparent counterexample of nourishment (as "nutrition"), which (like *ERCE*) it explains as a series of synchronous causes.[23] In contrast, his writings evince relatively little interest in the central topic of *EPEU* Part I—our knowledge that there is an external material

---

[21] Shepherd's page citations of the *Treatise* correspond only to a "new edition" published in 1817 (Hume 1817), however, so those, at least, must have been made in or after that year; see "Short Titles and Forms of Citation" in this volume.

[22] Shepherd's page citations to *Lectures* correspond to the first edition, and not to the editions that appeared in 1822 and 1823.

[23] On the other hand, the positive account of inductive reasoning elaborated in Whewell's books bearing directly on that topic (Whewell 1837 and especially 1840b) does not appear to be greatly indebted to Shepherd, even though they share some notable points in common. Letter 9, which she wrote to thank him for a gift copy of his *History of the Inductive Sciences* (Whewell 1837), judges his discussion of the nature of inductive reasoning in that work to be insufficient and to stand in need of doctrines that she had—in fact, although she does not mention it—already stated more than a decade earlier in *ERCE*.

world—or in many of the varied additional topics of Part II. Three of his brief *Aphorisms* (§§LXV–LXVII in Whewell 1840a and 1840b) do mention the apparent paradoxes of "single" and "upright" vision, which are also topics of the final essay in *EPEU* (as well as of Shepherd's follow-up article of 1828), but in a letter to him thanking him for sending the *Aphorisms*, Shepherd singles out his remarks on that topic as unsatisfactory (Letter 11).

Essays on the Perception of an External Universe (1827)

Essays on the Perception of an External Universe, and Other Subjects Connected with the Doctrine of Causation (included in Shepherd 2020, edited by Antonia LoLordo) was published in London in 1827 by John Hatchard and Son. Unlike its formally anonymous predecessor, the volume credits its author on the title page as "Lady Mary Shepherd, author of '*An Essay upon the Relation of Cause and Effect*.'" The book has two distinct parts. Part I is a single multi-chapter work, "Essay on the Academical or Sceptical Philosophy as Applied by Mr. Hume to the Perception of External Existence," while Part II comprises fourteen "Short Essays on Several Subjects."

Shepherd states in the Preface to Part I that it was originally intended as an appendix to *ERCE*, one that would contain "some inquiry into the nature and proof of the existence of matter, and of an external universe" because it is "necessary in order to the more enlarged comprehension of *that manner of action exerted in causation which renders it 'a producing principle*,' to have a right understanding of the idea of an *external* object." Ultimately, however, the "notions that suggested themselves" exceeded "the limits of that work" and she determined that they required a work of their own (*EPEU* 29/xi–xii).[24] *EPEU* Part I clarifies the "manner of action exerted in causation" by distinguishing between (1) the "internal existence" of our own "sensations" (taking the term 'sensation' in a generic sense "comprehending every consciousness whatever" [*EPEU* 33/6]); and (2) the "external existence" of things not in the mind, things which nevertheless "exhibit their qualities" by causing sensations in the mind when conjoined with the mind and with sense organs. Although the intrinsic natures of external objects cannot be known as they are in themselves, Shepherd asserts, the fact that there *are* such external objects is known even by very young children, through a process

---

[24] It seems that Shepherd must therefore have begun drafting Part I in or before 1824. See her reference to "a future Essay on the nature of external objects" in her footnote at *ERCE* 88/137.

of "latent" reasoning involving the Causal Principle. In this way, Shepherd notes, the central doctrines of *EPEU* depend on the principles previously established in *ERCE*, while at the same time they clarify the understanding of *ERCE* by showing more distinctly how those principles apply. In this way, the two works throw "a mutual light upon one another" and comprise an integrated whole.

The title of *EPEU* Part I alludes to the final section (Section 12) of Hume's *Enquiry*, entitled "Of the Academical or Sceptical Philosophy."[25] That section states simply that the mind is "carried, by a natural instinct or prepossession . . . without any reasoning . . . [to] suppose an external universe, which depends not on our perception" (*Enquiry* 12.7). The earlier *Treatise*, however, devotes a great deal of attention to an elaborate explanation of the prepossession, one that attributes it to operations of the imagination (*Treatise* 1.4.2). According to this account, the imagination successively attributes to what are in fact some of its own sense perceptions an existence that is (1) *continued* even when not perceived, (2) *external* to the mind, and (3) *causally independent* of the mind. (Philosophers, recognizing that our sense perceptions in fact lack these features, are later forced by the imagination, Hume holds, to postulate causes resembling our sense perceptions to which these features will apply.) Because of this greater detail, Shepherd undertakes "in this essay as in the former one [*ERCE*] to consider Mr. Hume's notions as expressed first of all in his [*Treatise*] and afterwards as resumed in his [*Enquiry*]." Her method, however, is "to conduct the argument rather by stating what I conceive to be truth, than by a minute examination of his reasoning" (*EPEU* 31/xvi).

Shepherd agrees with Hume that the mind attributes the three features he identifies, and in that order, but she disagrees about both the source and the object of the attributions. Thus, after a brief "introductory" chapter stating the question at issue, she devotes the first three numbered chapters of *EPEU* Part I to her own positive accounts of the attributions of "continued, external, and independent" existence, respectively, through reasoning from the Causal Principle and the Causal Likeness Principle. These attributions, she holds, are made from the very outset to objects different and distinct from our sense perceptions. (Ironically, however, the mind often comes *later* to conflate these perceptions with the external objects. This tendency, she holds, is convenient as a matter of practice, but still philosophically misleading.)

---

[25] 'Academical Philosophy' refers to the school of skepticism that developed in the later history of the Platonic Academy. Hume takes this kind of skepticism to be moderate or mitigated, in contrast to what he understands to be ("excessive") "Pyrrhonian Scepticism."

The next four chapters of *EPEU* Part I concern, respectively, objections to our knowledge of external existence drawn from the phenomenon of dreams; the proper way to understand the roles of contributing and whole causes in sense perception; the use of the term 'idea', with particular attention to memory; and applications of these doctrines to several further topics, including the existence of God and the relation between mind and body. The final chapter is a useful "recapitulation."

EPEU Part II often elaborates on topics that are considered only in passing in *EPEU* Part I and/or *ERCE*, and it adds substantially new topics as well. In a footnote, Shepherd explains the origins of *EPEU* Part II as follows:

> The substance of these minor essays were addressed to several friends who considered some objections overlooked in the larger essays, and who permitted the insertion of the answers they approved of, and which they considered useful. (*EPEU* 159n1/314n)

The frontmatter of *EPEU* describes the contents of Part II specifically as "Essays Containing Inquiries Relating to the Berkeleian Theory; the Comparison of Mathematical and Physical Induction; the Union of Color and Extension; the Credibility of Miracles; The Nature of a Final Cause and of Mind; the Reason of Single and Erect Vision"—although these are not the only topics. Of the fourteen essays, the first three are said to be "against Bishop Berkeley," the next two against "Mr. D. Stewart," the next three "against Mr. Hume," the next five "against several modern atheists" (who remain unnamed), and the last one "against Dr. Reid."

Later Essays (1828–32)

"On the Causes of Single and Erect Vision" (1828)

"On the Causes of Single and Erect Vision" was first published in the June 1828 issue of *The Philosophical Magazine, or the Annals of Chemistry, Mathematics, Astronomy, Natural History, and General Science*. It was reprinted the following month—divided into two parts and described as being "From the *Philosophical Magazine*"—in the "Scientific Notices" section of the July 15 and 22 issues of *The Kaleidoscope; or, Scientific and Literary Mirror*. It greatly expands on the final essay (Essay XIV) of *EPEU* Part II. That essay is listed in the table of contents for *EPEU* as "The reason why we see objects single instead of double, and erect instead of inverted—against Dr. Reid." The title given at the head of the essay itself is even more explicit about its topic: "On the reason why objects appear single although painted on two retinas, and why they appear erect although the images be inverted on them."

In the *EPEU* essay, Shepherd begins by asserting, in response to the first stated problem, that the mind can perceive a figure by sight only if there is "painted" on the retina both the color of that figure and a different surrounding color, and that the mind can perceive *two* figures by sight only if there is also the sensation of a "line of demarcation" between them. Although a single object will paint a figure with surrounding color at corresponding points on two retinas, it will not paint a line of demarcation between two figures, and hence, she argues, the mind can at most superimpose the sensory images from the two retinas into one sensory image. In response to the second stated problem, she asserts that objects can be perceived as "inverted" only if their images are painted on the retina as inverted *relative to those of other objects*. Since this does not generally occur, objects are not perceived by the mind as inverted but as erect. She contrasts these explanations with those offered by Thomas Reid. Like Stewart after him, Reid drew a sharp distinction between mere brute *sensations*, which do not themselves involve any conception of objects, and *perceptions*, which do include the conception of objects. According to Reid, our sensations merely "suggest" perceptions of objects to the mind in a way that is ultimately inexplicable and could have been otherwise. Shepherd criticizes this view as appealing to an "original law of our constitution" rather than to "the very nature of things" (*EPEU* 411/199).

The 1828 essay "On the Causes of Single and Erect Vision" defends what are fundamentally the same explanations for the two phenomena in question, but it aims to do so "with greater nicety" and "further detail"—resulting in an essay more than three times as long as the original. In the new essay, Shepherd embeds her explanations in the context of five "metaphysical positions in relation to vision" and three "optical facts"; provides additional arguments, examples, and elaborations (including one about the causes of double vision of a single object); and brings into discussion the published views of the Scottish-American physician William Charles

Wells (1757–1817) and the Scottish scientist and inventor David Brewster (1781–1868).[26] Indeed, Shepherd may have been prompted to write the longer essay, at least in part, by the treatments of single and erect vision in Brewster's pamphlet entitled *Optics* that was published in 1827 or early 1828 as part of the popular Library of Useful Knowledge series.[27]

The importance as well as the interest of the topic of single vision to Shepherd is indicated by two of her letters. To William Whewell, she writes of "the views of single and erect Vision, a right doctrine concerning which is so intimately connected with the whole laws & faculties of the human Mind" (Letter 11). In her letter to Robert Blakey, she remarks:

> This "Essay" [*ERCE*] and that on "Final Causes" [*EPEU* II.9: "On the objection made to final causes as ends, on account of the existence of physical efficient means"][28] together with that on "Single and Double Vision,"[29] are the three whose secret principle, I think, you will not find in any other authors named in your prospectus. They confute modern Atheism. (Letter 12)

Exactly how she believes that her treatment of single vision confutes modern atheism is a matter of interpretation, but the remainder of the letter suggests that it may be by explaining single vision not through a merely arbitrary "theory" (like that of Reid) but as an example of divine "final causes" operating as "physically efficient means" in a way that is "deducible from the general laws of causation" as established in *ERCE*. For an explicit connection between vision and final causes, see "Lady Mary Shepherd's Metaphysics" (Shepherd 2020: 209/701).

---

[26] Brewster was especially known for his work in optics, but he was also an early contributor to the *Edinburgh Review* and subsequently the editor of the *Edinburgh Encyclopedia*. In connection with the Leslie Affair, Brewster wrote a satirical piece in defense of Leslie (Brewster 1806). He was also a disappointed candidate to replace Leslie as Professor of Natural Philosophy at Edinburgh upon Leslie's death in 1832.

[27] See Brewster 1829.

[28] This is the title heading the essay itself. The table of contents for *EPEU* II deletes the comma and adds "—Lord Bacon's ideas concerning a final cause noticed." This is one of the essays described as being "against several modern atheists."

[29] The intended reference is presumably to Essay XIV of *EPEU* II, since the title of that essay as listed in the table of contents includes the phrase 'Why we see objects single instead of double', whereas the title of the 1828 essay does not include the term 'double' at all; as noted, however, the explanation for the phenomenon is fundamentally the same in both essays.

"Observations by Lady Mary Shepherd on the 'First Lines of the Human Mind'" (1828)

"Observations by Lady Mary Shepherd on the 'First Lines of the Human Mind'" was published, without Shepherd's prior knowledge or approval, in 1828. It is a short critique of the book *First Lines of the Human* (Fearn 1820), written by the self-taught Scottish philosopher and former naval officer John Fearn (1768–1837), and it was solicited from Shepherd by Fearn himself. It appeared in Volume I of *Parriana: or Notices of the Rev. Samuel Parr, LL.D. Collected from Various Sources, Print and Manuscript, and in Part Written by E. H. Barker, Esq. of Thetford Norfolk* (Barker 1828: 624–27). Samuel Parr (1747–1825) was a schoolmaster, minister, and writer who had been something of a mentor to Fearn, and Fearn took the opportunity of contributing to a volume of miscellaneous writings devoted to Parr's memory to publish over one hundred pages of material. Some of this was correspondence with Parr himself, but a good deal more of it was correspondence with Dugald Stewart centering on Fearn's repeated claim (already made public in *First Lines of the Human Mind*) that Stewart had dishonorably harmed him by ignoring his priority over Stewart in proposing the specific thesis that "visible figure can only arise as the result of conscious contrasting colors." Following the Stewart correspondence, Fearn turns to Shepherd's "Observations." He prefaces them with a letter to the volume editor, E. H. Barker, explaining why he is providing for publication a critique that Shepherd had sent to him, at his request, in private correspondence (Barker 1828: 622–23), and he asserts that Shepherd had left the decision about publication up to him. Following the "Observations" is his own much longer "Reply to the Criticisms of Lady Mary Shepherd on the 'First Lines'—With Observations on her Ladyship's Views with regard to the Nature of Extension, as contained in her 'Essays on the Perception of an External Universe'" (Barker 1828: 628–50). He concludes by adding a synopsis of a different book of his, on linguistics.

In the "Observations," Shepherd fully grants the truth and importance of the thesis that "visible figure can only arise as the result of conscious contrasting colors"—a thesis that also figured prominently in her own essays of 1827 and 1828 on single vision.[30] However, she emphatically rejects his further thesis *"that the sensations of color and of touch are themselves* EXTENDED *as well as the mind, in which they inhabit."* (In fact, Fearn held that the mind is an "extended

---

[30] She later indicates, in "Lady Mary Shepherd's Metaphysics" that, while she had claimed no originality for the thesis, she had written without knowledge of Fearn's assertion of it.

sphericule," i.e., small sphere.) This, she argues, confuses the sensations *of* extension that are produced in the mind with the external causes of those sensations—two very different kinds of things than must therefore have different "definitions." The latter really are extended, she argues, but the former are not; and to suppose otherwise leads to many "absurdities," such as that the sensation of a fat man is itself fat, and that having a sensation of a fat man requires more space than having the sensation of a thin man. She also rejects Fearn's further distinctive claim that the external causes of our sensations are simply "energies of the Deity."

"Lady Mary Shepherd's Metaphysics" (1832)

"Lady Mary Shepherd's Metaphysics" (included in Shepherd 2020, edited by Antonia LoLordo) was published in *Fraser's Magazine for Town and Country* in 1832. A footnote indicates that it contains "the Substance of Two Letters addressed to Mr. Fearn, originally written September 1828." Shepherd begins by expressing her surprise, and initial anxiety, at the publication in *Parriana* of "a paper, not really intended for the public eye." As described in the footnote, the article contains three elements. The first is "a Refutation of Mr. Fearn's Doctrine relative to the Extension of Mind." In addition to elaborating on her previous criticisms of the doctrine that sensations are extended, she rebuts Fearn's argument in his "Reply" in *Parriana* that she is herself committed to the mind's being really extended by her view of the omnipresence of God. Her response appeals to her definition of 'extension' as "the capacity for receiving unperceived motion." (By "unperceived motion," she means motion as it is in itself, in contrast with the *sensation* of motion.)

The second stated element of Shepherd's essay is "A Vindication of Mr. D. Stewart against the imputation of literary injustice towards Mr. Fearn." She defends Stewart's integrity on the grounds that he, like Reid but unlike Fearn, draws a sharp distinction between sensations and perceptions, so that the coincidence of his view with Fearn's is not as great as the latter supposes; she adds that Stewart likely had not attended to Fearn's views about perception because of the absurdity of the doctrine that the mind is an "extended sphericule." Shepherd then goes on, in connection with Fearn's view that the external causes of our sensations are simply "energies of the Deity," to provide a very valuable summary of many of her own positive metaphysical views.

The third and final element is "the Rectification of an erroneous allusion of Mr. Fearn's to Sir I. Newton's doctrine of Causation." In his "Reply" in *Parriana*, Fearn had interpreted Shepherd as disagreeing (at *EPEU* 148-49/288-89) with Isaac Newton's well-known statement that God may "vary the Laws of Nature, and make Worlds of several sorts in several Parts of the Universe. At least I see nothing of Contradiction in all this" (Newton 1730: 379-80). She explains that she agrees with Newton, properly interpreted, that God could have created a different world with different "laws," but only by creating different kinds of objects with different powers, not by giving different laws or powers to the kinds of objects that actually exist—which would be a contradiction.[31]

Letters (1824[?]–43)

Of the twelve letters written by Shepherd known still to exist, the majority were sent to her close friend Charles Babbage (1791–1871). He was educated at Cambridge University and later held the position there of Lucasian Professor of Mathematics (the same chair previously held by Isaac Newton) from 1828 to 1839, although he continued to live in London. He spent a considerable part of his life developing and seeking to build what he called the "Difference Engine" and the "Analytical Engine"—digital programmable machines whose design is now often regarded as the origin of computer science. Shepherd's letters to him are warmly sociable, and they demonstrate her interest in mathematics as well as her willingness to press her own philosophical views in detail.

Three of the letters were written to William Whewell (1794–1866), whom her daughter described as one of the "persons who, besides my father, most thoroughly entered into my mother's mind and followed where she led into great and wide depths of abstract enquiry" (Brandreth 1886: 119). The son of working-class parents, he excelled as a student at Cambridge and rose through positions as a lecturer in mathematics and Professor of Minerology to become the Knightsbridge Professor of Moral Theology, Casuistical Divinity, and Moral Philosophy (as the position was then called); from 1841, he served as Master of Trinity College, and twice took a turn as Vice Chancellor of the University. Now regarded as the pre-eminent British philosopher of science prior to John Stuart Mill, he had an impressive command of the history of the various sciences and sought to introduce broadly Kantian

---

[31] For an analysis of the exchange with Fearn, see Atherton 2005.

a priori elements into his account of reasoning about the world. Each of the three existing letters from Shepherd was sent at least partly to thank Whewell for sending publications, on which she always comments.

The final letter was sent to Robert Blakey (1795–1878), a writer, philosopher, and political radical who published two books on moral science and a four-volume *History of the Philosophy of Mind* (Blakey 1848); he also served from 1849 to 1851 as Professor of Logic and Metaphysics at Queen's College, Belfast. The letter concerns specifically her inclusion in his *History of the Philosophy of Mind*, but Blakey reports in his memoirs that

> I had, about this period, several personal interviews with Lady Mary Shepherd, who had written, some years before, on metaphysical topics, with no inconsiderable portion of credit to herself. . . . Her lengthened sentences, uttered with great distinction, were quite stunning, and filled one with amazement at the subtility of her mind. (Blakey 1879: 160)

He comments that the letter reprinted there is only one "among others received from her."

Indeed, the evidence shows that Shepherd must have written other letters of philosophical interest that are now destroyed or lost as well. For example, although a portion of Letter 2 anticipates to some extent the content of Essay V of *EPEU* Part II, her explanatory footnote at *EPEU* 159n1/314n implies that other essays may have involved additional correspondence with friends as well. Her daughter's memoir mentions a series of "long letters" over several years between Shepherd and the scientist and philosopher Thomas Forster (Brandreth 1886: 114), and it includes brief letters to Shepherd from Sir William Henry Maule (a prominent judge), Sydney Smith, and Richard Whately—with all but Whately writing in response to their receiving or reading *ERCE* (Brandreth 1886: 206–10). Tantalizingly, the memoir also mentions having a letter "from Elizabeth Barrett [Browning] to my Mother, with some remarks on one of her metaphysical Essays" (Brandreth 1886: 182). In *Parriana*, John Fearn alludes to correspondence prior to the publication of "Observations by Lady Mary Shepherd on the 'First Lines of the Human Mind,'" and "Lady Mary Shepherd's Metaphysics" summarizes two letters that she wrote to him subsequently. Letter 9, to Whewell, mentions a letter to the mathematician and scientist Mary Somerville concerning induction and instinctive belief. It is therefore to be hoped that additional letters may still be found.

AN ESSAY UPON THE RELATION OF CAUSE AND EFFECT,

CONTROVERTING THE DOCTRINE OF MR. HUME,
CONCERNING THE NATURE OF THAT RELATION;

WITH OBSERVATIONS UPON THE OPINIONS OF DR. BROWN
AND MR. LAWRENCE,
CONNECTED WITH THE SAME SUBJECT.

LONDON: PRINTED FOR T. HOOKHAM,
OLD BOND STREET, 1824.

ADVERTISEMENT TO THE READER.

In the work now presented to the public, I have endeavoured to set down the suggestions, which at different times have occurred to me upon the theory of the relation of Cause and Effect, adopted by Mr. Hume, Dr. Brown, and Mr. Lawrence; and to unfold the train of reasoning which has led me to regard their arguments as illogical, and their conclusions as untrue.

I am fully aware of the difficulties attending such an undertaking, arising both from the popularity of those authors, as well as from the nature of the subject.

Every one must be conscious that the particular forms of expression, in which thoughts of an abstruse and subtle nature are introduced to the imagination, and grow familiar there, are so intimately associated with them, as to appear their just and accurate representative.—But these forms of expression, though clear and satisfactory to the person in whose mind they are so associated, may yet fail in conveying the same ideas with sufficient precision to the understandings of others. In the statement of facts, in moral discussions, in declamation or poetry, this inconvenience can scarcely arise, since they rarely present to an intelligent reader any image which has not under some modification previously passed through his mind, and is not connected with his reflections or experience. But in the subtlety of metaphysics it is otherwise; and moreover, language which was originally framed to suit the commonest occasions of life, is ill fitted, even under the application of the most accomplished intellect, to express the nice abstractions of that science.

These difficulties are the only excuse I can offer for many obscurities of expression, which I fear will be found in the following dissertation, which consists of little more than marginal observations, upon what I cannot but regard as fallacies of the above-mentioned writers, without any pretence of composition or laboured arrangement.

PREFACE.

It is attempted, in the following pages, to controvert Mr. Hume's doctrine on the "Nature of the Relation of Cause and Effect," as set forth in several sections of his "Treatise on Human Nature;"[1] and as confirmed in three sections of his "Essays."[2] —The former work is taken notice of only in as far as it forms a foundation for the latter. But, in as much as some propositions are taken for granted in these latter sections, which serve as the support of all the argument, it could neither be so well answered, nor brought so clearly within the reader's comprehension, as by exposing the fallacies of those assumed premises on which it is founded, and which are to be found at large in the earlier work.

In this respect, Mr. Hume cannot fairly avail himself of the higher esteem he has called upon us to grant to his "Essays" above his juvenile "Treatise;"[3] for, as the conclusions are the same in the Essays as in the Treatise, and as the *medium* arguments used in the Essays are the *conclusions drawn in consequence of great detail of previous discussion in the Treatise*, it is both fair and necessary to examine these details.

It may be, as is hinted in the Advertisement to the Essays,—"that *these details* contain some of those *negligent reasonings that he could have wished not to acknowledge in after life.*"

I shall not, however, readily allow of the advantage of such an excuse; for, as long as the premises that support his matured opinions are only to be found regularly deduced in this unacknowledged work, it is incumbent upon one attempting an Answer to expose them; for, there is no little art, in refusing to adopt the "negligent reasonings of youth," in a state of advanced judgment, yet covertly making use of a material proposition (that might pass as true, even in many an acute mind, in reading these popular and elegant Essays), which is only supported by the sophistical reasonings of the youthful

---

[1] [Shepherd is referring to David Hume's *A Treatise of Human Nature* (Hume 1817). I henceforth cite this work as *Treatise*; see Short Titles and Forms of Citation in this volume.]

[2] ["Essays" refers to David Hume's *An Enquiry concerning Human Understanding*, which was initially published as *Philosophical Essays concerning Human Understanding* and subsequently included (under the revised title) in his *Essays and Treatises on Several Subjects* (Hume 1800). I henceforth cite this work as *Enquiry*. See Short Titles and Forms of Citation in this volume.]

[3] [In a 1776 "Advertisement" added to Volume II (containing *An Enquiry concerning Human Understanding*) of existing and subsequent editions of his *Essays and Treatises on Several Subjects*, Hume describes *A Treatise of Human Nature* as a "juvenile work, which the Author never acknowledged" and declares that "Henceforth, the Author desires, that the following Pieces may alone be regarded as containing his philosophical sentiments and principles." The "Advertisement" is discussed and quoted more fully in the introduction to this volume.]

Treatise, and is evidently adopted in consequence of them. It is also possible, that Mr. Hume might not intend to deny his opinions, in every particular that regarded these points, as he continued to hold the consequential doctrine deduced from them; therefore there may be the less infringement upon the wish he expresses, "*not to be considered as publicly avowing any doctrine not contained in his latter Essays.*"

"That Nature may be conceived to alter her course, without a contradiction,"[4] is the material proposition (elicited in the Treatise, and subsequently assumed in the Essays), on account of which the reader's patience is principally intended to be intruded upon; and which is mentioned in this place, in order that he may perceive the importance of its investigation, previously to his consideration of the more avowed objects brought under his notice, in the answers to the three sections of the Essays, entitled, "Sceptical Doubts concerning the operations of the Understanding;"—"Sceptical Solutions of these Doubts;" and "Of the Idea of necessary Connexion."[5]

The doctrines contained in these last, lead directly to a scepticism of an atheistical tendency, whose dangerous nature can require no comment, nor any apology for its refutation. Nevertheless, did there seem but sound argument for their support, whatever might be the unhappiness of the opinions that could be inferred from them, I would leave them unnoticed and uncontroverted, imagining there might possibly be an error in the argument, beyond the reach of my discovery; and should content myself in withholding an assent to propositions which my understanding might be unable to refute. Nor at this time of day does the intention of entering into this controversy appear to be useless. It is not many years since Mr. Hume's notions were the occasion of much dispute, on the very ground on which I have undertaken it; a dispute which nearly lost the mathematical chair in one of our universities to the present possessor of it, on account of his favouring this doctrine. His opinion, however, as far as it related to any countenance it might afford to the principles of atheism, was defended from the insinuation, by a learned treatise, from the then Professor of Moral Philosophy in the same university.[6]

---

[4] [Shepherd is loosely paraphrasing *Treatise* 1.3.6.5: "We can at least conceive a change in the course of nature; which sufficiently proves, that such a change is not absolutely impossible."]

[5] [These are, respectively, *Enquiry* Sections 4, 5, and 7.]

[6] [Shepherd is referring to the so-called Leslie Affair of 1805 at the University of Edinburgh. The "present possessor" to whom Shepherd refers is John Leslie (1766–1832), although he had actually exchanged the Chair of Mathematics for that of Natural Philosophy in 1819, five years before the publication of *ERCE*. The "then Professor of Moral Philosophy" to whom she refers is Thomas Brown (1778–1820), although he actually became Professor of Moral Philosophy only in 1810. The "learned treatise" is Brown's *Observations on the Nature and Tendency of the Doctrine of Mr. Hume, concerning*

This treatise, whilst it controverts Mr. Hume's opinions in some respects, denies that atheistical inferences may be deduced from them: but I shall endeavour to show, that, in this respect, the author wanted observation and acuteness: neither perceiving the corollaries that go along with the doctrine, nor detecting the sly and powerful sophistry of the reasoning by which they are supported.

Also a modern and living author, of great celebrity, Mr. Lawrence, in his late Lectures,[7] has adopted Mr. Hume's and Dr. Brown's notions of the relation of cause and effect, as containing a proof of the materiality of the soul;— a doctrine of sufficient importance to justify a further investigation of the argument on which it is supposed to be well founded.

In every controversial work, much obscurity appears in an author's arguments, on account of the opinions of his adversary not being distinctly understood; owing either to partial quotation, or mistaken statement: I therefore mean to obviate all chance of any misunderstanding on that ground, by giving the adversary's opinions upon the controverted doctrine in his own words; taking care to leave out only extraneous matter, and to alter the arrangement in such a manner as to form at once a clear and concise, a fair and intelligible view of the whole subject.

---

the Relation of Cause and Effect, second edition, enlarged (Brown 1806). For details and explanation, see the discussion of ERCE in the introduction to this volume. I henceforth cite this work as Oberservations.]

[7] [Shepherd is referring to William Lawrence's Lectures on Physiology, Zoology, and the Natural History of Man, delivered at the Royal College of Surgeons by W. Lawrence, F.R.S. (Lawrence 1819), which she later calls his "Physiological Lectures." I henceforth cite this work as Lectures.]

AN ESSAY, &c.

INTRODUCTORY CHAPTER.

The plan I mean to adopt, in order to give a clear view of Mr. Hume's doctrine of the relation of Cause and Effect, in the most concise manner possible, is; first to arrange such quotations from the "Treatise of Human Nature," as will show the opinions there held; and afterwards select some others from the "Essays," in which they are corroborated, and enlarged upon; and which will be sufficient to show, that the doctrines contained in the Treatise are there repeated; with the *addition* of an application of them to the affairs of ordinary life; as affording a ground of scepticism concerning the powers of the understanding having any part to perform in the regulation of her expectations.

The quotations from the Treatise will first show, "what is the doctrine enquired into;" Secondly, the argument, by which Mr. Hume attempts to confute the opinion of the necessity of a Cause, for every beginning of existence; and also the argument he employs in aid of his own doctrine, concerning the ideas we have of the *necessary connexion of Cause and Effect*; and of the *belief* there is placed in such necessary connexion.—Thirdly, the definition of the relation of Cause and Effect; this definition being the object aimed at by the whole argument.

The doctrine enquired into is the necessary connexion of Cause and Effect, and is divided into these two general propositions or queries;

First, "For what reason we pronounce it necessary, that every thing whose existence has a beginning should also have a Cause?"

Secondly, "Why we conclude, that such particular Causes must necessarily have such particular Effects; and what is the nature of that inference we draw from the one to the other, and of the belief we repose in it[8]?"

Mr. Hume's method of answering these questions is by adopting a new and sceptical view of the subject, and by attempting to confute those philosophers who were of a different opinion from himself concerning it, by asserting, that it is "neither *intuitively* nor *demonstratively* certain that every thing which begins to exist must have a cause; for in order to show that neither intuition, nor demonstration, proves the maxim that *whatever begins to*

---

[8] See Treatise on Human Nature, Vol. 1, Part 3. Concluding Sentences of Sect. 2d, page 116. Sect. 3d, 5th, 6th, 7th, part of Sect. 8th, page 150 to end. [The quoted "queries" are from *Treatise* 1.3.2.14 and 1.3.2.15, respectively. *Treatise* 1.3.3 begins to address the first query, while Shepherd treats *Treatise* 1.3.5–7 and 1.3.8.13–17 (perhaps also including 1.3.8.12) as addressing the second.]

exist must have a cause for existence, let us consider that all certainty arises from a comparison of ideas, and from the discovery of such relations, as are unalterable so long as the ideas continue the same. These relations are, resemblance, proportions in quantity, degrees of any quality, and contrariety; none of which are implied in this proposition, *whatever has a beginning has also a cause of existence*; that proposition therefore is not intuitively certain." "That the proposition is incapable of demonstrative proof, we may satisfy ourselves by considering that all *distinct* ideas are *separable from each other*; and as the ideas are separable from each other, and as the ideas of Cause and Effect are evidently distinct, it will be easy for us to *conceive* any object to be *non-existent this moment and to be existent the next*, without conjoining to it the distinct idea of a Cause, a productive principle." "The separation therefore of the idea of a cause, from that of a beginning of existence, is plainly possible for the imagination, and consequently the *actual* separation of these objects is so far possible, that it implies no contradiction, nor absurdity; and is, therefore, incapable of being refuted by any reasoning, from mere ideas; without which it is impossible to demonstrate the necessity of a cause." "Accordingly every demonstration which has been produced for the necessity of a cause, is *fallacious and sophistical.* They all presuppose the existence that begins to be an *effect*; but this does not prove that *every sort of being must have a Cause*."[9]

"As the opinion, therefore, that every existence must have a Cause, is not derived from knowledge, or scientific reasoning, it must necessarily arise from observation and experience; the next question therefore is, *how experience gives rise to such a principle?* This question I shall sink in the following: Why we conclude that such particular causes must necessarily have such particular effects? Because the *same answer will serve for both questions.*"[10]

The next subject, therefore, which is considered is "necessary connexion;" where it is shown in what way *experience* becomes the foundation of our expectations of similar effects rising from similar causes. The reader must remember that this discussion is supposed to contain the answer to the question, concerning the idea we have of the necessity of a Supreme Cause; else he might be apt to forget that he has the author's authority for considering the *custom and habit of the mind, arising from an association of ideas, as the only ground of our belief* in the necessity of a *cause* for the beginning of any

---

[9] [Shepherd's characterizations of Hume's claims in this paragraph are drawn, often with identical wording, from *Treatise* 1.3.3.1–4. The final sentence, however, is a summary that does not directly correspond to any passage in the text.]

[10] [Shepherd is slightly paraphrasing, with an omission, *Treatise* 1.3.3.9.]

existence; and consequently for any notion of the necessity for a great Author, Contriver, and Arranger of the universe.

Mr. Hume goes on, "The next question therefore is, whether experience *produces* the idea by means of the *understanding* or *the imagination*, whether we are determined by *reason* to make the transition, or by a certain association (of ideas) and relation of perceptions."[11]

"If reason determined us, it would be on this principle—*That instances of which we have had no experience must resemble those of which we have had experience; for that the course of nature continues uniformly the same.* Now there can be no demonstrative arguments to prove that those instances of which we have had no experience resemble those of which we have had experience."[12]

15 "*We can at least imagine a change in the course of nature*; reason therefore can never show us the connexion of one object with another, though aided by experience; when, therefore, the mind passes from the *idea* or *impression* of one object to the idea or belief of another, it is not by *reason*, but by certain principles, which *associate together the ideas of these objects*, and unite them in the *imagination*.—The inference, therefore, solely depends on the *union of ideas*;[13]—for,

"After we have observed resemblance in a sufficient number of instances, we immediately feel a determination of the mind to pass from one object to its usual attendant, and to consider it in a stronger light on account of that relation. The several instances of resembling connection lead us into the notion of *power and necessity*."

16 "Necessary connexion, therefore, is the effect of this observation, and is nothing but an internal action of the mind, or a determination to carry our thoughts from one object to another."[14]

"The efficacy or energy of Cause, therefore, is neither placed in the Causes themselves, nor in the Deity, nor in the concurrence of these two principles, but belongs entirely to the soul, which considers the union of two or more objects in all past instances. Thus objects have no discoverable connexion together, nor is it from any other principle, but *custom operating on the imagination*, that we can draw any inference from the appearance of one, to the

---

[11] [Shepherd is quoting almost exactly from *Treatise* 1.3.6.4.]

[12] [Shepherd is drawing from *Treatise* 1.3.6.4 and 1.3.6.5.]

[13] [Shepherd's initial clause quotes *Treatise* 1.3.6.5 (replacing 'conceive' with 'imagine'), while the remainder of the passage draws closely on *Treatise* 1.3.6.12.]

[14] [In these two short paragraphs, which are intended to continue the preceding quotation, Shepherd is quoting with some changes ('necessary connexion' for 'necessity') and omissions from *Treatise* 1.3.14.20.]

existence of the other; and all BELIEF in this connexion consists *only* in a lively idea *associated to a present impression;* for belief is nothing but an idea that is different from a fiction in the *manner* of its being conceived. *A present impression,* transports the mind to such ideas as are related to it, and communicates to them a share of its *force* and *vivacity.*"[15] The definition of the relation of Cause and Effect, follows this analysis of it; and may be observed to be conformable to this notion of a *custom of the mind* being its only foundation.

Thus, 3dly, "We shall now give a precise definition of Cause and Effect.— There may be two definitions given of this relation, which are only different views of the same object, and make us consider it either as a philosophical or as a natural relation: either as a comparison of two ideas, or an association between them."

"We may define a cause to be *an object precedent and contiguous to another, and where all the objects resembling the former are placed in like relations of precedency and contiguity to those objects that resemble the latter.* In the latter sense, *a cause is an object precedent and contiguous to another, and so united with it, that the idea of the one determines the mind to form the idea of the other, and the impression of the one to form a more lively idea of the other.*"[16]

I now refer the reader to the three Sections already mentioned, as found in the 2d Vol. of Mr. Hume's "Essays;" namely,

"Sceptical Doubts concerning the operations of the Understanding."

"Sceptical Solutions of these Doubts;" and, "Of the Idea of necessary Connexion."

From these I have arranged some Extracts that will enable us to observe that these doctrines are repeated there, with the addition of an application of them to the affairs of ordinary life, as affording a ground of scepticism concerning the powers of the understanding, in the regulation of its expectations.

That "Nature may be conceived to alter her course, without a contradiction,"[17] is the material proposition in both Essays; used as an *argument* to prove, that it is "*custom*" only which forces the "imagination" to *fancy* there is a "necessary connexion between Cause and Effect," with a liveliness, and vivacity of conception, equal to a *firm belief founded on reason.* In the Essays, *the whole of these notions* are supposed to derive their support from the

---

[15] [Shepherd quotes the first sentence of this paragraph with only minor changes from *Treatise* 1.3.14.23. The second sentence draws from *Treatise* 1.3.8.12, 1.3.7.5, 1.3.7.7, and 1.3.8.2.]

[16] [These two paragraphs draw from the last sentence of *Treatise* 1.3.14.30 and the first portion of *Treatise* 1.3.14.31.]

[17] [*Treatise* 1.3.6.5 states: "We can at least conceive a change in the course of nature." *Enquiry* 4.28 states: "It implies no contradiction, that the course of nature may change."]

argument, that as we have no knowledge, either *à priori*, or *à posteriori*, concerning the "secrets of Nature;" so our observation of the action of a Cause, affords no ground for the conclusions of reason respecting it.

That the idea of causation is only derived from custom, becomes therefore the premises from which the conclusion is deduced, that "beings can begin their existences of themselves;" which proposition, though not formally repeated in the Essays (and which immediately renders void that for the necessity of a great first Cause, and "*productive principle*" of all things), must tacitly in these Essays be considered as well grounded, because, *as every* foundation whatever, for supposing *any cause* necessary for *any effect*, is denied, and only an influence of "custom on the imagination" is allowed as suggesting a "*fancy of it*[18];" it necessarily follows, that nothing beyond what this influence suggests can be assigned as any reason why there should be any productive principle for all the contrivances and ends that take place in the universe; it must therefore, I think, be understood that this "juvenile reasoning" was adopted, and acknowledged but too surely, in the latter Essays.

The extracts from the "Essays" are intended to be a counter-part to those taken from the "Treatise," which "show the argument Mr. Hume employs in favour of his own doctrine concerning the necessary connexion of Cause and Effect, and of the Belief reposed in it."[19]—As also the definitions of this relation, which the notions give rise to, and which, with a single exception, will be observed to be little varied from the former ones.

I begin the subject with those reasonings which are reckoned the support of the main argument, "Nature may be conceived to alter her course, without a contradiction."

First.—Says Mr. Hume[20], "I shall venture to affirm, as a general proposition, which admits of no exception, that the knowledge of the relation of Cause and Effect is not in any instance attained *à priori*. Experience then is the foundation of all our reasonings concerning that relation."

"And, as the first imagination of a particular Effect is *arbitrary*, where we consult not experience; *so must we also esteem the supposed tie or connexion between the Cause and Effect which binds them together*, and renders it impossible that any other Effect could result from the operation of that Cause[21]."

---

[18] Had ideas no more *union in the fancy*, than objects seem to have to the understanding, we could never draw any inference from Causes to Effects, nor repose belief in any matter of fact.—See Treatise on Human Nature, vol. i. part 3d, p. 134 [*Treatise* 1.3.6.12].

[19] [Shepherd is closely paraphrasing from *ERCE* 36/10 of this Introductory Chapter.]

[20] Hume's Essays, Vol. 2, Part 1, Sect. 4th, p. 27, 33, 37, &c. [*Enquiry* 4.6, 4.14–15, 4.20, etc.] Part of Sect. 5. [*Enquiry* 5] Sect. 7 [*Enquiry* 7].

[21] Ibid. p. 30 [*Enquiry* 4.10].

Secondly,—"After Experience of the operations of Cause and Effect, our conclusions from that experience are not founded on reasoning, or any process of the understanding; for Nature has kept us at a great distance from all her secrets, and has afforded us only the knowledge of a few superficial qualities of objects, while she conceals from us those powers and principles on which the influence of these objects entirely depends."[22]

Thirdly.—"But notwithstanding this ignorance of natural powers and principles, we always presume, when we see like sensible qualities, that they have like secret powers, and expect that Effects similar to those we have experienced, will flow from them." "This is a process of the mind or thought of which I would willingly know the foundation;" "but enumerating all the branches of human knowledge, I shall endeavour to show that none of them can afford an argument, whence reason may draw a conclusion, that the future must necessarily resemble the past; for all reasonings may be divided into two kinds; namely, demonstrative reasoning, and that concerning matter of fact and experience. That there are no demonstrative arguments in the case seems evident, since it implies *no contradiction that the course of nature may change*; and that an object seemingly like those we have experienced may be attended with different or contrary effects;"[23]—for,

"May I not clearly and distinctly conceive that a body falling from the clouds, and which in *all other* respects resembles snow, may have the taste of salt, or feeling of fire. Is there any more intelligible proposition than to affirm, that all the trees will flourish in December and January, and decay in May and June?"[24] "The bread which I formerly ate nourished me; but does it follow that other bread must also nourish me, &c.?"[25]

"From causes which appear similar we expect similar effects—this is the sum of all our experimental conclusions—but it seems evident that if this conclusion were formed by reason, it would be as perfect at first, and upon one instance, as after ever so long a course of experience; but the case is far otherwise."[26]

"Nothing so like as eggs; yet no one, on account of this apparent similarity, expects the same taste and relish in all of them. Now, where is that process of reasoning, which from one instance draws a conclusion so different from

---

[22] [Shepherd is combining statements from *Enquiry* 4.15 and *Enquiry* 4.16.]
[23] [Shepherd is drawing, with minor additions, on *Enquiry* 4.16–18.]
[24] [Shepherd is quoting almost exactly from *Enquiry* 4.18. She puts a period after 'fire' where Hume has a question mark.]
[25] [Shepherd is quoting, with an omission, from *Enquiry* 4.16.]
[26] [Shepherd is quoting with only minor changes from *Enquiry* 4.20.]

that which it infers from a hundred others? When a man says, I have found in all past instances such sensible qualities conjoined with such secret powers, and when he says, similar sensible qualities will *always* be attended with similar secret powers, he is not guilty of a tautology, nor are these propositions in any respect the same. You say the one proposition is an inference from the other; but you must confess the inference is not intuitive, nor yet is it demonstrative; of what nature is it then?"[27]

25 "This principle is custom and habit: for wherever the repetition of any particular act produces a propensity to renew the act, we always say this propensity is the effect of custom. Custom is the great guide of human life; and when we say, therefore, that one object is connected with another, we mean only they have acquired a *connexion in our thoughts*; and *our belief* (in this necessary connexion,) is *nothing more* than a conception more intense and steady than attends the fictions of the imagination; and this manner of conception arises from a *customary conjunction* with something present to the memory or the senses."[28]

The definition of the relation of Cause and Effect is much the same as in the "Treatise;" it is this:

"We may define a Cause to be an object *followed* by another; and where all the objects similar to the first are followed by objects similar to the second; or, in other words, where, if the first object had not been, the second never had existed."

26 And again, he has a third definition: "The appearance of a cause always conveys the mind by a customary transition to the idea of the effect. Of this also we have experience; we may therefore form another definition of a cause, and call it an object followed by another, and whose appearance always conveys the thought to that other."[29]

---

[27] [Shepherd is drawing from *Enquiry* 4.20 and the latter part of *Enquiry* 4.21.]

[28] [Shepherd is combining, with some changes, material from (in order) *Enquiry* 5.5, 5.6, 7.28, and 5.13. In the context of *Enquiry* 5.13, Hume's examples of beliefs arising from customary conjunction are beliefs in particular "matters of fact," such as the impending movement of a billiard ball. Neither there nor elsewhere does he write specifically of "belief in [a] necessary connexion." However, he does often refer to the ascription or supposition of a necessary connection between cause and effect, and holds that the idea of necessary connection arises only after experience of constant conjunction and a transition of thought due to custom.]

[29] [Shepherd is quoting these definitions almost exactly from *Enquiry* 7.29. She counts Hume as giving *three* definitions of 'cause' because she treats the phrase 'or, in other words, where, if the first object had not been, the second never had existed' as a *second* definition. Hume, in contrast, treats this phrase simply as a part of or a commentary on the first definition, which he has just given in the preceding portion of the sentence; hence, he treats what Shepherd calls his "third definition" as his second and last definition (for example, by including it in his subsequent reference to "both definitions").]

CHAPTER THE SECOND.

HAVING now made an abstract of Mr. Hume's Treatise and Essays on the subject of the relation of Cause and Effect, I shall proceed to examine each part in as regular an order as I conveniently can; and endeavour to answer the two questions first proposed, in a more popular, and, I hope, not more illogical method than Mr. Hume has followed, by attempting to prove,

FIRST, That *reason*, not *fancy* and "custom" leads us to the knowledge, That every thing which begins to exist must have a Cause.—SECONDLY, That *reason* forces the mind to perceive, that *similar causes* must necessarily produce *similar effects.*—THIRDLY, I shall thence establish a more philosophical definition of the relation of Cause and Effect.—FOURTHLY, show, in what respects Mr. Hume's definition is faulty.—FIFTHLY, proceed to prove that Nature cannot be supposed to alter her Course without a contradiction in terms; and, finally, show, that *Custom and Habit* alone are not our guides; but chiefly reason, for the regulation of our expectations in ordinary life.

After this, I shall endeavour to point out some material faults in Dr. Brown's reasoning, tending rather to support Mr. Hume's erroneous arguments, than to repel them: arguments which Mr. Lawrence avails himself of, in the Physiological Lectures, at present before the public; which have drawn so much of its Notice; and upon which I shall not consider it irrelevant to make a few remarks.

SECTION THE FIRST.

First, then, let me show, why Mr. Hume's argument, in favour of the possibility of beings commencing their own existence is sophistical; as well as his attempted confutation of those philosophers who have argued to the contrary. Mr. Hume says, the proposition, "that whatever has a beginning, has also a Cause of existence," cannot be demonstrated, because the ideas of Cause and Effect are "distinct" and "separable;" and it will be easy to conceive "any object to be non-existent this minute," and "existent the next;" without "conjoining to it the idea of a Cause, or a productive principle."[1]—This imagination is plausible, and may perhaps appear well founded until thoroughly sifted. On a first impression, Causes and their Effects may seem separable, because two things are mentioned; one is distinct from the other, and may be *imagined* separated from it.

They may also *seem* to follow one another, and *time* to elapse between the *operation of the Cause*, and the *appearance of the Effect*; so that during the interval of the supposed period, the effect might be *imagined in suspense*,[2] and so indifferent to existence or non-existence; but upon a strict and rigid attention to the real nature of a thing in opposition to its accidental appearances, one cannot, for a moment, suppose that the circumstances here mentioned, namely, of antecedency of Cause and subsequency of Effect; or of that *distinctness of language* which occasions two words to be used for two ideas; should in any degree render it possible for causes and their effects to exist apart in nature. That it is impossible for them to do so, without involving a direct contradiction in terms, is a proposition I hope to prove in the course of this Essay.

But before examining into this notion, concerning the possibility of effects being held in suspense, and then of being liable to begin their own existence, or, in Mr. Hume's words, "of the separation of the idea of a cause from that of a beginning of existence,"[3] it will be necessary to render the expressions in which it is conveyed more intelligible. This can in no way be done so long as the *definition of the word effect* presupposes a cause; for the supposition of the objection lies, in its being possible for *effects* to be held in suspense: but in order that this should be possible, the meaning of the word *effect* must be altered. Then, if the ideas are altered that lie under the term, according as the varied occasion seems to require, there can be no philosophy; and it never can be insisted on, that the *effects*, which are *supposed to be conjoined* with their causes at one period of time; and to require, in order to their exhibition, those causes or others; and to receive the name of *effects*, on account of requiring

---

[1] [Shepherd is drawing from *Treatise* 1.3.3.1–3. Hume uses the phrase 'productive principle' as a synonym for 'cause' in *Treatise* 1.3.3.3, 1.3.3.5, 1.4.5.1, and 2.1.2.4; Shepherd invokes it often for the same purpose.]

[2] [Hume writes in *Treatise* 1.3.3.4: "The points of time and place, say some philosophers, in which we can suppose any object to begin to exist, are in themselves equal; and unless there be some cause, which is peculiar to one time and to one place, and which by that means determines and fixes the existence, it must remain in eternal suspence." This is his only use of the term 'suspense' or 'suspence' in connection with causation. In a footnote, Hume cites Thomas Hobbes as an intended referent.]

[3] [Shepherd takes this phrase from *Treatise* 1.3.3.3.]

causes; can again, upon another occasion, not be *effects*, not require *causes*, be held in suspense, and be *imagined* capable *of beginning their existence by themselves*, without conjoining to them the distinct idea of any "productive principle."—It might as well be reckoned sound reasoning, after defining the figure 2 to be a sign signifying that two units are necessary to its composition, to maintain, that because it stands *singly*, it can be *imagined an unit itself*, without a contradiction; so that it *does not* stand in need of 2 units to its composition:—that is, a word may be taken in two contradictory senses, and then it may be reasonable to predicate of each, affections that belong only to the other; and so to form any contradictory scheme in the world. To make, therefore, any thing like a rational meaning in this sentence of Mr. Hume's, nothing more can be intended by it, than that we should imagine, those existences which we always observe conjoined with others in such a manner, that they *appear* to be their effects, properties, or qualities, to owe them *no real existence or dependence*; and therefore capable of being independent objects, and of beginning their own existence. In like manner, it may be said of *causes*, that although the word signifies something calculated to introduce a certain quality, yet that in fact it does not introduce a new quality; thus naming the object in one sense, and imagining its essence in another sense.

This also is as though we should agree to designate each unit by the figure 1; and to assert, that the union of two units introduces a compound notion, which shall be made known by the sign 2; and on account of this relation, the union of the units shall be called the cause of the compound quality two, under a single term; and the sign 2 shall be named its *effect*; and afterwards assert, that we can *imagine* the *cause*, that is the *union of the two units*, to exist without, and separate from, the effect, the result 2. All this cannot take place whilst we assign the same meaning to our words; and if we use the terms in different senses, there can be no philosophy.—Therefore, to make any meaning whatever of the proposition, "We may imagine causes to exist separate from their effects;"[4] the objects we call *causes* are not to be imagined as *causes*, but may be supposed *not to cause any thing*, but to exist without *determining their own effects*, or *any others*; that is, causes and their effects are so evidently distinct, that they may be imagined to be unconnected objects, that are *not causes and effects*, and to exist separately without a contradiction, though they are named expressly as signs of the ideas we have, that they are necessary to one another.

---

[4] [Shepherd is loosely paraphrasing *Treatise* 1.3.3.3.]

Thus, the original question, namely, "Whether every thing which begins to exist requires a cause for its existence?"[5] resolves itself into two others; viz.

First, Whether objects called EFFECTS, necessarily require causes for their existence? or, whether they may begin to exist with, or without them indifferently?—As also,

Secondly, Whether any objects whatever, without being considered as having the *nature of effects*, can begin their existences?

It may be plainly seen, that the first of these questions is sunk in the latter, because, if objects *usually considered as effects* need not be considered as effects, then they are forced to begin their existences *of themselves*: for, conjoined or not to their causes, we know by our senses that they do begin to exist: we will, therefore, immediately hasten to the consideration of the second question, which may be stated in the following terms: Whether every object which begins to exist must owe its existence to a cause?

Let the object which we suppose to begin its existence of itself be imagined, abstracted from the nature of all objects we are acquainted with, saving in its capacity for existence; let us suppose it to be *no effect*; there shall be no prevening[6] circumstances whatever that affect it, nor any existence in the universe: let it be so; let there be nought but a blank; and a mass of whatsoever can be supposed not to require a cause START FORTH into existence, and make the first breach on the wide nonentity around;—now, what is this starting forth, beginning, coming into existence, but an action, which is a quality of an object not yet in being, and so not possible to have its qualities determined, nevertheless exhibiting its qualities?

If, indeed, it should be shown, that there is no proposition whatever taken as a ground on which to build an argument in this question, neither one conclusion nor the other can be supported; and there need be no attempt at reasoning.—But, if my adversary allows that, no existence being supposed previously in the universe, existence, in order to be, must *begin to be*, and that the notion of *beginning an action* (the being that *begins* it not supposed yet in existence), involves a *contradiction in terms*; then this *beginning* to exist cannot appear but as a *capacity some nature hath* to alter the presupposed nonentity, and to act for itself, whilst itself is not in being.—The original assumption may deny, as much as it pleases, all cause of existence; but, whilst in

---

[5] [The first of two questions posed by Hume in *Treatise* 1.2.14–15 is, "For what reason we pronounce it *necessary*, that every thing whose existence has a beginning, shou'd also have a cause?" This question then constitutes the main topic of *Treatise* 1.3.3, "*Why a cause is always necessary.*"]

[6] ['Prevene', a chiefly Scottish term that is now obsolete, meant "to precede or come before."]

its very idea, the commencement of existence is an effect predicated of some supposed *cause, (because the quality of an object* which must be *in existence to possess it,)* we must conclude that *there is no object which begins to exist, but must owe its existence to some cause.*

For this reason it is, that the answers to Dr. Clarke and Mr. Locke are unsound, in as far as they are an endeavour to show, that their arguments are altogether sophistical.—Mr. Hume objects to them, that the existence supposed to begin by itself, "is not to be considered as an *effect*; and that these authors assume what is not granted, viz. that the existence in question requires *a cause*;" as where Dr. Clarke shows it is an absurdity to imagine an object its *own cause*, and Mr. Locke asserts that it is equally so, to conceive of *nothing* as a cause.[7] It is undoubtedly true, that these authors assumed that which was in question; namely, that every existence must have a cause: but, as every thing not yet in existence, *to exist at all*, must *begin*, and as the *beginning* of any thing must always be supposed, by the *nature of the action*, to be a quality of something in existence, which existence is yet DENIED by the statement of the question, these philosophers felt the involved absurdity so great, that they passed over the first question as too ridiculous, probably, to consider formally; then showed, that the mind of man was forced to look upon all things which begin to exist as *dependent* QUALITIES; and thus, that an object could neither depend upon *itself for existence*, nor yet upon *nothing*.

Let it be remembered, too, that although Mr. Hume inveighs against this method as sophistical, by conceiving it begs the question, yet his own argument, the whole way, consists in the possibility of imagining an *effect* "*non-existent* this minute," and "existing the next;" and does not himself consider any other "sort of being" possible; and has no other way of supporting his own notion of the beginning of existence by itself, except under the *idea of an effect in suspense*; which is still a *relative term*, and begs the question for the necessity of its correlative, i.e. its *cause*, just as much as he asserts his adversaries do, whom he declares to be illogical reasoners.

If then (as I hope I have shown) all objects whatever, which *begin to exist*, must owe their *existence to some cause*, those we usually consider as *effects* CANNOT be held in suspense; suddenly alter their nature; be "*non-existent* this minute, and existent the next;" and, though always introduced as *qualities of*

---

[7] [Shepherd is paraphrasing Hume's criticisms, at *Treatise* 1.3.3.5–8, of Samuel Clarke (1775–1829) and John Locke (1632–1704). Hume mentions each in a footnote, but provides no citations. He is evidently referring to Clarke 1998: 12 and *Essay* 4.10.3, respectively.]

other objects, be easily separated from the ideas of their causes, and require no "productive principle."

"That Cause and Effect are distinct and separable;" so "that any object may be conceived, as therefore *capable of beginning its own existence*,"[8] must be considered as among the notions adopted in *the Essays*: what else is the meaning of such propositions as these: "There appears not throughout all nature, any one instance of connection, as conceivable by us;" "one event follows another," "but we never can observe *any tye between them*, &c.[9]" Indeed, the not admitting "*any relations of ideas*," or "*any reasonings a priori*," (so as to be capable of supporting the idea of CAUSATION as a *creating principle* absolutely necessary in the universe) is but repeating "the *juvenile ideas*" of the Treatise, and "*casting them anew in these later pieces*[10]."

Before I proceed further, I wish my reader to grant the proposition, "That a Being cannot begin its existence of itself;" because I mean to make use of it in my further reply to Mr. Hume's doctrines; and, unless this step is allowed, I can make no further progress in this argument.

SECTION THE SECOND.

We will now proceed to the second part of the original inquiry; that is, Why "we conclude that such particular Causes must necessarily have such particular Effects; and what is the nature of that inference we draw from one to the other, and of the belief we repose in it?"[11] The question, however, ought to stand thus, "why LIKE CAUSES must necessarily have LIKE EFFECTS?"[12] because what is really enquired into, is the *general notion of necessary connexion*, between *all like* Cause and Effect; and by thus putting the question respecting *particulars only*, although they might be included in an universal answer, yet no answer applicable to them MERELY, could authorize an *universal axiom*.

---

[8] [Hume invokes the distinctness and separability of ideas of causes and effects when arguing in *Treatise* 1.3.3.3 that a thing may be conceived to begin to exist without a cause, but Shepherd's formulation in terms of a thing's "*beginning its own existence*" (using 'begin' as a transitive verb) is her own.]

[9] Essays, Sec. 7. p. 77 [*Enquiry* 7.26].

[10] See advertisement to the Essays. [Shepherd has already alluded to this advertisement at *ERCE* 33/1; see also footnote 3 there.]

[11] [Shepherd is quoting from *Treatise* 1.3.2.15.]

[12] [Hume identifies the general principle that "the same cause always produces the same effect" as part of his fourth "rule by which to judge of causes and effects" (*Treatise* 1.3.15.6). His account of how the mind comes to accept this principle on the basis of experience is given in *Treatise* 1.3.8.14, 1.3.12.5, and *Enquiry* 8.13.]

The manner of stating the enquiry in *the Essays*, is also too vaguely expressed, (although it be evident that it is the *general relation* which is enquired into.) Mr. Hume says, "we will now enquire, how we arrive at the *knowledge of Cause and Effect*[13]." It ought to be stated, how we arrive at the knowledge of the *necessary connexion*, between *like* Cause and Effect?

Let it be remembered, that Mr. Hume says, "this principle is nothing but custom and habit;"[14] that "belief in necessary connexion is nothing but an intense and steady conception, arising from the customary conjunction of the object with something present to the memory or senses; that when flame and heat, cold and snow, have always been conjoined together, there is such a customary conjunction between them, that when flame and snow are anew presented to the senses, the mind is carried by custom to expect heat and cold."[15]

"That *reason* can never show us the connexion of one object with another, though aided by experience; for we can at least *conceive a change in the course of nature*. That necessary connexion is nothing but an internal act of the mind, determined to carry its thoughts from one object to another."[16] Thus *necessary connexion* of cause and effect is only a custom of the mind! *Power* is only a custom of the mind! Expectations, and experience, are only customs of the mind! The consequence of which doctrine is, that as a *custom of the mind* is entirely a different circumstance from the *operation of nature*, we may "*conceive*" at least the contrary of what we have been accustomed to may take place,—we may conceive the "course of nature to change."

Now it is my intention to shew, in contradiction to these ideas of Mr. Hume, that it is *Reason*, and not *Custom*, which guides our minds in forming the notions of necessary connexion, of belief and of expectation[17].

---

[13] Essays, Sec. 4. p. 27 [*Enquiry* 4.5]. [Shepherd writes "will now" in place of Hume's "must."]

[14] [In characterizing the psychological principle responsible for the mental transition of inference from the idea of a cause to the idea of an effect, or vice versa, Hume writes in *Enquiry* 5.5: "This principle is CUSTOM or HABIT. For wherever repetition of any particular act or operation produces a propensity to renew the same act or operation, without being impelled by any reasoning or process of the understanding; we always say, that this propensity is the effect of *Custom*." Treatise 1.3.8.10 offers a similar definition.]

[15] [Shepherd's paraphrase draws first from *Enquiry* 5.13 and then from *Enquiry* 5.8. In these paragraphs, Hume discusses beliefs as they result from causal reasoning, but he does not mention a specific "belief in necessary connexion."]

[16] [Shepherd is combining elements of *Treatise* 1.3.6.12, *Treatise* 1.3.6.5, and *Treatise* 1.3.14.20.]

[17] I conceive it impossible to have a complete conviction that every Effect is inherent, or contained in its Cause, until the mind be imbued with the knowledge, that objects are but unknown circumstances in Nature, when unperceived by the senses; which when perceived, exhibit their appropriate qualities accordingly; and which then appear in certain defined masses, as to the different senses they affect, as to their figure, &c.; and receive an arbitrary name for their assemblage. They must have also among each other certain proportions. When these unknown circumstances, (or

43   In order to this let us bear in mind the reasoning already adduced in the foregoing Chapter, and it thence immediately follows, that objects which we know by our senses do begin their existences, and by our reason know they cannot begin it of themselves, must begin it by the operation of some *other beings* in existence, producing these new qualities in nature, and introducing them to our observation. The very meaning of the word Cause, is *Producer* or *Creator*; of Effect, the *Produced* or *Created*—and the idea is gained by such an observance of nature, as we think is efficient in any given case, to an *experimentum crucis*.[18]

Long observation of the invariableness of antecedency, and subsequency, is not wanted; many trials are not wanted, to generate the notion of *producing power*.

One trial is enough, in such circumstances, as will bring the mind to the following reasoning.

Here is a new quality, which appears to my senses:

44   But it could not arise of itself; nor could any surrounding objects, but one (or more) affect it; therefore that one, (or more) have occasioned it, for there is nothing else to make a difference; and a *difference* could not "*begin of itself.*"

This is an argument, which all persons, however illiterate, feel the force of. It is the only foundation for the demonstrations of the laboratory of the chymist; which all life resembles, and so closely, in many instances, that the philosopher, and the vulgar, are equally sure of what cause is absolutely necessary to the production of certain effects; for instance, each knows that in certain given circumstances, *the closing of the Eye* will eclipse the prospect of nature; and the slight motion of reopening it, will restore all the objects to view. Therefore, the Eye (in these circumstances,) is the *Cause* or *Producer of vision*. ONE trial would be enough, under certain *known*

45   circumstances[19]. Why? not from "*custom*," because there has been *one trial*

---

affections, or substances,) in nature, *mix*, and are thereby *altered, the qualities which affect the senses are in the same proportions* altered, and are necessarily included in those objects as their Effects. But this part of the subject, is of such moment that a separate consideration of it is intended. [Shepherd is referring to what became her 1827 book, *Essays on the Perception of an External Universe (EPEU)*.]

[18] [An "*experimentum crucis*" ("crucial experiment") is an experiment that shows which one of the available explanatory hypotheses is correct. The concept was described by Francis Bacon (1561–1626), and the term was popularized by Robert Boyle (1627–1691) and Isaac Newton (1643–1727), among others. Hume uses the term himself in *An Enquiry Concerning the Principles of Morals*, which was also included in *Essays and Treatises on Several Subjects* (Hume 1777, 1800), as does Thomas Reid (1710–1796) in his *Inquiry* (Reid 1764, 1997).]

[19] When more trials are needed than ONE, it is in order to *detect the circumstances, not to lay a foundation for the general principle,* that a LIKE Cause repeated, a LIKE Effect will take place.

only; but from *Reason*, because vision not being able *to produce itself, nor any of the surrounding objects by the supposition*; it is the *Eye* which must necessarily perform the operation; for there is nothing else to make a difference; and a different quality could not "*begin its own existence.*" It is this sort of REASONING UPON EXPERIMENT, which takes place in every man's mind, concerning every affair in life, which generates the notion of Power, and necessary Connexion; and gives birth to that maxim, "*a like Cause must produce a like Effect.*" The circumstances being supposed the same on a second occasion as on a former one, and carefully observed to be so; the Eye when opened would be expected to let in light, and all her objects. "I observe (says the mind) in this or any other case, all the prevening circumstances the same as before; for there is nothing to make a difference; and a difference cannot arise without something to occasion it; else there would be a *beginning of existence* by itself, which is impossible."

It is this compound idea, therefore, *the result of the experience of what does take place upon any given trial*, MIXED with the *reasoning that nothing else could ensue*, unless on the one hand, *efficient causes were allowed for the alteration*; or, on the other, that things could "*alter their existences* FOR THEMSELVES;" which generates the notion of *power* or "*producing principle,*" *and for which we have formed the word.*

It is in vain to say that a habit of association of ideas from observing "*contiguity in time, and place,*" between objects is all we know of *power*; a habit of the mind will not *begin existence*, will not *introduce a quality*. The really philosophical method of viewing the subject is this: that objects in relation to us, are nothing but masses of certain qualities, affecting certain of our senses; and which, when independent of our senses, are *unknown* powers or qualities in nature. These masses change their qualities by their mixture with any other mass, and then the corresponding qualities determined to the senses must of course also change. These changed qualities, are termed *effects*; or *consequents*; but are really no more than NEW QUALITIES arising from *new objects*, which have been formed by the *junctions of other objects* (previously formed) or might be considered as the *unobserved qualities* of *existing objects*; which *shall be observed when properly exhibited*.

If then an existence now in being, *conjoined with any other*, forms thereby *a new nature*, capable of exhibiting *new qualities*, these new qualities must enter into the definition of the objects; they become a part of their natures; and when by careful experiment, or judicious observation, no new prevening circumstances are supposed to make an alteration in the conjunction of the same bodies, the *new qualities*, that are named *effects*, are expected without a doubt to arise upon every such conjunction; because, they as much belong to this *newly combined nature*, as the original qualities did to each separate nature, before their conjunction. So little is custom the principle of cause and effect, that if upon the *first* and original trial of the element of fire, all surrounding circumstances were put away from having any influence over it, saving the body it destroyed; that power of *discerptibility*[20] would be ever after considered as one of its qualities; as much as its colour or its light, or its warmth, without the presence of which, it would not be fire.

This conjunction with a grosser material than itself, is the new circumstance, on which it exhibits its essential and permanent quality of discerptibility to the senses; now if the trial be complete, when upon a second occasion an object having the same sensible qualities as fire hath, known also to have been elicited from the same prevening circumstances, meets with the same gross body as heretofore, it must of *necessity* consume it. There is nothing to make a *difference*. A *difference* is an *Effect*, a *change of being*, an *altered existence*, an existence which *cannot "begin of itself"* any more than any other in Nature; could the fire be supposed not to consume the gross body, there would be a *difference* of qualities, that is, new qualities, which by the data there is no cause for. The original circumstances, of which fire is the compound Effect, from which it results as a *formed object*, are supposed to be ordered the same as on a former occasion; these are necessarily compelled to be attended with the same effects or combined qualities; otherwise there would be the *"beginnings* of *existence"* by themselves, which has before been shown to be impossible. But the *combined qualities*, are the whole qualities that fire in every circumstance, is capable of producing. Meeting, therefore, with a gross body, which on any one occasion, in certain circumstances, it once consumed; under the same circumstances, it must necessarily again consume it. That DIFFERENCES OF EXISTENCE cannot begin of themselves; is therefore the second conclusion supposed to be established.

"*Antecedency* and *subsequency*" are therefore immaterial to the proper definition of "Cause and Effect;" on the contrary, although an object, in order to act as a Cause, must be in Being antecedently to such action; yet when it *acts as a Cause*, its *Effects are synchronous with that action*, and are

---

[20] ['Discerptibility' generally means "divisibility into parts"; here Shepherd evidently means "the ability to separate into parts."]

included in it; which a close inspection into the nature of cause will prove. For effects are no more than the new qualities, of newly formed objects. Each conjunction of bodies, (now separately in existence, and of certain defined qualities,) produces upon their union those new natures, whose qualities must necessarily *be in*, and *with them, in the very moment of their formation.*

Thus *the union of two distinct natures*, is the *cause, producer* or *creator* of another; which must instantly, and immediately, have all its peculiar qualities; but the cause has not acted, is not completed, till the *union* has taken place, and the new nature is formed with all its qualities, *in*, and *about it. Cause producing Effect*, therefore, under the strict eye of philosophical scrutiny, is a *new object* exhibiting *new qualities*; or shortly, the formation of a new *mass of qualities*. A *chain of conjunctions of bodies*, of course, *occupies time*; and is the reason why the careless observation of philosophers, enabling them to take notice only of some one distinct effect, (after perhaps innumerable successive conjunctions of bodies,) occasions the mistake, by which they consider *subsequency of effect*, as a part of the *essential definition* of that term; and *priority*, as *essential* to the nature of Cause.

As a short illustration of the doctrine unfolded, let us take the idea of nourishment, considered as the effect, subsequent to the taking of food, its cause. Here the *nature* of nourishment, is *a process* which begins to act immediately that food is in conjunction with the stomach. "That we are nourished;" is only the last result of a continuous chain of causes and effects, in formation from the first moment the food enters the stomach, to that, in which every particle is absorbed and deposited in the proper place in the body. Here, the capacity of food to exhibit certain qualities, when in conjunction with the body, is shown; the nature of the human body, to exhibit certain other qualities, in consequence of that conjunction, is also shown; but the *effect of nourishment*, being *subsequent* to, and at such a distance of time from, the original Cause, is only so, on account of its being the effect of a vast number of causes, or unions of objects in succession, of which the union of the stomach and the food was first in order.

Our deficient observation, is apt to prevent our taking notice of the 2d, 3d, or indefinite number of effects; which arise in consequence of as many conjunctions of objects.

But the first, and other *effects* successively, are as much and entirely synchronous with their *causes*, as any other quality of any single object, which is always exhibited along with it.

2dly.[21] It is also quite immaterial to the definition of this relation, whether an untried, or unobserved quality, be called *quality*, or *effect*. The unknown or at present undetermined quality, which is termed an effect, might always change its place with some *known quality*, and not bear the name of effect; and *vice versa*: Thus, a blind man may call the object which warmed, or burned him, fire; but his eyes being supposed suddenly to open, he would consider the flame and its brilliant colour as the *effects* of fire; whilst he who sees fire constantly, being able always to take notice of its flame and colour, considers them as the constant and unvarying *qualities* of fire, and which render the substance before him worthy of bearing that name; but the quality of burning, which he does not *constantly* experience, he names an *effect* or *consequence* of fire previously being in existence. But the true method of looking upon the subject is this—that fire, in order to deserve the name it bears, must comprehend all its qualities *tried* and *untried; observed* and *unobserved; determined* and *undetermined*; it deserves the name only on account of its being a certain defined object; *elicited from certain causes observed to be efficient to its production*; and by the very conditions of the question, is allowed to be *the same*. But an object is nothing else (in relation to *us*,) than a mass of peculiar qualities; and when observations inform us, that any known mass is produced by similar circumstances, on various occasions; such mass or object must necessarily contain all its qualities, and be equal to exhibit all its effects in hitherto untried events. Upon any occasion where we are either certain, or have a high probability, that an object presented to us is truly similar to a former one, and was created by the same causes; we expect all tried qualities to be the same as before, and any *untried* quality, (that is, any quality not in present operation, though previously ascertained,) must belong ever after to its definition. All that is necessary is to be correct, as to the prevening or influencing circumstances which gave *birth to the object*. They being the same on any two or more occasions, the object elicited must necessarily be the same—but it is not the same, unless it hath all its *qualities*, and no other than its qualities. Therefore fire, in order to have a right to the sign of the word fire, for an expression of its attributes, in order to be a "*like cause*," must of necessity burn as much as it must be red, otherwise the red object were not fire; and *could not have been produced by those causes that elicit that element*.

I mean therefore to conclude, that Effects are but the qualities of an object not

---

[21] [Presumably, Shepherd writes "2dly" because she has already declared "antecedency and subsequency" to be immaterial to the definition.]

experienced by some of the senses of the human frame, whilst certain others at present touch it; *the knowledge of which last*, being joined to the observation of the WHENCE the object was produced, beget the knowledge of what new untried qualities may be expected in future under given circumstances. It becomes therefore part of the definition of fire to burn certain bodies, to melt others; of bread to nourish the human body; of snow to be cold, and white; and these qualities they must have, in order to compose that entire *enumeration of qualities*, for which appropriate names have been formed, and to the exhibition of which similar and efficient causes have been in action.

If it should be said, that in considering objects as masses of combined qualities, the *result* of like Causes previously in action, we beg the question not yet supposed to be granted,—I answer; that *like* Causes, that is, *like* objects, are by the supposition admitted, and then the question arises, whether it is demonstrable they must have like effects or qualities, *under like circumstances in future?* I answer, they must have like effects, or qualities, because there is nothing else *given* that can be supposed to make a difference; and a difference of qualities could not arise of *itself*, could not begin its own existence; and I add, not only, there is nothing else *supposed* that can make a difference; but that when we also know that in the FORMATION of any object no difference took place; then, *there is no ground whatever*, for imagining the *possibility* of an *alteration* in *the effects of that object*. But although it be very difficult in the analysis of this question, not to use the word *cause* in its intended sense, before the definition of the word is given, and although it be true that in this last observation I may have done so in saying, *that objects must be the same which are elicited from like causes*, i.e. *from the junction of like prevening circumstances*; (and which position will be fully borne out in the process of the argument;) yet a fastidious reader may omit every such reference to the notion of Cause; for the argument is perfect without it, and stands thus:

Effects are nothing but those *same conjunctions of qualities*, which in other words are admitted as *similar causes*, in the supposition of the question. The objects (whose *union is necessary* to a given result,) must certainly exist, *antecedent* to such an union. But it is *in their* UNION, there exist those *newly formed objects*, or masses of qualities called *Effects*, which are therefore *identical* with the *similar cause*; for in *this union*, Cause and Effect are *synchronous*, and they are but different words for the same *Essence*. Fire and wood must be antecedent to combustion, no doubt; but in the *union of Fire and Wood*, there exists immediately *combustion* as a new event in nature;—also in this union exists the similar *cause* allowed by the *data*, whilst combustion is also termed the *Effect* of the union of Fire and Wood; but, however termed, an *effect*, is in fact a new but similar object as heretofore. A *similar* mass of qualities, in kind, which cannot therefore be a *different* mass of qualities in kind.—Equals added to equals upon any two occasions, the whole must be equal; add equal qualities to equal qualities, the sum of the qualities must be equal upon every repetition of the junction;—and the *sum* must be the *same result* taken *twice over*, not two *different*, or possibly *altered sums*. Therefore I repeat, that in the consideration of the nature of Cause and Effect, it is immaterial whether the yet unframed qualities of objects, previous to their junction, be named *effects*; they are to be considered as qualities; and qualities may be considered as *effects*, under any circumstances that prevent their usual exhibition. Effects when developed are no more than qualities; and qualities previous to their developement are in our imagination considered as Effects.

3dly. Again, it is immaterial to the definition of the relation of Cause and Effect, that we are not acquainted with the "secret powers" of natural objects, either before or after experience; for when we find, that in any distinct and given circumstances they put on certain qualities to the senses, their secret powers and properties must be qualified in all *like circumstances* to be the same, and are obliged to be so; because no contrary qualities could "begin their existences of themselves;" and by the *supposition* there is no *cause in the circumstances*, to give rise to any *differences in the qualities*. Indeed, Mr. Hume makes a great mistake in supposing it necessary to demonstrate, in every particular instance, what *particular* Effect must necessarily flow from its object, in order to gain the idea of *necessary Connexion*. The *how* and the *why* have nothing to do with the general reasoning affecting the general proposition; for "whether like Causes shall produce like Effects" is *not* a question exactly the same as whether "such particular causes shall have such *particular* effects?" which Mr. Hume seems to consider as precisely of the same import[22]; whereas *one is a general* question, which however answered, in the *affirmative* or *negative*, would apply to *particulars*. But supposing in each *particular* instance under our notice, we could descry the "*secret powers of nature*," the general question concerning *all* like causes would still remain unanswered; and an universal conclusion could not logically be deduced

---

[22] Compare Sec. 4. p. 30 [*Enquiry* 4.10–11], with Sec. 4. p. 34 [*Enquiry* 4.16].

from the particular premises concerning it: as will be more fully argued in the discussion upon Dr. Brown's reasoning.

If it should be asked, (as Mr. Hume presently does,) how is it known when objects are similar upon any two occasions; the "sensible qualities may be the same, and not the *secret powers, upon which the Effects depend?*"[23] I answer, this is to *shift* the question from the examination of *like Causes supposed*, to the consideration of the *method whereby their presence* may be *detected*[24]. But this difficulty is met, and considered in, its proper place; I shall only here say, that as the *secret powers* are the real external unknown Causes in Nature, which determine the sensible qualities, as well as *every other Effect*; so when we find the sensible qualities the same on any two occasions, we are sure the secret powers are similar *thus far*, and therefore fitted to exhibit their further similar effects;—(or *combined secret powers and sensible qualities*;) and although some *unobserved* cause might creep in to alter the object, whilst appearing the same, yet this we do not *imagine* when we are not aware of it, especially in cases where the same sensible qualities have been regularly exhibited along with like secret powers; for this regularity is perceived as an *Effect*, for which there must be a proportional *Cause*, and begets a proportional belief accordingly.—We argue from the *regular Effects*, (the sensible qualities;) to the *regular Causes*, (the secret powers;) which having been equal to certain other *Effects or properties*, we expect again the same, under similar circumstances.—We argue from the regular *ends* nature keeps in view, up to nature's God, who ordained them, and who must be supposed still to continue true to those ends; and along with the grander operations of nature, we may often in many cases observe our own actions, and those of others, conspiring *only* to fashion similar objects. But when the *secret powers*, and sensible qualities, are known, *or supposed the same*, the conclusion is demonstrative; *so must be the Effects*. Whilst, were it possible to know the secret powers in each *particular* past instance, *universal* truth would not thence result. Neither has Mr. Hume any right to make this argument; because to conceive "there may be secret powers which may change the Effects, dependent on them," is to make use of the relation between Cause and Effect, as of a really necessary connexion, in order to oppose his adversary: a principle

---

[23] [Shepherd is characterizing *Enquiry* 4.16 and *Enquiry* 4.21.]

[24] I should not here have taken notice of this objection, but that as Mr. Hume does suddenly shift the question, so I would not appear to avoid an answer to it: otherwise it is something too early to enter upon the subject; obliging me to make use of my argument previously to its complete developement. But the reader may pass over to the next Section if he please.

which he previously refuses to admit. Also the objection forms an illogical argument in another way. For it virtually draws a general conclusion from *two negative premises*. To assert, that like sensible qualities merely, will NOT produce like Effects; and, that *like sensible qualities* are NOT *like Causes*, is to separate the middle term both from the subject and from the predicate of the general question. By *such an argument* Mr. Hume is certainly right in supposing, that REASON cannot support "*our conclusions concerning the operations of Cause and Effect.*"

63 Having thus cleared a way, towards the comprehension of this relation of Cause and Effect, we will proceed to a definition of those terms in the next Section.

SECTION THE THIRD.

A Cause, therefore, is such action of an object, as shall enable it, in conjunction with another, to form a new nature, capable of exhibiting qualities varying from those of either of the objects unconjoined. This is really to be a producer of new being.—This is a generation, or *creation*, of qualities not conceived of, antecedently to their existence;—and not merely an "*idea always followed by another*," on account of a "customary association between them."

An Effect is the produced quality exhibited to the senses, as the essential property of natures so conjoined. Necessary connexion of cause and effect is the obligation qualities have to inhere in their objects, and to exhibit their varieties according to the different human senses with which they come in contact. Power is but another word for efficient cause, or "productive principle;" and signifies the *property* which lies in the *secret nature of objects*, when unobserved by the senses, and which determines the qualities that can be exhibited to them upon every new conjunction.—An *object* may be defined, a *combined mass of qualities*; the result of proportional unknown circumstances in nature, meeting with the human senses.

64

But Mr. Hume's three definitions of the relation of Cause and Effect are, in many respects, faulty, and not borne out by his own arguments; for he defines a Cause "an object followed by another, and where all the objects similar to the first are followed by objects similar to the second."[25]—Now, if he means

---

[25] [Shepherd is quoting from *Enquiry* 7.29, changing only some punctuation.]

an object that will in *future*, as in *past* times, be always followed by another; an *invariable* necessity in the antecedent to be followed by its subsequent, his whole argument tends to prove the *contrary*, and to show that experience has power to answer for the *past* only, and cannot for the future; for, that we may conceive a "change in the course of nature," and that imagination supplies only the notion of *invariable* expectation from "custom;" that this is the sense of the passage containing the original definition, we may be sure of, from what follows; for he goes on to say, "or in other words, where if the first object had not been, the second never had existed;"[26] but this idea expresses a much stricter necessity of connexion than does the relation of any number of objects, which had only followed each other in *past time*, however often their antecedency and subsequency had been repeated. Such a necessity is contradicted the whole way by the argument. It is quite another sentiment, from that which arises from the ideas of always *before and after*. That which requires another object to its existence, must be *necessarily connected* with it; and I contend that it is so connected, as a *new quality* of an altered mode of existence. But Mr. Hume says, it is only connected, as an invariable subsequent, must always be understood to require its invariable antecedent.—But I retort, Why does the definition assume more than the argument can possibly bear out?

How can the *invariableness* of the future be answered for by the experience of any invariableness in the past? It is truly impossible that it should be so. Custom can only, at the most, lead us to *expect* that the future would be similar to the past; but it never could so sufficiently answer for it, as to enable us to form a definition concerning its *absolute* INVARIABLENESS *of phænomenon*.

Indeed, in many cases there are *single* exceptions to *universal* experience, and to any habit of expectation founded on it; which at once proves Mr. Hume's definition to be erroneous; for hence the *invariableness* of the sequence becomes altered, and custom shown to be utterly incapable of affording an *universal definition*, of the relation in question.—Now, *experiment* is what decides as to a real and necessary cause, under given circumstances.—When an event happens under one set of circumstances,

---

[26] [As noted previously, Shepherd counts this sentence from *Enquiry* 7.29 as Hume's *second* definition of 'cause', out of three in total. However, Hume regards himself as offering only two definitions in total and treats the sentence beginning "in other words" as an alternative formulation or elaboration of the first. See also *Treatise* 1.3.14.31, which provides two similar definitions but does not include this formulation. The *Treatise* versions each include a requirement of contiguity between cause and effect, as well as one of temporal succession.]

not under another in all respects the same, save ONE; *that one* is a *true cause*, and a *necessary one*; and under the same circumstances, it must be invariably wanted to that end; and every mind feels it so, because it perceives that an *alteration* could not begin of itself. This, and nothing but this, is a *strict necessity*, and can enable the mind to predicate for the future as for the past.

But the first definition is also faulty in another instance; because in every just definition, the ideas that are included in the terms, must not suit any other object. Now many objects are invariably antecedents and subsequents, that are not Causes and Effects; and it can be no good definition, to warrant the arguing in a circle, which *this definition* evidently does.

The second definition is also erroneous, because although similar causes must have similar effects, yet *diverse* causes may produce the same effects also—therefore the *second object might exist* without the first, by the operation of any other cause efficient to it[27]. The third definition, viz. "an object followed by another, and whose appearance always conveys the *thought to that other*," does not differ materially from the first—yet it is worthy of observation, that the thought always being carried by the appearance of one object to the idea of another, proves nothing but *an accidental, though strong association of ideas*; and is in like manner objectionable, on account of *suiting other objects than the thing defined*. Every *Andrew* is not necessarily "Simon Peter's Brother," although my thought always recurs to that idea, upon every mention of the name of *Andrew*.[28]

SECTION THE FOURTH.

It follows then from the definitions given in the preceding section, and the reasonings on which they are formed, that were a body, in all other respects resembling snow, to have the taste of salt and feeling of fire, it would be an extraordinary phœnomenon, no doubt; and one which might for ought we know take place, but it would not be snow; and such a body could not fall

---

[27] I make this remark however, rather with respect to Mr. Hume's notion of Cause than my own; in order to shew there is an inconsistency between his argument and his definition; for *diverse antecedents* might invariably be *followed* by *similar subsequents*; then, in each separate case the second object might exist without the first. [In *Treatise* 1.3.15.6, Hume states as the second part of his fourth "rule by which to judge of causes and effects," derived from experience, that "the same effect never arises but from the same cause." The *Enquiry* does not explicitly state such a principle, however.]

[28] [According to the Gospels, the apostles Andrew and Peter ("Simon who is called Peter") were brothers; Andrew was the first to meet Jesus and is traditionally regarded as the first to be called by Jesus to be an apostle.]

from the clouds but by new causes efficient to its formation;—it would, therefore, be entirely a different object, and would require a new name; and the phœnomenon could offer no ground for the conclusion, that *reason* does not afford an argument, for the expectation of similar effects from similar causes.

Nature, it is true, varies all her operations; but not in a manner that can ever make it appear otherwise than a contradiction to reason, that it should be through interferences with her regular course. For instance, something similar to the case imagined does take place; we all know that various substances fall from the clouds; but they are all named by various names accordingly; they are known *by reason* to be different *masses of qualities*, different objects, which must have been produced by different circumstances. Such variety, therefore, offers no contradiction to our REASON, our EXPECTATIONS, or our TERMS. Yet Mr. Hume seems to think that nature, without a contradiction to our ideas, may be supposed to alter her course in the *determination of her qualities*; and occasion contrary and different qualities, from otherwise similar objects. Nature, no doubt, preserving in many objects certain appearances to some of the senses, may vary the remaining qualities.

But this cannot be, without her using prevening causes of an altered kind, efficient to the new production; and then it is a new object and must be *newly named*. Such events as these, which are nothing else than all the various events, in the universe, (for all things are *alike* to some of the senses, and *diverse* in others;) nature is full of; but this does not prove, there is not a *necessary connexion* between CAUSE AND EFFECT; and that *custom* only guides our expectations. On the contrary, it is because there can be no "*beginnings of existences*" by themselves, that we know, when new phenomena arise, from *apparently* similar circumstances, that we must lie under a mistake; and that the new objects cannot be *the same objects altered*, and elicited from similar circumstances. We might as well deem meteoric stones to be snow, as a body, which had the taste of salt and the feeling of fire. Nature, therefore, cannot, when employing *like* causes in action, alter her course in determining different and contrary "*Effects*" from otherwise similar objects; because in such a case, these *new qualities* would absolutely be *uncaused; different* qualities would be exhibited from *precisely similar conjunctions of bodies*, i.e. *different* and *contrary* qualities, (or Effects) from otherwise similar objects, (or Causes) which is impossible.

Should it be said that nature is supposed to be employing *different* causes in action; by altering the "*secret powers*" (whilst the "*sensible qualities*" remain the same,) that it is in this way she changes her course—then the prevening *conjunctions of bodies* which produced these secret powers, being supposed different; the *natures* of the objects are different; they are truly *other* objects, and there is no astonishment at the production of their altered Effects; *there is no alteration in the course of nature*; and the Phenomena will not support Mr. Hume's argument *against* REASON, and in favour of CUSTOM only; it follows, therefore, that if "we imagine the course of nature *may change*," it must be under the notion of a *cause equivalent to it:—in which case there is no contradiction offered to the notion of causation as founded on* REASON. But for nature otherwise to change, and to vary either her "*Effects*," or "*Secret powers*," without varying the causes or prevening circumstances whose junction formed the objects, whence these result;—is so obviously impossible, that we cannot even suppose the will and power of the Deity to be able to work the *contradiction*. He could not make a finite quality, *dependent* upon himself or some other cause for its exhibition, to become *independent* and able to *exist of itself*; he could not otherwise than by himself altering the determination of the causes that form the objects; then there is a cause for the alleged change—the objects are not *similar* objects; the *whole* prevening circumstances are not the same; and it is only *unlike* causes again that beget *unlike* effects; unlike objects that vary in their qualities.

But the following sentence[29], which contains the passage alluded to, involves an ambiguity of expression, which ought to be noticed, lest it should appear as though I had mistaken it, and consequently my answer not appear sufficiently applicable, viz. "Nature may be supposed to change her course since it implies no contradiction, that an object SEEMINGLY like those which we have experienced, may be attended with different or contrary Effects." There is here an ambiguity of sense on account of the expression "SEEMINGLY;" for it may either intend, *an alteration in the determination of Effects from objects, in* ALL OTHER *respects similar, save in these* CONTRARY *effects*; or *an "*ARBITRARY" *change in the "secret powers" "which mix with the sensible qualities; and on which the effects entirely depend"* in either sense, such an arbitrary change in the course of nature, is a "CONTRADICTION TO REASON" and an IMPOSSIBILITY.

Mr. Hume however seems to use it in either of these senses, as the occasion serves, and without conceiving there is much difference between them.

The former sense however appears to be that in which it is used, as applicable in the instance concerning the changes upon snow. Compare

---

[29] Sec. 4. p. 36. [Shepherd is quoting from *Enquiry* 4.18 with some initial paraphrasing.]

CHAPTER THE SECOND   63

these *passages*[30], "may I not distinctly conceive, a body *in all other respects* resembling snow having the taste of salt, and feeling of fire"—with[31], "Every Effect is a distinct event from its Cause; and ever after it is suggested, its conjunction must appear *arbitrary* with its Cause, since there are always many other effects, which to *reason* might seem fully as consistent and natural." But it is in the latter sense, viz.: in the "*arbitrary*" alteration of the "*secret powers*," *(in order to form* DIFFERENT *Causes for the determination of* DIFFERENT *Effects)*, which must explain the following passage[32]: "Let the course of nature be allowed hitherto ever so regular proves not that for the future it will continue so." "The secret nature of objects, and consequently all their effects and influences, may change without any change in the sensible qualities;" In either of the senses in which Mr. Hume uses the notion in question, it is equally absurd; for as *Cause* is not by him granted, nature must be supposed to change her regular march *uncaused*; whether in striking off *different* and *contrary* qualities, from objects in *every other* respect similar, *save in these arbitrary and contrary determinations*; or in the mixing *different secret powers* amidst the *sensible qualities*. Nor will it answer for Mr. Hume to shift his position, and say; that the "secret powers" may be considered, as *changed* by the *regular operations of nature*; and that, on account of our inability to detect them, we are necessarily obliged to consider, the *sensible qualities* ONLY, *as like Causes*; thereby concluding the *Effects* will be *similar* upon *insufficient grounds*; and thus REASON, not able to support the idea of a *really* necessary connexion between them.

For upon this supposition, the *real relation* of Cause and Effect, is *assumed as granted*—

1st. In order to account for the change in the secret powers.

2dly. To account for the change in the effects dependent upon them.

And this is at once yielding the whole argument to the adversary[33]! enabling him justly to retort, that he makes use of the general principle concerning Cause and Effect (which is now granted), and which he supports

---

[30] Essays, Vol. 2. Sec. 4. p. 36. [In what follows, Shepherd is again quoting with some alteration from *Enquiry* 4.18.]

[31] Ibid. p. 30. [In what follows, Shepherd is quoting with changes and omissions from *Enquiry* 4.11.]

[32] Ibid. p. 39. The method in which this idea begs the question, has been taken notice of before. [In the two sentences that follow, Shepherd is quoting, with some changes, from *Enquiry* 4.21.]

[33] This sort of argument forms a sophism which logicians term "*ignoratio elenchi*;" "something being proved which is not necessarily inconsistent with the proposition maintained:" See W. Logick. p. 240. [Shepherd is paraphrasing Isaac Watts, *Logic*: 240.] And this is the real gist, of the whole of Mr. Hume's argument (a *posteriori*) and which is generally considered, I believe, as both acute and *logical*.

upon "*general reasoning*" whereby in many instances to *suspect*, and in many others to *detect*, UNlike secret powers amidst the sensible qualities, by which means it becomes applicable, as an AXIOM founded on REASON, wherewith to try every kind of experience both in philosophy and common life—whilst also he can maintain;—that unless it were for the knowledge of such a general principle, *no knowledge* of the "secret powers of nature" in ever so many *past* instances, could be of any material service to us *for the future*.

All mathematical demonstration is built upon the notion; that where quantities, or diagrams, resemble each other, the relations which are true, with respect to ONE of each kind will be true with respect to *all* others of a *like* kind; ONLY *because there is nothing else to make a difference among them*. So, if in all *past time*, such *secret powers* could be shown necessarily connected with such *sensible qualities*; yet *in future* it could not thence be proved to continue so, *unless supported by the axioms;—that* LIKE *Causes must* EXHIBIT *like* Effects, and that DIFFERENCES CANNOT ARISE *of themselves*.

Upon the whole, therefore, Mr. Hume must be understood to mean, that as we know nothing of "*Cause and Effect*," or of the "*secret processes of nature*," so she might be supposed indifferently to strike off contrary Effects from similar prevening Causes, or else to alter their "secret powers," whilst their FORMATION was produced by the same means as usual. Thus that exactly the same circumstances might prevene the falling of snow, (precisely the same objects might unite to produce that object,) upon any two occasions, yet, it might have the taste of salt or feeling of fire! That the "secret powers" of vegetation might in future be altered; although the seasons should roll the same as before; and every power in nature be only equal to the contrary supposition!

To all which I answer, nature cannot alter her course when she is employing *similar means* in the formation of objects, by changing any of the "Secret powers," or altering any Effects; because the prevening circumstances being supposed in any two cases similar, there would be no assignable reason for the difference. A difference, or change, *either* in the "*secret powers*" of objects, or the *Effects* of Causes, (other things remaining the same) is exactly equal to the CREATION of so *many new qualities*, which could not, without a CONTRADICTION, *arise of themselves*.

I can conceive it said by some, although Mr. Hume would have no right to do so, that a miraculous interference might alter the course of nature; not so, not in determining the production of dissimilar objects from similar causes. No miracle could form an *uncaused* change in nature (which is the notion in question).

A miraculous interference, that is, an interference of God as a cause, might alter the production of objects, yet still there is a *cause* equivalent to the *change*, and again *unlike* objects beget *unlike* qualities: I therefore draw a conclusion from the whole of this reasoning, exactly contrary to Mr. Hume's inference from his; admitting indeed with him, that before experience we cannot know what *particular* effects will flow from given causes; yet *after experience* I judge that it is "*reason* which guides us in our expectations; because it convinces us, that instances" (of *Effects*,) "of which we have had no experience must resemble" (when Causes are similar) "those of which we have had experience, for that the course of nature must continue uniformly the same,"[34] *by the regular determination of like Cause and Effect*.

The same kind of answer will serve for other paradoxical questions which Mr. Hume puts in these Essays.

Is there, says he, any more intelligible proposition than to affirm, that all the trees will flourish in December and January, and decay in May and June?[35] Certainly not, to those who conceive that the "course of nature may without an implied contradiction alter the determination of Effects that proceed from like Causes," or, which is the same thing, exhibit different or contrary qualities, from similar objects. But according to the method I have laid down of viewing the operations of nature, there cannot be a more *unintelligible proposition* than to assert of those trees, which have usually flourished in May and June, that they may cease to do so, and only thrive in December and January.

So far from the mind being able distinctly "*to conceive*" such a change in their qualities, when the proof has been once afforded, that it is their nature to require warmth for their growth; and that cold kills their blossoms; it must be ever after considered impossible for these objects to affect qualities not originally included in their *natures*;—or, for their *natures* to alter, without a cause equivalent to the alteration—or a cause equivalent to it to be *supposed*, without REASON being the foundation of the whole principle of CAUSATION.

To suppose that the circumstances which at first stamped them the objects they are, could enable them to preserve themselves similar objects, and yet arbitrarily put on wholly contrary qualities, seems to be about as reasonable as to assert that black may become white, and white become black, and yet each colour merit its original name, of *black* or *white*; whilst, at the same time, these changes take place on account of such a "change in the course

---

[34] [Shepherd is quoting, with minor changes, from *Treatise* 1.3.6.4.]
[35] [Hume poses this question in *Enquiry* 4.18.]

of nature," as determine that although all the causes in action are sufficient only to produce black, yet white shall appear; and *vice versa*. Indeed, before "*nature could be conceived to alter her course;*" the question about which Mr. Hume is *examining experience* (namely, whether she will support the knowledge of the necessary connexion of like objects and their qualities,) must be supposed to be *already* answered in the *negative*; and that it is KNOWN *that nature may be supposed* to exhibit *similar* antecedents *followed* by *different* subsequents, or in other words that there is *no necessary connexion* between like objects and like qualities; which is begging the question; and in a different way from that in which he means to answer it, for he means to support the doctrine of necessary connexion, though upon principles peculiarly his own. Should it be said that I assume the contrary position, I answer, I do not *assume* it; but have previously proved the general conclusion, that "all like causes must have like effects;" (because otherwise, *objects would begin of themselves*:) in order purposely to show that "nature cannot alter her course." Mr. Hume makes also a great mistake in supposing because we can conceive in the fancy the existence of objects contrary to our experience, that therefore they may really exist in nature; for it by no means follows that things which are incongruous in nature, may not be contemplated by the imagination, and received as possible until reason shows the contrary. Indeed, the fallacy, on which his whole sceptical doctrines are *built*, may be seen at the very outset of his first Essay. He imagines it impossible to conceive the *contrary* to any *known relation* in quantities; but that we may *conceive* the *contrary of every matter of fact as possible*—impossible, under *the same circumstances*, and if the *circumstances alter*, the fact is a *different fact*; but not a *contrary one*— any more than the *different* relations of various quantities are not *contrary* to each other. Mr. Hume did not perceive that all objects whatever in relation to us, are but masses of certain qualities elicited from certain prevening circumstances, and therefore incapable of having different qualities, (or of showing diverse effects) whilst yet they remain similar objects *born under like circumstances*. He did not perceive that the "*productive principle,*" or *the Cause of an Effect*, is to be found *in the junction of objects already existing*, by which new objects are formed; but conceiving the nature of the operation of this principle to be wholly unknown, he imagined and alleged all things to be only "*conjoined, and not connected;*"[36] and that they might change their

---

[36] [Hume writes in *Enquiry* 7.28 that all events "seem *conjoined*, but never *connected*." Shepherd's previous reference to "the very outset of his first Essay" is to *Enquiry* 4.1–2.]

places fortuitously; custom only connecting them in the fancy; and a contrary fancy as capable of unconnecting them again.

Strange philosophy! "Effects may be supposed non-existent this minute, and existent the next;" (and so in suspense,) and may therefore "begin their existence by themselves."[37]—If this be so, undoubtedly we want no Causes for our Effects; our Rose-trees may suspend their blossoms in June; the flower require no warmth for its expansion, and remain non-existent till December!

That different objects have different qualities, all are well acquainted with;—The Chinese rose, and the holley, can thrive in Winter; but the same kind of rose, that hitherto has grown only in spring, and flourished in summer, can no more put forth its leaves and expand its blossoms in winter, than the mercury in a *tried* thermometer can suddenly contract to the freezing point, in a burning summer's day.

Let us however, before quitting this important and interesting argument, chuse an example to prove, that "nature cannot without a contradiction be imagined to alter her course." Let a receiver[38] be imagined void of every substance whatever; and nothing but an *uncoloured space* within it. Now it is surely the "course of nature," for this uncoloured space to *remain as it is*, without some *cause steps in to alter it*; and if *some cause steps in to alter it*, "nature does *not* alter her course." Then let nature be supposed to alter her course, and a *scarlet colour uncaused* to enter. Does not every reader perceive the impossibility that scarlet uncaused could enter? that it could "start of itself into existence?" yet such is the idea that is veiled under Mr. Hume's argument;—that different and contrary qualities can take place in similar circumstances; that a rose may blow[39] in winter, when the causes were efficient to its blowing only in June! No circumstances are supposed changed; and yet "*of itself*," the nature of the rose may change!—and so may a new phenomenon take place in an *empty receiver*, as the entrance of a scarlet colour, or of a dove, or any other imaginable being, without an equivalent change of circumstances for its introduction.

The sum of Mr. Hume's argument is, that we knowing nothing of the "secrets of nature," we cannot know there is really a necessary connexion between objects; but *imagining* there is, this *imagination* arises, from a

---

[37] [Shepherd is glossing, but not quoting from, *Treatise* 1.3.3.3.]

[38] [In this use of the term, now historical, a *receiver* is an airtight glass container from which the air has been emptied by an air pump.]

[39] ['Blow', in this sense, means to blossom or bloom.]

CUSTOMARY OBSERVATION, of *the invariableness of their antecedence and subsequence*;—which invariableness, however, does not prove, that each connexion may be more than an *insulated casual event*; not obligatory in nature; therefore *other subsequent* events might, without a contradiction, be imagined to happen after *similar antecedents*, and a *different order of events* might be supposed in the "course of nature."

Now shortly the whole of this reasoning concerning the *possibility of nature altering her course*, is but a circle! for the argument is invented to show that CUSTOM *not* REASON, must be the only ground of our belief in the relation of Cause and Effect.—But it is *impossible to imagine such a change in nature*, unless *reason* were previously excluded as the principle of that relation;—*and it is impossible to exclude reason as the principle of that relation*, except by supposing *that nature may alter her course.*—Thus the idea of *causation*, is founded only on *experience*[40], experience is supplied with arguments by *custom* not by *reason*[41] and custom is supported in her authority by a supposed change in nature[42], *impossible* to any idea of causation[43], *unless* ALREADY SUPPOSED TO BE MERELY THE EFFECT OF CUSTOM[44].

Nor must we conclude this branch of the subject, without observing the contradiction that lies in the very endeavour to persuade the world that *custom is the true* "CAUSE *of* BELIEF" *in necessary connexion*, when before assenting to such a doctrine it must give up all usual habits of thinking upon the subject, and believe upon Mr. Hume's reasoning, what it never before believed!—

Mr. Hume himself recapitulates his argument thus:

"Every idea is copied from some preceding impression (idea being an Effect *derived* from impression as its Cause). In all single instances of the operation of bodies there is nothing that produces, nor consequently can suggest the idea of necessary connexion. But when *many* instances appear, we

---

[40] "The opinion that a cause is necessary to every new production arises from experience."—TREATISE. [Shepherd is closely paraphrasing from *Treatise* 1.3.3.9.]

[41] "All inferences from experience are Effects of *custom* not of *reasoning*."—ESSAYS. [Shepherd is quoting almost exactly from *Enquiry* 5.5.]

[42] "Since it implies no contradiction that the course of nature may change, there can be no demonstrative arguments in the case."—ESSAYS. [Shepherd is closely paraphrasing from *Enquiry* 4.18.]

"Wherever there is a propensity without being impelled by any reasoning we say this propensity is the *Effect* of custom."—ESSAYS. [Shepherd is closely paraphrasing from *Enquiry* 5.5.]

[43] "If *there* were nothing to bind objects together the inferences from present facts would be entirely precarious."—ESSAYS. [Shepherd is quoting with a minor change from *Enquiry* 4.4.]

[44] "Our belief in *causation* is the Effect of custom."—ESSAYS. [Shepherd is alluding to *Enquiry* 5.8, where Hume describes beliefs that result from causal inference as being due to custom. He does not use the specific phrase 'belief in causation'.]

feel a new impression, a customary connexion in the thought, between one object and its usual attendant[45]."

Now this method of placing the argument is but the statement of *another circle*; for *causation* is used as the very principle which lies at the foundation of the whole system; and afterwards we are desired to search for the impression, which is the CAUSE of that EFFECT, viz. the *idea causation*.

And it is no answer to say that the notion of causation is spoken of in his own sense, not in his adversary's; for in either sense it is equally illogical, to prove the conclusion by the premises, and the premises by the conclusion.

What should we think of an author, who, in attempting to account for the original discovery of metals, proved that it was effected by the use of instruments framed from a material termed *iron*, drawn from the bowels of the earth?

In like manner there is *a want of logical precision* in referring all the principles which connect our ideas to three kinds of associations amongst them; of which *causation* is ranked as one;—and then (in order to account for causation,) shew the power that lies in the associations of ideas. Such a notion ends in the formation of a mere identical proposition; *viz.* a certain association of ideas is causation; and causation consists in an association of ideas.

But there is still another passage in Mr. Hume's Essays, of greater consequence than any I have quoted, or argued on; and which I shall yet detain the reader for a few moments in order to consider; it is this following:

"As reason is incapable of any variation, the conclusions which it draws from one circle, are the same which it would form from surveying all the circles in the universe. But no man having seen one body move after being impelled by another would infer, that *every body* will move after a like impulse[46]."

This passage I consider as containing the whole gist of Mr. Hume's error, and therefore it points out where my answer should meet it. The error consists, in making an *incomplete comparison*, between the two subjects compared. *Every body* is taken in an indefinite sense for every *kind of body*; but *circle* is

---

[45] Compare the Treatise and Essays,—in both works *impressions* are considered as absolutely necessary to *cause* ideas—to create them;—to *produce* them;—they are considered as the truly "productive principle" of ideas—*Objects* without which they could not exist. [Shepherd draws Hume's "recapitulation" directly from *Enquiry* 7.30.]

[46] Essays, Vol. 2. Sec. 5, p. 47. [Shepherd is paraphrasing closely from *Enquiry* 5.5, substituting 'would infer' for Hume's 'could infer'.]

not taken for every *kind of figure*. The reason whence the CONCLUSIONS concerning all circles are *general*, is upon the very principle of Cause and Effect; for I know by experience, that upon the first study of Mathematical science, I found much difficulty in a philosophical objection I could not easily answer; namely; that the relations of the quantities in one figure did not seem *necessarily* applicable to *all* of a like kind; until I perceived that the affections of *all*, were INVOLVED in *one* of *each kind*; as there was nothing to occasion a *difference* amidst their relations. Now then let the data be the same, and the IMPULSE *given* not only be *like*, but the BODY *given be like*; and I conceive that every man, and every child, would expect, upon a second trial, that the same body would move in the same manner as before. The inference would be drawn from the mind perceiving, (in the first instance,) that no motion would have taken place except from the conjunction of the body with the impulsive force; and in the second case would add to the memory of this Effect, the reasoning, that there being nothing else to make a difference, a like Effect would again take place. Nay, I am persuaded, that reason might go so far as, from calculating the proportions of the impulse used, and the body moved, to conclude the varieties, which would take place under proportionably different circumstances.

Mr. Hume draws two inferences of much consequence from his doctrine; 1st, that as our *custom of thinking* is not the *operation of nature*, so we have no positive proof, that a cause is wanted for the existence of the universe as of a truly "*productive principle.*" 2dly, That it is *unreasonable to believe in miracles*, because it is foolish to allow of our *customary habits of thinking*, which arise from "experience in the course of nature," to be interfered with by an "*experience of a less frequent occurrence*;" which dependence upon testimony can only afford. This latter inference he professes in his Essay against Miracles.[47] The former opinion is less openly acknowledged; not being stated in explicit terms, but of immediate inference from the doctrine; and which he was well aware of, was the case.

The sum of my answer and argument is, that although we know not the "secrets of nature," yet we know that nothing can "begin its own existence;" therefore there must truly be a "productive principle," a cause necessary for every new existence in nature;—that we gain the knowledge of a "necessary connexion between Cause and Effect," by an *experimentum crucis*, and therefore no greater number of invariable antecedents and consequents are

---

[47] [Shepherd is referring to *Enquiry* Section 10, "Of Miracles."]

wanted, than what is necessary, in order *to observe* what circumstances *affect each other, or the contrary.* That neither *fancy* nor *custom* creates the notion by an association of ideas; but the UNDERSTANDING gains it, by an observation of what is *that circumstance, without which a new object does not exist.* Things therefore could not change their places, nor nature alter her course, without a contradiction.

Hence it is that a cause is wanted in the universe equivalent to the change from non-existence to existence! And also that it is not more unreasonable to believe in miracles than in any other extraordinary phenomena in nature, when we may suppose, that *efficient Causes have been in action,* towards their production; and that *final causes* are of *sufficient weight to justify the altered work of Providence!*

But a minute investigation of Mr. Hume's Essay on Miracles is much wanted. The purport of it, and the method by which it is drawn out as a consequence from the three preceding Essays, has not (that I know of) been observed by the learned. One would think at first sight that Mr. Hume, in admitting that the "course of nature might change," conceded much to the Christians. Instead of which he adroitly turns round upon them, and says, "so it may in fact;" but in "custom" you *think it cannot,* therefore it is absurd to allow this custom of thought to be overthrown by testimony. In this struggle of fancy, against fancy, the more powerful must and ought to prevail!—If these pages should find favour before the public, an examination of the Essay on Miracles is intended to follow them; without which the answer to these on Cause and Effect is hardly complete.[48]

Should an objection arise to my doctrine, that on account of supposing causes to act as the junctions of different qualities, and yet by pushing back all causes to the ONE UNCAUSED ESSENCE; I thereby prevent the idea of him being reposed in as a Cause; as he forms ONE object only: I answer, that the uncaused essence, however mysterious in his nature, and however awful and distant to our speculations, must nevertheless have attributes; or in other words, its own peculiar qualities, which required no former beings, to *give birth to them.*

The unions of such qualities among themselves, might well be equal to the going forth of the great Creation! The union of *wisdom,* with benevolence;

---

[48] [Shepherd's essay entitled "That human testimony is of sufficient force to establish the credibility of miracles" is Essay VIII of *EPEU* Part II. By 'the three preceding Essays', she means the three "Essays" of Hume's that she has been directly discussing—that is, *Enquiry* Sections 4, 5, and 7.]

and of these with the "*power*" arising out of the inexhaustible resources of his essence, might well occasion the "starting forth" of innumerable beings; the highest orders of which, without the slightest philosophical contradiction, might be considered as coeval and coequal with the Father "as touching the Godhead."[49] But after this, the wide universe, with all its gradations of wonderful beings, with all its powers of life and heat, and motion, must have come out from him according to the laws with which they were endowed. And although the original undivided essence, whose qualities were equal to such creation, must be considered as antecedent to his own work; yet the *operation* of that essence must ever have been the same from all eternity; and in that point of view, the *junction* of wisdom and benevolence, with whatever "*capacities*" of that essence were efficient to their ends, must have been accompanied with their instant synchronous Effects;— the *formation of inferior beings*. "Let there be light," said God, "and there was light."[50]

Thus God, the universal Father, and with him any noble *manifestations* of his essence; then archangel, and angel; man (or beings analogous to him) and animals; mind, and matter; may be considered as having existed eternally, coming forth from him, living in him, and supported by him; whilst an analogous state of being must be expected to continue eternally, in like manner— and it may also be expected as a circumstance consistent and probable with the whole of so grand an arrangement, that some inferior orders of beings may be raised in the scale of nature, to be inhabitants of a kindlier world than this; with enlarged capacities for happiness and virtue.

The consideration of the method the understanding has recourse to, in order to judge of the probable presence of similar causes on the contrary, will come under our view in the next Chapter.

---

[49] [This phrase alludes to the Christian *Athanasian Creed*.]
[50] [Shepherd is quoting *Genesis* 1:3.]

CHAPTER THE THIRD.

I SHALL now proceed to apply the principles already laid down, to the examination of the question concerning the guidance of our expectations in ordinary life, which question forms the subject of the Essay entitled Sceptical Doubts concerning the operations of the Understanding. The question itself might be shortly stated thus:—why does the operation of the apparent qualities of an object upon the senses, lead the mind to expect the action of its untried qualities, when placed in fit circumstances for their operation?

Why should bread, on account of its formerly nourishing the body, be expected to nourish it again? why may it not, whilst it preserves "its colour, consistence, &c." nevertheless destroy the human frame?

In my answer to these questions, I shall allow to Mr. Hume, that the memory of the sensible and *apparent* qualities of any object, is necessary to the acknowledgment of it as the same body, upon every acquaintance with it; also that the *memory of what its qualities will be*, when conjoined with any other, is also requisite to the *expectation* of any farther qualities arising from it.

The idea of these must be associated with the sensible qualities; but the knowledge that they will assuredly take place, when existing in like circumstances, is founded upon much stronger principles than those of custom and habit.

It is founded—

First,—Upon a quick, steady, accurate observation, *whether the prevening causes are the* SAME, *from which an object is elicited in any* PRESENT *instance, as upon a* FORMER *one*;—and,

2dly,—Upon a demonstration, that if the observation hath been correct, the result—(i.e. the *whole* effects or qualities,) must necessarily be the same as heretofore; otherwise contrary qualities, as already discussed, would arise without a cause, i.e. a *difference begin of itself*, which has been shown to be impossible[1]. Thus the first step the mind takes, in order to be satisfied that

---

[1] It has already been shown upon mathematical principles, that a *difference* in the *result* of equal unions, can no more arise out of the *mixtures of any other qualities of objects*, than from the *junctions of those of number*. If ONE added to ONE, bear out the result TWO, *once*; it must ever do so; and if a

the same *apparent qualities* in any object will be attended with like "*secret powers,*" is the consideration, from the surrounding circumstances, of what the prevening causes were, which gave *birth to the object*; and therefore whether the *apparent qualities* are *truly* the accompaniments of the *same nature* or not.—As for instance, we can form a notion almost with certainty, whether the substance placed upon the table has been truly elicited from such causes, as could alone produce the compound object bread. Whether the pure liquid offered, be the result of such circumstances as render it water, or of such others, as may prove it, (notwithstanding its apparent quality to the eye,) to be spirits of ammonia? &c. It is not the *mere* appearance of the external qualities, which can determine the mind to expect certain effects; it is only that *appearance in conjunction with the recollection of the probable causes, that have produced the objects in question*, and which lead the mind to suppose the said objects to be truly bread, water, or hartshorn;[2] and therefore impossible not to be capable of exhibiting all their qualities, and none other than their qualities.

The first step belongs to those combined qualities of mind called good sense; and will always be made with an assurance and propriety in proportion to it. The nature of its operation is this;—the mind knows that different objects have the same apparent qualities to some of the senses, which cannot afford a sufficient test concerning the farther exhibition of others;—but observation enables it to judge, when an object is presented, what *causes have been used in its formation*; and if it perceives that the causes have been similar, it *knows* that the whole effects or qualities must necessarily be similar; otherwise there might be an uncaused "change in the course of nature;" which, although sometimes *philosophers* imagine possible, *no ordinary minds* ever do, because they never think a *change* can take place of itself; or in other words, qualities begin their own existences.

It is nothing but this reasoning concerning the *causes*, used in the *formation of an object*, which makes us argue to the "secret powers," and the similar appearances only guide us, in as far as they form a proof that they are truly the same objects, with respect to those appearances; for SIMILAR *objects could not have different appearances.*

The way to try the case is to observe the action of the mind, when two objects are presented of precisely similar appearance, but which may be

certain proportion of *blue and yellow particles*, form a mixture termed GREEN, *once*; GREEN in like manner shall ever *thence* result.

[2] ['Hartshorn' was a common term for the horn or antler of a male deer, and also for the ammonia that was frequently obtained from it, especially as that substance was used in an aqueous solution.]

thought, on account of the uncertainty as to the circumstances which elicited them, possibly, to possess different properties.

We always enquire, in such cases, as to some *leading circumstance*, which may enable us to judge what causes were used in their formation.

If an ignorant person, for instance, whom we perceived could not read, were about to serve us in a chymist's shop with *Epsom salts*; we, being aware that *oxalic acid* had the same *apparent* qualities, should not feel an assurance in the "*secret powers*;" but would cautiously enquire for some mark, by which to be guided in our notion as to their *original* FORMATION;—i.e. as to what mass of qualities *apparent*, and *secret*, had been combined by the hand of nature, or art, in the object before us. It is here that Mr. Hume's mistake is evident in the statement of what he deems an irresolvable difficulty, concerning the method of the mind in the *guidance* of its expectation with respect to the *untried qualities*, or "Effects," of the objects presented to it.

These are his words,—

"The two following propositions are far from being the same; I have found that such an object has always been attended with such an Effect; and I foresee that all other objects, in *appearance similar*, will be attended with similar effects."[3] The connexion between the two propositions is not intuitive; of what nature is it then? I answer, WE NEVER DO MAKE THE CONNEXION— *we never do foresee that objects similar in appearance* ONLY, *will be attended with similar Effects.*—But as *truly similar* objects, must necessarily *appear* the same, we combine these acknowledged similarities, with the circumstances which we are aware of, as *most probable to have been used in their formation*, and thence judge whether the object be *truly* a mass of similar Effects or qualities, elicited from like causes in action, or the contrary.

If the causes in action have been the same; (and we are pretty good judges if they have, or have not, in the vast variety of ordinary cases with which we have to do,) then the objects in question must necessarily possess the whole qualities which belong to their natures, whether taken *singly*, and acting *alone* on the senses; or acting in *conjunction with another object*, and exhibiting those *further qualities*, which are usually termed "*Effects.*"

Thus Mr. Hume's statement—"I have found such an object has always been attended with such an effect; and I foresee other objects, in *appearance similar*, will be attended with similar effects;" is not the state of the human mind in any given circumstance. It should rather run thus, (although the

---

[3] [Shepherd is quoting, with minor changes, from *Enquiry* 4.16.]

familiarity we have from infancy with the objects of life prevent the notion from being so distinctly formed, much less expressed, as to be easily detected when called upon.)

107 Here is an object which has been the result of LIKE CAUSES IN ACTION, *now as formerly*. The *whole* mass of Effects, which *those causes once* produced, must necessarily *be again* capable of being exhibited in like appropriate circumstances.

It may also be added, that when an object in nature is, on account of some governing circumstance relating to it, considered as a similar object with another; because that governing circumstance points out the creating causes of it; then the "Effects" as well as the *apparent* qualities, enter into its definition, and *bread* stands as a sign of *all the ideas under the term*, and of *nothing but the ideas*.

It receives that name on account of its *tried qualities*, and it retains it, when *known to have been formed by those creating causes*, that necessarily can only determine *similar effects*.

If the human body is in the same state on any occasion, as on that when bread nourished it; there is as great a necessity it should again *nourish*, as that it should be *white*.

108 Thus all experimental reasoning consists in an *observation*, and a *demonstration*, as has before been shown;—an *observation*, whether the circumstances from which an object is produced, and in which it is placed, are the same upon one occasion as upon another;—and a *demonstration*, that if it is so, *all its exhibitions will be the same*. But Mr. Hume asks in another question of the same nature, why we judge *otherwise* concerning the "Effects" (or untried qualities), following the apparent qualities, in some other objects.

"Nothing, says he, so like as eggs; yet no one, on account of this apparent similarity, expects the same taste and relish in all of them;" "Now where is that process of reasoning, which from one instance, draws a conclusion so different from that which it infers from a hundred others?"[4]

The reason is, because it is one of the *tried, known, qualities* of eggs, to become soon changed in their flavour; without any great indication of such 109 change becoming apparent to the eye;—therefore again, there is *not* a connexion between the apparent qualities, and "secret powers," and we should enquire if *we doubted*; concerning *some circumstance before tasting* that might afford a *discreet judgment*, some ground for conceiving that *only*

---

[4] [Shepherd is quoting both sentences, with minor changes, from *Enquiry* 4.20.]

those causes, had hitherto been in action, which had been likely to produce *fresh eggs*.

This instance forms an argument on my side of the question, rather than on Mr. Hume's; as it shows there is not an absolute connexion, (and that the mind never thinks there is,) between *the mere* APPEARANCES, and the "*Effects*" *of an object*;—but that we judge concerning the probability of the method in which an object has been *formed*, and of *the circumstances it may have been placed in afterwards, as likely or not to alter it*; before we announce, whether the *apparent* qualities are indications of those "*secret powers, on which the Effects entirely depend*."[5]

Thus I not only assert, that *these are* "the steps" the mind takes, from *experiment* to *expectation*; namely, ONE OF A HIGH PROBABILITY, that the prevening circumstances which determine those *masses of Effects*, (or qualities) called *objects*, have rendered them *the same* upon a present occasion, as upon a past; AND ONE OF DEMONSTRATION, that IF they are the same objects, *all* the *unexhibited* qualities, or *effects*, must also be THE SAME; but I also affirm, that "*custom*" is not, cannot, be the principle on which the notion of necessary connexion between Cause and Effect is really founded; and that with respect to the most familiar objects of our life it has only a partial operation, in governing our expectations of the future. I grant that custom or an association of ideas, arising from those habits which infix ideas in the mind, is the foundation of all *memory*; and therefore similar appearances, suggest the *remembered unexhibited accompanying qualities* of objects; but it will not suit *all* the phenomena; it will not give the *assurance* that the accompanying untried qualities, must of necessity take place; and that the object in question merits the name assigned to it. In order to prove this proposition, let us try any of the various strongly associated circumstances, which govern the mind, where clearly the suggestion to the imagination, can arise from nothing else but association of ideas. The ideas of these may always be disjoined from each other, without any apparent inconceivableness to the fancy; which is always the case in endeavouring to imagine a *similar cause* to take place with *one we have before known*, and a *different Effect* follow, from *that* which had *previously followed it*.

Let any school-boy, who always joins the first two lines in Virgil together, endeavour to imagine one line only written, without the other; he can do it; or that Virgil might have made another line, the first remaining the same; he

---

[5] [Shepherd is loosely paraphrasing from *Enquiry* 4.16.]

can; one is not the *cause* of the other; nor, are they necessarily connected. But when he says, twice 2 are 4, he finds that the consequence of two units being taken two times over, necessarily exhibit four units to the mind; and cannot be disjoined from that result, while the terms are spoken of in the same sense.

Like Causes necessarily *include*, and therefore *produce* and *exhibit* their *Effects*. The mind indeed may be forced from every recollection of habit, and consider the qualities of an object apart from each other, as in any other association: but the mind never can consider them as *possible* to exist *apart in nature*; it never for a moment supposes it but *inconceivable*, and impossible, that they should be "non-existent this moment," and "existent the next" without conjoining to them the idea of a cause or "productive principle."

The only difficulty the mind has to do with, in forming a right judgment concerning its expectations of the qualities of objects, is the probability, or the contrary, whether the circumstances which formed them, are the same as heretofore or not.—But this part of the question, we always consider with more or less nicety of induction; and do not believe them to be so, from external appearances only, but from those circumstances which enable us to know, what *course nature was taking, when she stamped them such as we see them*.

We judge in short that nature, in the continuance of her plan, is constant still to her own great ends; where the first beginnings of the work are wholly out of our cognizance.

We judge from the memory, of the parts we have ourselves taken in the disposition of Causes.

We judge from the knowledge we have had of the actions of others, and of the parts they have also been performing in their disposition; and when these are all in the affirmative, towards the probability of like Causes having been in action, in the formation of any object immediately concerning us; then we judge that the similar appearances, are qualities, of a like object, which only remains to be tried, to justify the assumption that *it is the same*; and that it deserves *the name* which has been bestowed on it accordingly. I think this answers the whole argument, and is sufficient to prove, that "*reason*" not "*custom*" is the great guide of human life; convincing us, that the "instances of which we have had no experience, must resemble those of which we have had experience, for that the course of nature must continue uniformly the same."[6]

---

[6] [Shepherd is quoting from *Treatise* 1.3.6.4, somewhat modifying Hume's final phrase, which is: "and that the course of nature continues always uniformly the same."]

SECTION THE SECOND.[7]

In the course of writing these pages, I have met with some passages in the works of Mr. Locke, which when compared with the whole of Mr. Hume's argument, (*à posteriori,*) must be considered as forming the basis of that elaborate and inconclusive reasoning. Mr. Locke says, "there is a supposition that *nature works regularly* in the production of things, and sets the boundaries to each species;—whereas any one who observes their different qualities, can hardly doubt that many of the individuals called by the same name, are in their *internal constitution* different from one another."[8]

Again; "Let the complex idea of gold, be made up of whatever other qualities you please, malleableness will not appear to depend on that complex idea. The connexion that malleableness has with those other qualities, being only by the intervention of the real collection of its insensible parts; which since we know not, it is impossible we should perceive that connection, &c."[9]

In another place he has; "But we are so far from being admitted into the *secrets of nature,* that we scarce so much as ever approach the first step towards them."[10]

The parallel passages in Mr. Hume's writings I need not again quote, especially as, if the reader has been interested in the course of this discussion, they will immediately recur to his memory.

Now Mr. Locke never meant to say that the differences of species could take place, excepting by the *regular operations of* CAUSES, *necessarily connected with their* EFFECTS; for he considered the sensible qualities of bodies, as dependant upon their internal constitution; which is both to acknowledge the relation of Cause and Effect, as also to conceive the *sensible qualities,* to be the EFFECTS of the *secret powers*[11].

Both of these principles Mr. Hume denies; saying expressly of the latter—"It is acknowledged on all hands, there is no connection between the sensible qualities, and those secret powers of objects, on which the effects entirely

---

[7] [Although there is no heading 'SECTION THE FIRST' in this chapter, presumably all of Chapter 3 up to this point may be considered to be the first section.]

[8] [Shepherd is quoting, with minor changes and omissions, from *Essay* 3.10.20.]

[9] [Shepherd is quoting, with changes and omissions from *Essay* 4.6.9. Presumably as a slip, she has 'real collection of insensible parts' where Locke uses his common phrase 'real constitution of insensible parts'.]

[10] [Shepherd is quoting from *Essay* 4.6.11 but substitutes 'step' for Locke's word 'entrance'.]

[11] "That every thing has a real constitution, whereby it is, what it is, and on which its sensible qualities depend, is past doubt."—Locke's Essay on the Human Understanding [*Essay* 3.10.21].

depend."[12]—Which latter remark I consider not only as erroneous, but astonishing! in as much as the ideas in this part of his Essay, are an obvious expansion of those of Mr. Locke, who is an *exception* to the notion of an universal agreement to this opinion; (being *one*, at least, and in authority equal to many, who does not acknowledge it.) The doubt however which Mr. Locke throws out, although it does in no respect affect the general principles concerning causation; yet it regards the difficulty there is in the *detection* of like objects, on account of our inability to form a judgment concerning their *internal constitutions*, from the *mere appearance* of their sensible qualities.

I consider Mr. Locke renders the difficulty something greater than it need be; although he acknowledges that a similarity in the sensible qualities forms an argument of high probability, (though short of demonstration,) in favor of the presence of truly similar objects.

For as the secret, external, unknown powers or qualities, in nature; determine the sensible qualities as their *effects*, as well as every other effect, or property; so when we perceive the sensible qualities in any instances to be *like*, we know that *as far as they go*, they are LIKE *Effects*, from like SECRET *constitutions*; which *secret constitutions* having been once able to determine certain effects, may do the same again; and not only *may*, but *must* do so again, *unless something has* occurred unobserved to make a difference among them.

In order to form a judgment if any thing is likely to have occurred towards making such an *alteration*; the mind has recourse to several observations and reasonings.—For considering that a certain figured, limited, portion of extended matter in nature, does by the action of the *self same particles*, exhibit different qualities, according to the different senses they meet, or variety of objects, with which they mix; so it applies these masses to the examination of more senses than one, for an higher certainty in this matter: knowing it to be very rare, but that a diversity is detected among the particles, by some *one* sense, at least. The senses, therefore, are considered capable of *nearly* detecting the similarity of internal constitutions; and this upon such a *regularity in fact* of the course of nature, which must itself be looked upon as a general Effect, from a general Cause.

Nevertheless the proposition founded on these trials, is but a probability, although a high one.

---

[12] [Shepherd is quoting, with a significant omission, from *Enquiry* 4.16, which actually reads (emphasis added): "It is allowed on all hands, that there is no *known* connection between the sensible qualities and the secret powers; and consequently, that the mind is not led to form such a conclusion concerning their constant and regular conjunction, by anything which it knows of their nature."]

But, 2dly. The mind has always a regard to the *method* taken by *nature* and *art* in the FORMATION of an object. When these are similar; the MASSES of *Effects*, or *objects*, are necessarily similar; and SUCH therefore will be *their* Effects in *their turn*. Then these *forming objects* are still silently traced backwards; in order to perceive if their production hath been similar—till we rest at last in those grand objects and operations in nature, which we have found so universally regular to certain ends, that upon the *general relation* of Cause and Effect, (as applicable to this particular case,) we *conclude,* that such a *regular like Effect*, can only be the result of a *like* continual cause; which shall not alter as long as the GREAT FIRST CAUSE doth not alter his pleasure therein. Thus we trace the *sensible qualities* of bread to the SECRET CONSTITUTIONS which have partly been put in action, by the sower and reaper of corn, the operations of the miller and the baker; and beyond these to the influence of the air, the sun, and the juices of the earth; which objects as they originally seem to have "come forth from the Father of man"[13] for his use, so have they ever continued too true to their destination, not to be considered as dependant on that "God of seasons," who has ordained the nourishment of his children to arise from "*bread, earned by the sweat of their brow.*"[14]

It is, on account of these reasons, (that in answer to Mr. Hume) I say, that "other bread" will also nourish, when a body of a like colour and consistency has frequently done so; and which remains free from the suspicion of any other beings having been concerned in its FORMATION than those alluded to. *Frequency of repetition*, abstracted from the *principle of* CAUSATION *as a* CONCLUSION *already drawn* from "*general reasoning*," is not a circumstance sufficient to generate such a principle, either from *custom*, or aught else; but being previously known and believed in; *frequency of repetition* becomes legitimately to be considered as an *Effect*, from a *Cause*, equally constant and general in its exhibition; and thereby begets a *reasonable*, as well as a customary dependance, upon the *necessary connexion*, that is between such regular Cause and Effect.

Thus the most ignorant conceive; *first* that qualities cannot begin of themselves; for there is as quick and accurate a perception, of natural contradictions in terms, amidst the least as the most learned of men: they therefore believe in *Cause*, as a "productive principle" in general. Secondly, they believe that regularity in nature is an Effect whose *Cause* they may

---

[13] [At John 16:28, Jesus says, "I came forth from the Father."]
[14] [This idiom may be traced to Genesis 3:19: "In the sweat of thy face shalt thou eat bread."]

regularly depend on, as a corollary with the preceding principle. Thirdly, they believe there is the intimate connexion of Cause and Effect between the secret powers, and sensible qualities of objects; conceiving that an OUTWARD *indefinite object*, which when it meets with the eye presents to it a certain colour, and with the touch a certain consistency, and which they believe to be FORMED from certain materials, will *also*, upon trial, be palateable to the taste, agreeable to the stomach, and nourishing to the body.

122   Thus when Mr. Hume says, "I require *for my information* what reasoning it is that leads men, from the mere sensible qualities of things to expect their future Effects?"[15] he requires the statement of an argument, which in fact is never made; for men conceive that it is *something indefinite*; i.e. a certain mass of particles determined into that mass by forming powers equivalent to it, which meeting with the eyes, is seen of a defined colour, with the touch yields the sense of a certain consistency, and when entering the stomach shall be enjoyed as a satisfaction to hunger[16]. *None ever suppose*, that it is what is *first* seen and felt—that it is *colour and consistency* which *afterwards* NOURISHES.—*They suppose it is that which is sown and reaped, and kneaded and baked*; which seen, or *unseen*; touched or *untouched*; is FITTED TO NOURISH; but being seen, shall be white or brown; and being felt, shall be of

123   a less or greater compressibility. The *sensible* qualities are only considered as SIGNS of the secret powers,—which *secret powers* are understood to be determined by certain similar processes of *art*, mixed with the grand and regular operations of nature. When the *formation* of objects can be less accurately detected; their similarity of internal constitution becomes more doubtful, from the mere appearance of *some* of the sensible qualities only;—for, the greater number of qualities which are exhibited as similar to the senses, the higher does the proof become, of the secret powers being also similar.

Fourthly.—The mind, (of ordinary persons especially), though appearing to reason upon this subject in a *circle*, yet in reality escapes the sophism and proceeds by a method involving much practical result and rational evidence. For instance; if there were an *appearance* of fire, doubted, as to its being more than a *mere* appearance of it;—the moment it were known to have been elicited from the concussion of flint and steel, there would no longer be

---

[15] [Shepherd is loosely paraphrasing *Enquiry* 4:20.]
[16] This part of the subject again touches upon the Berkleyan theory, concerning external nature; and the opinions ordinary minds have of the *external existence*, or the contrary, of the sensible qualities: upon *which point* Hume and Berkeley are at variance. [George Berkeley (1685–1753) asserted that sensible qualities cannot exist outside of all minds, and he maintained that this was compatible with common sense. Shepherd discusses his views at length in *EPEU*.]

a doubt on that matter. Then if in any case did the question arise, whether those objects usually considered as *flint and steel*, were truly such, it would be thought a proof in the affirmative, if upon their concussion they could elicit a *sensible* spark. Philosophers might imagine the *secret powers* of the *whole* to be altered; but plain understandings would consider the *entire coincidence* to be too great and remarkable to arise from *chance*. Such *sensible causes*, giving birth to such *sensible effects*, they would suppose formed a connection of the highest probability, whence to form a judgment, that the whole secret powers of each were similar. And in cases of high probability the mind is as much *determined* to action, as by demonstration. It cannot stand hesitating, and therefore "takes a step" (in arguing from the sensible qualities to the future effects of things,) governed by a *high probability* founded on REASONING "that *they* ARE" connected with like secret *powers, on which the Effects entirely depend.*

Nor is this argument in a circle, for the mind does not reason from the Effects to the Causes; and from the Causes back again to the Effects, but considers in each of these cases, that the *invariable regularity* of nature is a POWER that may be depended upon; and from which fact of *invariableness* the reasonable argument is framed, that the same secret powers will accompany the sensible qualities which have ever done so, when elicited from like *apparent Causes*. It is an additional proof added to the APPEARANCE *of fire*, that it is REALLY such, if found to be the result not only of *apparently* like Causes in action, but of such that have *never been known to* MISS FIRE, when they have *seemed* to kindle it. Whilst should the temper of steel lie under any suspicion, of incapacity as to the determination of its Effects; if upon trial, the spark be immediately emitted, the conclusion is as immediate that this Effect is similar in the secret powers, which nature in no instance ever failed, to determine along with such sensible qualities.

In moral feelings also, I might argue that had I a friend whose absence might suggest a dread, lest the *powers* of his friendship had become weakened; if upon his return I observed the same *sensible manifestations* of regard as heretofore I should have very reasonable ground to judge, that they were the symptoms of a *heart*, as true to me as ever, whose faith was always found to shew itself *in similar demonstrations of kindness*.

It is one of the most ordinary modes of reasoning that the generality of mankind possess; to consider invariability of recurrence as incapable of arising from *chance*.—The meaning of which is, that having the principle of general causation already in their minds, they judge that invariable regularity cannot be *undesigned* and without an end in view, (as well as that it is itself an *Effect*, and must therefore have its own Cause, i.e. a *regular* invariable Cause of whose very *essence* it is, only to determine similar Effects.) And it is remarkable that this idea and in the *very same language* expressing it, is used at the beginning of Mr. Hume's "*Treatise*," as the sole foundation of a system expressly undertaken to prove that the mind never *reasons*, from experience to expectation. His words are to this purpose; "*this coincidence*," (viz. of an IDEA always requiring an IMPRESSION to prevene it,) "IS TOO GREAT TO ARISE FROM CHANCE!"[17]

To return to Mr. Locke, he merely meant to say, that nature in her regular and usual modes of operation, from Cause and Effect might form *irregular collections of qualities*, not to be detected by mere appearances; and therefore unworthy *on that account only*, of retaining the *names* of regular species, which are *also named* on account of their *tried* Effects and properties. But every man acquainted with Mr. Locke's writings must consider him, as far from wishing to authorize in future times such a scheme as that of Mr. Hume's. Nor do I think he would dissent from my notions, that the method the mind takes to judge of the kind of objects which are present is:

1stly.—By tracing the *manner* of their formation.

2dly.—By considering an invariable regularity in nature as reasonable to be depended upon, being itself an invariable effect from an equal Cause.

3dly.—By the application of various senses to the affections of the particles.

4thly.—By the consideration that the sensible qualities being similar is a presumption in favor of similar secret powers, as *truly* similar objects would necessarily *appear* the same.

5thly.—That in like manner when *Effects* are *apparently* similar a presumption is formed in favor of apparently similar causes, having given birth to *like secret powers* in the EFFECTS, as well as *their sensible qualities*.

6thly.—That the mind quickly and habitually surveys these things; so that the understanding being *accomplished* in such latent, and constant reasoning; may uniformly blend and use it, although it may find a difficulty of analyzing it when called for.

7thly.—That after the application of an exact experiment, it is impossible to imagine a difference of qualities to arise under the same circumstances.

It is strange that a system at once so unstable and confused, as Mr. Hume's, should ever have been built upon any notions of Mr. Locke, whose

---

[17] [Shepherd is paraphrasing *Treatise* 1.1.1.8: "Such a constant conjunction, in such an infinite number of instances, can never arise from chance; but clearly proves a dependence of the impressions on the ideas, or of the ideas on the impressions."]

moral conclusions are so much at variance with his. Divest Mr. Hume's ideas of the air, of science and grace, which he throws around them, and present them in a plain and popular manner, they will appear thus.[18]—

"The mind cannot become acquainted with the knowledge of a necessary connexion between Cause and Effect; for there exists no relations amidst things, of which an *idea* can be conveyed to it, except by the means of an original *impression*."

"But in nature events are entirely *unconnected*, therefore not capable of conveying an *impression* of *necessary connexion*, or of POWER; yet men conceive that events, are *not thus unconnected*—in which idea they are mistaken; as *experience*, which is the ONLY field for their observation in this matter, merely offers to view certain similar sensible qualities, which are *frequently*, although not *invariably* followed by other similar sensible qualities. In certain cases, however, there have been such *invariable* sequences (though "of *loose, casual, unconnected events*") that a definition of Cause and Effect, as of an *invariable* sequence, may be *framed thereon*."

"In as much as it is only like sensible qualities with which we are acquainted, so they alone are considered as like *Causes* or *antecedents*; and they have *no connexion* with the *secret powers of objects*,—which secret powers, are *nevertheless the only true Causes on which the Effects entirely depend*;—therefore *like* sensible qualities NOT being like Causes might be followed by *different* Effects."

"Hence the *Custom* of the observance of those sequences of sensible qualities, which are similar, can alone convey the *impression*, whence the *idea* of causation results; and thence *necessary connexion* is a "fancy of the mind," not a relation in nature."

"To prove that *Custom* is the only "*Cause*" of our *belief in causation*; it is perfectly *reasonable* to suppose, that such an *invariable sequence might be interrupted*, for there is no contradiction in imagining an "ARBITRARY" *change in the course of nature*. Yet should a contrary *imagination* resist *reason*, and not conceive *in fact* this interruption as possible to take place; she may again *reconsider* the possibility of nature altering her course, forming no contradiction to *reason*."

I appeal to those who are acquainted with Mr. Hume's Essays, if this statement be not the sum of the argument—and I also appeal to every man

---

[18] [Shepherd intends the remainder of this paragraph and the four paragraphs that follow as a summary of Hume's general line of thought, not as quotations or close paraphrases of specific passages.]

capable of logical accuracy, if it doth not involve every species of illogical sophistry; for,

1st.—There is drawn a general negative conclusion; from an examination of particular instances only. If the adversary may not draw from particular experience the general affirmative conclusion, that *there is a necessary connexion*; neither can Mr. Hume infer a general negative position, that there is *not a necessary connexion* between Cause and Effect. He also deduces a general affirmative conclusion, viz. *"that the future shall invariably resemble the past;"* from *particular* instances only[19].

2dly.—The mind is directed to infer a conclusion against the general relation of Cause and Effect, by the demonstration of a proposition in nowise inconsistent with it; namely, that *like* sensible qualities, NOT being *like* Causes, might be followed by DIFFERENT Effects[20].

3dly.—A general negative conclusion is in fact drawn from negative premises, merely;—(however the illogical method may be disguised both as to manner and diction), for it is concluded there is no proof for the existence of the general relation of Cause and Effect between objects;—because experience shows that like sensible qualities are *not* like Causes; and are therefore *not* necessarily connected with like Effects[21]!

4thly—The question is *shifted* from the examination of the general relation of Cause and Effect, to that of the criterion for ascertaining the presence of like Causes[22].

5thly.—The very proposition is admitted, which is in dispute; in order to serve the purpose of his argument;—first, in the statement that *impressions are the productive Causes of ideas*;—secondly, in supposing the secret powers of an object to be alone *the real productive Causes of its future properties*;—thirdly, in conceiving Nature may alter her course for the express purpose of changing the secret powers; *and that they are changed by such alteration*;—and

---

[19] See p. 66, of this Essay [*ERCE* 59/66].
[20] See p. 76, ibid. [*ERCE* 63/76].
[21] It may be seen, that on account of these *particular* and *negative* propositions, (which after all include *that proposition which is in question*) he *really* deduces *there is no such existence, in this relation* AMIDST THINGS—for in the place of the *reality of its existence in nature*, (supposed by their statement to be disproved to reason, and therefore disproved altogether) *a "fancy of it in the mind alone"* is obliged to be substituted in its stead. This "FANCY" is *no connexion* between objects. [Despite Shepherd's use of quotation marks, no phrase like '*fancy of it in the mind* alone' occurs in Hume's texts. However, *Treatise* 1.4.7.5–7 declares that the "connexion, tie, or energy" of causes is "nothing but [a] determination of the mind," and the passage strongly implies that the illusory aim of finding a "connexion, tie, or energy" in causes themselves is a "trivial suggestion of the fancy."]
[22] See further, p. 60, and 62, of this Essay [*ERCE* 57/60 and 57–58/62].

lastly, in alleging *custom to be the sole Cause* (i.e. producing generating principle) *of the* IDEA *of causation*[23,24]

6thly.—The proposition "that the course of nature may be supposed to change," is used *ambiguously*, signifying indifferently either an uncaused alteration of the SUBSEQUENT *sensible qualities* or of the ANTECEDENT *secret powers*[25].

7thly, and lastly.—The two chief propositions of the argument are in opposition to each other; for Mr. Hume attempts to establish, *that* CUSTOM *not reason is the principle of causation*, whilst he allows REASON to be the sole ground and necessary Cause of this belief.

In presenting the foregoing observations to the reader's attention, I have endeavoured, I hope, without presumption, to show that Mr. Hume's reputation for logical correctness has been overrated. The effect of his work is to astonish by its boldness and novelty;—to allure us by its grace and lightness; his propositions are arranged so artfully, that their illogical connexion is not perceived, and the understanding, without being satisfied, is gradually drawn into inferences from which it would *gladly* but cannot *readily* escape.

If any reader should agree with me in conceiving this scheme to be fallacious, when minutely analyzed, and is thereby enabled to overcome its influence on his mind, I shall consider myself more than repaid for the labour of thought spent in an endeavour towards so desirable an end.

---

[23] In these several instances it cannot be contended that Mr. Hume's idea of Cause, is only that of an antecedent; IMPRESSION is supposed not merely *to go before*, but to *create* IDEA; i.e. to be an object absolutely necessary and completely efficient to its production, &c.
[24] See pages 76, 90, and 146, &c. of this Essay [*ERCE* 63/76, 69/90, 92/146, etc.].
[25] See p. 73, ibid. [*ERCE* 62/73]

CHAPTER THE FOURTH.

OBSERVATIONS ON DR. BROWN'S ESSAY ON THE DOCTRINE OF MR. HUME.

DR. Brown's theory[1] merits a particular investigation, and I shall follow him very shortly through each observation he makes on Mr. Hume's doctrine, which he states in *five* propositions. He first of all begins however with his own definition of the relation of Cause and Effect; which does not differ materially from that of Mr. Hume; and has the same inconvenience attending it; viz. *that it will apply to other regular sequences,* than *those which belong to this relation.* "A cause," says he, "is an object, which immediately precedes any change, and which existing again in similar circumstances, will always be immediately followed by a similar change."[2]

And again, "invariableness of antecedence, is the element which constitutes the idea of a cause."[3]

But I ask, how do you get acquainted with this fact? Mr. Hume says he knows it; "because of the habit arising from past custom, carrying the thought to an expectation of the future, with a liveliness of conception equal to the experience of the past,"[4] i.e. there is *uncertain certainty*; for, a lively idea hath not, in a *waking* any more than in a *sleeping* hour, CERTAIN EXISTENCE for its resemblance, without some *other notion* than merely its vivacity to support an *argument for its reality*[5].

---

[1] [The "Essay on the Doctrine of Mr. Hume" to which Shepherd refers is Thomas Brown's *Observations on the Nature and Tendency of the Doctrine of Mr. Hume, concerning the Relation of Cause and Effect,* second edition, enlarged (Brown 1806). I cite this work as *Observations.*

[2] [Shepherd is quoting with minor changes from *Observations* 44–46.]

[3] [Shepherd is quoting, with a significant omission, from *Observations* 46, where Brown writes, "Priority in the sequence observed and invariableness of antecedence in the future sequences supposed, are the elements which constitute the idea of a cause." However, *Observations* 36 describes "invariableness of antecedence and consequence" as "the only essential circumstance of causation."]

[4] [Shepherd is giving a general summary of Hume's view, rather than quoting from a particular passage.]

[5] This notion is intended to be fully discussed in a future Essay on the nature of external objects. [Shepherd is referring to her "An Essay on the Academical or Sceptical Philosophy," published in 1827 as the multi-chapter first part of *EPEU*. In her preface to that essay, she describes an earlier

Dr. Brown says, "I know it *from instinctive belief*, arising from the observation of seeing in *any one instance*, certain Effects follow given Causes."⁶

Now I confess, I do not know what "*instinctive belief*" means, except as applied to the mysterious manner in which animals know of the qualities of bodies previous to experience, by some laws beyond our scrutiny; or at most our conscious belief, of the existence of a simple sensation.

Intuitive belief, I understand; and by it is meant,—that in the relation of the two members of a proposition, the truth is contained in the definition of the terms; and cannot be altered without altering the signs of the ideas, which have been just allowed to stand for them.—But to say that *instinctive*, or *intuitive* belief, can arise in the mind, as a *conclusive proposition*, when it requires *experience*, in order to form some DATA for its *premises*; is to say you believe a thing, without a *reason* for it, and that you are sure of it, because you are sure of it, *although you do want an experiment*, in order to form *a basis for the proposition*, which is to be a *reason* for your *instinctive* conclusion. This is Dr. Brown's Theory.

He is excellent in detecting some of Mr. Hume's fallacies; but in not allowing that the proposition, "like Causes must have like Effects," to be founded on *reason*, is equally guilty of a most important one himself.

The first proposition of Mr. Hume which he examines is, that the relation of Cause and Effect cannot be discovered *à priori*.⁷

To this Dr. Brown assents; and I grant, that the particular qualities which will arise, under new circumstances that bodies shall be placed in, cannot. But the exact nature of the question is here rendered very ambiguous: for the *general* relation of Cause and Effect, is the subject *in question*; but the *question answered*, is whether the *particular* Effects arising from *particular* Causes, can be known; and in *whichever way* it is answered, *it does not form an answer* to the GENERAL one;—for, like Causes in general, might *necessarily be connected* with *like Effects* (of whatever kind they might be); and this

---

intention to include in *ERCE* an appendix containing "some inquiry into the nature and proof of matter, and of an external universe," an inquiry that, because of its length, is instead "unfold[ed] ... in the following essay" (*EPEU* 29/xi). Section 2 of Chapter 1 of that essay contains a discussion of the difference between dreams and "realities."]

⁶ [Shepherd is giving a general summary of Brown's view, rather than quoting from a particular passage. Brown uses the terms 'instinctive' and 'intuitive' interchangeably to describe what he regards as a universal "belief" or "principle" that every change is invariably connected with certain immediately prior circumstances. This belief, he holds, allows the mind to make an inference after a single observed sequence of a particular kind without requiring (as Hume had claimed) repeated experience of a constant conjunction.]

⁷ [Brown examines this proposition in *Observations* 47–80.]

proposition known, from some *process of reasoning*; although neither *before* nor *after* experience, the *particular* kind of Effects from given Causes should be discovered. This ambiguity renders the argument nugatory, and it would be tedious and unnecessary to say any thing more upon it.

The second proposition of Mr. Hume's Theory is, that even "after experience the relation of Cause and Effect cannot be discovered by reason."[8] To this Dr. Brown also agrees. The same ambiguity, concerning the nature of the question again prevails; for *reason might be* able to teach us after experience, that the *same* qualities must arise out of the *same objects, when there was nothing to make a difference*, although she should not inform us of the "secrets of nature," and explain to us any better, the mode of the connexion in each particular instance; for if the contrary were true;—if we could know those "secrets" in every particular instance, it could not form a ground, for concluding that "*all like Causes must have like Effects.*"—*General conclusions* cannot flow from *particular* premises, whether they be formed by *reason*, or *custom*, or *instinct*.

But Dr. Brown's argument, *against reason*, must be examined more minutely; these are his words; "he who asserts that "A WILL always be *followed* by B, asserts more than that A always HAS BEEN *followed* by B; and it is *this addition* which forms the *very essence* of THE RELATION OF CAUSE AND EFFECT; neither of the propositions *includes* the other; and as they have no agreement, *reason*, which is the sense of agreement, *cannot be applied to them*."[9]

To represent the relation of Cause and Effect, as A *followed* by B, is a *false view* of the matter. Cause and Effect, might be represented rather by A x B = C, therefore C *is* INCLUDED *in the* MIXTURE OF THE OBJECTS called CAUSE. If C arises once from the *junction of any two bodies*; C must upon every other *like conjunction*, be the *result*; because there is *no alteration in the proportions of the quantities to make a difference*;—C is really *included* in the MIXTURE *of* A *and* B, although, to our senses, we are forced to *note down* (as it were) the SUM arising from their union, *after the observance of their coalescence*. In like manner the results of all arithmetical combinations are *included* in their statements; yet we are obliged to take notice of them separately and subsequently, owing to the imperfection of our senses, in not observing them with sufficient quickness, and *time* being requisite to bring them out to full view and *apparent* in some DISTINCT *shape*. Indeed my whole notion, of the relation of Cause and Effect, is aptly imagined, by the nature of the necessary results, included in the juxta-position of quantities.

---

[8] [Brown examines this proposition in *Observations* 88–94.]
[9] [Shepherd is quoting with minor changes from *Observations* 81.]

But as long as Cause shall be considered ONLY *as an antecedent*; the FUTURE can never be proved to be *included in the* PAST, which yet is truly the case.—For when it comes to be observed, that *Cause means, and really is the creation of* NEW QUALITIES, (from new conjunctions in matter or mind,) then it is perceived that the future is "involved in the past;" for when existing objects *are the same*, they must put on SIMILAR QUALITIES; otherwise *contrary qualities or differences*, would arise of themselves; and "begin their own existences," which is *impossible*, and *conveys a contradiction in terms*[10]. All that *experience* has to do, is to show us, by what passes within ourselves, that there is a *contradiction* in the supposition of *qualities beginning their own existence*; and A CONTRADICTION is never admitted in the *relation of any ideas* that present themselves. The very act of reasoning consists, in such a comparison of our ideas, as will not permit of *inconsistent propositions*[11]; which would be the case, if "like Causes could produce *other* than like Effects."

So then REASON does establish this beautiful and certain proposition, which is the foundation of all our knowledge;—*That like Causes must ever produce like Effects*.

The third proposition is;—that the relation of Cause and Effect is an object of *belief* alone.[12] To this Dr. Brown also agrees, saying, "any quality which is incapable of being *perceived,* or *inferred*, can result only from an *instinctive principle of faith*."[13] But I ask how do you know the *future* is invariable? You say from an instinctive principle of faith in observing the *present*. I reply, that it is as impossible to draw an INSTINCTIVE *general conclusion*, from *particular premises*, as a REASONABLE one. That A follows B, can no more form an *instinct* than a *reason*, for universal certainty of a similar sequence.

The fourth proposition, that the relation of Cause and Effect is believed to exist between objects only after their "*customary*" conjunction is known to us;[14] Dr. Brown combats with such ingenuity, reasons against with such severity of logic, and vanquishes with such skill and power, that all I should

---

[10] No mathematical reasoning can ever be driven further back, than by showing that the *contrary* of an asserted proposition *is a contradiction in terms*.

[11] The beginning of every quality is perceived to be only a *change*, upon some objects already in existence; and therefore cannot convey the same notion to the mind, as the *beginning of a quality*, supposed to be *independent of other objects* and NOT to be a change. THE BEGINNING OF EXISTENCE, therefore, cannot appear otherwise than *contrary* to the idea of its *independency* of those objects of which it is a *change*.

[12] [Brown examines this proposition directly in *Observations* 94. He further discusses the first three propositions in connection with the idea of power and the principle that every beginning of existence requires a cause in *Observations* 94–121.]

[13] [Shepherd is quoting with an omission and minor changes from *Observations* 94.]

[14] [Brown examines this proposition in *Observations* 121–42.]

attempt to say upon it, would be useless. I can only express my regret, that he could suppose, a notion of *belief*, founded upon the influence of the imagination, rather than of *reason*, to be a *rock*, on which we might build our house, without "*danger of the storm and tempest.*"[15]

Nor is Dr. Brown's "*blind impulse of faith*" a much more secure one. He imagines such a principle to be the foundation of all demonstrative reasoning;—but it is really not so. *Intuitive* propositions are those *included in the very terms*, given to our impressions; and are as true as *they* are, whose truth arises from *simple conscious feelings*, ARBITRARILY named. But INSTINCTIVE propositions, *not so grounded*, and which require some DATA, some *experience*, some *premises*, in which it is confessed they are *not included*, are an absolute contradiction to philosophy and common sense.

The fifth proposition is, "that when two objects have been frequently observed in succession, the mind passes readily from the idea of one to the idea of the other; the transition in the mind itself being the impression from which the idea of the necessary connexion of the objects as Cause and Effect is derived."[16]

This opinion, namely, "*that an easy transition of thought,*" is the only foundation of the idea of power, Dr. Brown also combats, and conquers; showing in a masterly manner the *illogical* CIRCLE in which Mr. Hume argues.—Indeed it is matter of surprise to reflect on Mr. Hume's reputation, *for logical* precision, when the whole superstructure of his work is built upon the denial of a proposition, which is *assumed as true in the premises*; for in the original inquiry, concerning the method by which we gain *ideas*; Mr. Hume says, it must be from IMPRESSIONS as their *Cause*; i.e. as a "productive principle;" for "their constant conjunction is too frequent to arise "from chance[17];" then

---

[15] [Psalms 55:8 and Isaiah 29:6 both use the phrase 'storm and tempest'. However, the primary reference here is perhaps to Luke 6:48: "He is like a man which built an house, and digged deep, and laid the foundation on a rock: and when the flood arose, the stream beat vehemently upon that house, and could not shake it: for it was founded upon a rock." In *Treatise* 1.4.7.2, Hume describes the "enmity of all metaphysicians, logicians, mathematicians, and even theologians" resulting from his philosophy as "that storm, which beats upon me from every side."]

[16] [Shepherd is quoting this proposition from *Observations* 142–43 with some omission. Brown examines the proposition in *Observations* 142–78.]

[17] "Let us consider how they stand with regard to existence, and of the impressions and ideas, which are Causes and which Effects." TREATISE.—"Such a constant conjunction can never arise from chance, but proves a dependence of the impressions on the ideas, or of the ideas on the impressions." TREATISE.—These notions, although not expressed in the *very same words*, are *plainly* found in the Essays. "Every idea is *copied*," or is "*derived*" from an impression, is precisely the same thought, and which as completely begs the question in dispute, as the passages do which I have quoted from the Treatise; evidently arguing that IMPRESSION is the "productive principle" of *idea*. [The first quotation slightly paraphrases *Treatise* 1.1.1.6; the second slightly paraphrases *Treatise* 1.1.1.8. Hume states that all ideas are copied or derived from impressions in *Enquiry* 2.5–6 and *Enquiry* 7.30.]

CHAPTER THE FOURTH 93

examining the nature of the idea of cause, or power; he asks, "from what impression (as its cause) this idea arises" (as its effect)?[18] Thus proving ideas to be "derived" from *impressions*, on account of the *necessary connexion* there exists between them; and then, *disproving* this doctrine of *necessary connexion*, from the *very* notions previously built upon it. It is considered, however, by Dr. Brown, that Mr. Hume's idea of power, although *false*, and only resolvable into a *strong imagination* founded on custom; "a belief not different from that we have in fiction, save in the vivacity of the conception of its objects;"[19] is nevertheless sufficient to guard the doctrine from any charge of excluding the necessity of *Deity for the creation of the universe*.

He seems to think, that as Mr. Hume got hold of the idea of POWER, by *some means or other*, it is immaterial by what means; as any idea of power whatever, would show that a Deity was alike necessary.

But this is false reasoning; if, according to Mr. Hume, we really did, from observing one object always follow another, fall into so strong a fancy, that one was *necessary to produce the other*, as to be unable to avoid the conclusion of their invariable and absolute dependence on each other; yet upon the supposition of once knowing this conclusion to be only the effect of a habit of mind, arising from an association of ideas; (a fancy, a custom of thought); we should nevertheless consider that the objects in nature might be perfectly independent of each other; and therefore could not draw any conclusion in favour of the necessity of a Creator, as the "productive principle" of the universe.

For should the circumstance of B following A, in all alphabets, generate in our minds the false notion that A *causes* B, yet if afterwards we should discover that these letters were not *truly necessary* to each other, and that in nature *any other letter* than B might *follow* A; although after such discovery, B might always be *suggested* on the *appearance* of A; yet not only would the notion of *causation* be really destroyed, if it arose from the *invariableness of their antecedence and subsequence*; but upon the supposition of the contrary, and that notwithstanding the conviction of the judgment, the *fancy of their mutual necessary dependence held its ground*; still we should not justify such an example as fit to be followed in ALL *our other expectations*; or thence conclude, that *all things we know of*, required necessarily their *antecedents*. No;— this *fancy of power*, without *knowledge of it*; this imagination of productive

---

[18] [Shepherd is perhaps alluding to *Enquiry* 2.9 and 7.30.]
[19] [Shepherd is evidently alluding to Hume's view of "poetical fictions" as presented in *Treatise* 1.3.10.6–11.]

principle, without an enlightened judgment concerning its absolute necessity, cannot be all that is necessary, to any arguments that are founded on the belief of "POWER."

A false and fanciful idea of power, of cause, and of connexion, is just as unsubstantial for their support, as though these words were absolutely "without any meaning."

The denial of the idea of power, as of truly a "productive principle," as of a *former and generator of new qualities in matter*, and the consideration of it as only "*a custom of mind*," does *not prevent the doctrine, as Dr. Brown seems to think it may, from involving the most dangerous consequences.*

How such an idea of power as Mr. Hume's, should give us the "consolation, and the peace, and the happiness, and the virtue of a filial confidence in the great Father of mankind,"[20] is hard to discover? A faith like this, would not go far in affording men that "security which has more to do with our happiness, than any present earthly enjoyment!"

---

[20] [Shepherd is quoting this phrase, with an omission, from *Observations* 195. The same paragraph describes this happiness as "measurable by no earthly enjoyment."]

CHAPTER THE FIFTH.

OBSERVATIONS ON MR. LAWRENCE'S LECTURES.

SECTION THE FIRST.

I shall now proceed to offer a few observations on a modern author, (Mr. Lawrence,) who in his Physiological Lectures,[1] eagerly seizes upon Dr. Brown's definition of the relation of Cause and Effect; which he imagines well adapted to an explanation of the properties of life.

In his 3d Lecture, p. 81, Mr. Lawrence says, "we can only trace, in this notion of necessary connexion, the fact of certainty or universality of concurrence; therefore it is we may assert the living muscular fibre is irritable, and the living nervous fibre is sensible. Nothing more than this is meant when a necessary connexion is asserted between the properties of sensibility, and irritability, and the structures of living muscular and nervous fibres."[2]

And again, page 79, "The only reason we have for asserting in any case that any property belongs to any substance, is the certainty or universality with which we find the substance, and the property in question, accompanying each other.—Thus we say gold is ductile, yellow, soluble in nitro-muriatic acid,[3] because we have always found gold when pure to be so—we assert the living muscular fibres to be irritable, and the living nervous fibres to be sensible for the same reason. The evidence of the two propositions presents itself to my mind as unmarked by the faintest shade of difference."[4] According to the theory of the foregoing pages of this Essay, there is the greatest difference between the evidence of the two propositions just quoted.

---

[1] [Shepherd is referring to Lawrence's *Lectures on Physiology, Zoology, and the Natural History of Man* (Lawrence 1819), which I cite as *Lectures*.]

[2] [Shepherd is drawing from successive paragraphs of *Lectures* III: 81. By 'irritable', Lawrence means "excitable to contraction." By 'sensible', he means "excitable to sensation."]

[3] ['Nitro-muriatic acid' is a now-obsolete term for a mixture of nitric and hydrochloric acids, which was also called *aqua regia* for its ability to dissolve gold.]

[4] [Shepherd is quoting, with minor changes, from *Lectures* III: 79–81.]

An object is here defined; "a combined mass of qualities, determined to the senses from unknown causes in nature, to which an arbitrary name is affixed." But *property* which is synonymous with Effect, "is the yet *untried*, or unobserved quality, which *will* arise upon the mixture of that mass with other objects."[5]

The *necessary connexion*, therefore, of a *name*, with the *qualities which it designates*, is no more than the connexion of an *arbitrary sound* with an *object*, or in other words with the *unknown causes in nature*, which determine the qualities that affect our senses; and which must be "necessarily connected with it" so long as we do not contradict ourselves in terms; or at least whilst we agree not to alter our terms. But the *necessary connexion* of an *object*, and its further *properties*, (or effects,) viz. those which are produced by its union with another object, arises from the obligation that certain combinations of qualities have to beget upon their *junction* with other combinations, certain NEW QUALITIES; and this *necessary connexion* must take place between the like objects on all future occasions, from the obligation that *like Causes have to produce like Effects*. The connexion of gold with fusibility, ductility, &c. is of the former kind of connexion, viz. that of a *name* for certain enumerated *qualities, en masse*[6].—The connexion of sentiency with the *live* nerve, is of the latter kind. The former is a *necessary* but *arbitrary* connexion; the latter is considered as a NECESSARY *Effect*, from certain combined and efficient *causes*.

SECTION THE SECOND.

Should it be objected, the word *gold*, does not stand as a mere *arbitrary* sign for *certain enumerated qualities*, but as a term, for *a portion of extended matter*, which will exhibit upon trial, *certain properties peculiar to itself*, I admit, that it is perfectly philosophical to consider the subject in this point of view; for either *a noun* as a *name*, may be considered as a sign, for *all* the qualities and properties understood to be under the term;—or as a sign, merely standing for the qualities of the genus;—then the noun is still only necessarily connected in the sense of an *arbitrary* connexion, *with the qualities which compose the genus*,—and the *mass of qualities*, which combine to

---

[5] [These definitions may be compared with those at *ERCE* 58/63–64.]
[6] See Locke's Essay on Human Understanding, Chap. 3. b. 6. Sec. 35 [*Essay* 3.6.35; there is no Book 6].

form this *object*, are afterwards necessarily connected as *a Cause*; when in its conjunction, with any other objects; it puts on further qualities, which then are its *effects*, or *properties*. In this sense, *gold*, mixed with light, (some of whose rays it reflects,) is necessarily yellow; mixed with heat, (in different degrees,) it is ductile, and fusible; mixed with N. M. acid, it is soluble.

If this should be the sense, which I do not think it is, of Mr. Lawrence in his passage on gold—it is true there may be "no difference between the evidence for the two propositions;" for both objects are *necessarily* and *invariably* connected with their effects or properties.

But neither of them are to be regarded, as *only* so connected with their properties *in future, because they have been invariably concurrent in past time.* 157

Mr. Lawrence, no more than Dr. Brown, or Mr. Hume, can predicate of *the* FUTURE, from *the past*, unless under the relation of Cause and Effect, as of a truly *productive principle, with a quality produced.*

I would further observe, that the arbitrary connexion of a name, with a certain number of similar enumerated qualities, requires no proof for its assertion; such qualities shall be gold, and such others lead and copper, if we please to call them so. But the necessary connexion of an object and its further *properties*, when combined with other objects, requires *experiment to prove its truth.*

Also the *definition* of the arbitrary name, is *absolute.*—Because the proposition in which it is contained is identical; such qualities, are gold—and gold is the enumeration of such qualities. But the definition of an object in respect to its exhibition of *further qualities in different combinations with* 158
other objects, is *conditional*; it being understood that it will not hold, unless the *circumstances are similar* upon each occasion, that have any *power to affect them*[7].

SECTION THE THIRD.

It is plain that Mr. Lawrence has overlooked these distinctions, where there are such manifest differences, on account of his "becoming acquainted with Dr. Brown's Essay on Cause and Effect," which he considers as "so simple and logical that any attempt at direct opposition would be utterly hopeless;"

---

[7] See Locke's Essay, Chap. 6. Book 4. Sec. 8 and 9 [*Essay* 4.6.8–9]; where unexpectedly I find he perfectly coincides with me.

and has quoted a long passage in a note as a proof of this, and as a support of the doctrine he is laying down in the text.[8]

In this passage are the three following sentences, which I shall not apologize for inserting; since the consequences of a hasty adoption, of what I consider FALSE *instead of* LOGICAL *deduction*, and *confused* instead of "simple" argument into important practical theories, cannot be too strongly deprecated, and I wish to give my reader full possession of the grounds of my reasoning.

The 1st consists in the definition of the relation of Cause and Effect, which I have already commented on, in the former Chapter against Dr. Brown.

"A cause is that which immediately precedes any change, and which existing at any time in similar circumstances, has been always, and will be always followed by a similar change."

"Priority, in the sequence observed and *invariableness* of antecedence in the *past* and *future* sequences supposed, are the *only* elements combined in the notion of a cause."

2dly. Of property, "the words property and quality admit of exactly the same definition, expressing only a certain relation of invariable antecedence and consequence in changes that take place on the presence of the substance to which they are ascribed."

3dly. "The powers, properties or qualities of a substance are not to be regarded as any thing superadded to the substance, or distinct from it. They are *only* the substance itself considered in relation to various changes that take place when it exists in peculiar circumstances."

Hence Mr. Lawrence concludes, p. 81, "That although induced to ascribe the constant concomitance of a substance and its properties to *some necessary connexion* between them, yet we can only trace in this notion, the fact of certainty or universality of concurrence. *Nothing more* than this can be meant when a *necessary connexion* is asserted between the properties of sensibility, and irritability, and the structures of living muscular and nervous fibres."[9]

Now I must shortly bring to my readers recollection, that I have already shown that Dr. Brown's definition which predicates *invariableness* in relation

---

[8] [In this and the immediately following paragraphs, Shepherd is quoting from a long footnote at *Lectures* III: 78–81; the footnote itself quotes extensively from pp. 15–21 of Brown's *Inquiry into the Relation of Cause and Effect* (Brown 1818). Lawrence cites it by that title, although Shepherd calls it simply "Dr. Brown's Essay on Cause and Effect." For further details and explanation, see the discussion of Brown and *ERCE* in the introduction to this volume.]

[9] [Shepherd is quoting here with minor changes from the main text of *Lectures* III: 81.]

to *future* sequences, is not supported by his argument, as no *past* experience *merely,* could prove it;—it being *illogical* to draw general conclusions from particular premises.—I have also, I think, shown that our knowledge of the *future,* arises from its being "*involved*" in the past; on account of *Cause being truly a productive principle,* and *Effects or properties* truly *produced* qualities, so that necessary connexion becomes a very different relation from either a *past or future sequence* of events, and signifies the "close bond" between the creator and created.

Had Mr. Lawrence, however, paid more attention than he has done to the *concluding* sentence I have quoted from Dr. Brown, he had not engrafted these errors into his system:—for nothing can be more just and beautiful than to say of the properties of a substance, "that they are only the *substance itself* in relation to *various changes* which take place, *when it exists in peculiar circumstances.*"—But such an idea is at variance with all his own previous definitions and arguments on the subject, for if "the powers, properties, or qualities of a substance are not to be regarded as any thing superadded to the substance, or distinct from it, but only the substance itself, considered in relation to various changes which take place when it exists in peculiar circumstances," then these properties and qualities cannot be *after* itself; but are *necessarily* connected *with,* because *inhering* in it, and brought out to view when *mixed* with the qualities of *other objects.*

SECTION THE FOURTH.

Now as the muscle and nerve can and do exist as organized beings, without irritability and sentiency when under death, so when as substances, they are placed under that condition called *life,* and are then only capable of putting on these qualities of irritability and sentiency, it must be by a *truly necessary connexion,* between life and these qualities. Irritability and sentiency are verily new powers and beings *created* by efficient, *creating* circumstances. *Sensation* and all its variety, is not an effect without a cause; and *life* is that object without which it will not exist in the *nerve;* and therefore according to the doctrine laid down in this Essay, is a true cause for it: being *one* of the objects *absolutely necessary* and efficient to *that* result in *certain circumstances;*— although what the WHOLE of those conditions may be, the *combination* of which is needful, may possibly ever remain beyond the scrutiny of man. Should Mr. Lawrence retort, that the phrase "the living nerve," stands *merely* as a *sign* of enumerated *qualities* and properties found together, in the way that I have said *gold* may stand as a *sign* for those that lie under that term; that it is in this sense he compares the two propositions concerning them; and in this sense, he alleges there is no difference in the evidence for the *only kind* of necessary connexion there exists between an *object* and its properties?

I answer the very statement of the proposition "the *living nerve* is *sentient*," *assigns a cause* and *producing principle* for sensation; for by placing an adjective before a noun, it becomes a *qualified noun*. And the qualities beneath the whole term are a mass of *altered* qualities, which alteration, is alleged to be *efficient* to the production of a new mode of existence; viz. that of sensation.

Thus (to use a familiar illustration) the saying a *bilious* man is *choleric*, assigns *bile*[10] as the *cause* of anger, and it would be puerile after such a proposition, to add, that "however strong the feeling may be, that there is the close bond of Cause and Effect between these objects, yet it is a mistake to suppose it." This would but be a subsequent denial of *what the statement previously asserted*.

Whereas *gold*, or any other noun, when it stands as a sign for any collection of qualities, and properties; is neither a cause nor an object; it is a word, a *name* merely, and when thus placed as the subject of a proposition, of which the qualities stand as the predicate, signifies, that by such a name, shall such masses, being found together and set apart from other collections, be signified[11].

This distinction between a *qualified*, and *unqualified* noun, on account of the different *nature* of the *connexion* of the predicate of the proposition, with its subject, Mr. Lawrence did not take notice of; or he would not have thought "there was not the faintest shade of difference" between the two propositions he states, in this respect.

SECTION THE FIFTH.

But this is not the most important error in Mr. Lawrence's system, arising from false notions, concerning the relation of Cause and Effect; for by a

---

[10] [The word '*vile*' in the text has been corrected to '*bile*' in accordance with Shepherd's obvious meaning.]

[11] See Locke's Essay in several places, especially Book 3. Chap. 8. Sec. 2. [*Essay* 3.8.2] compared with Chap. 9. Sec. 12, 13, and 17 [*Essay* 3.9.12–13 and 3.9.17] and Chap. 10. Sec. 20, 21, and 22 [*Essay* 3.10.20–22].

strange sort of contradiction, in philosophy, although he denies that *any cause* can be found, among those things which are invariably together, for the properties they exhibit; yet he makes no difficulty in inferring that the *whole causes* are supposed to be found from the mere circumstance of their invariable coalesence; insomuch that *no extraneous* cause need be sought for.—The sum of his argument is, "*There is no such thing as* CAUSE *and* EFFECT, *to be perceived between the objects with which we are acquainted. It is idle to say we have found a Cause; it is still more idle to look for it.*—*Objects are found to be amassed qualities and properties, which have invariably existed together in past time, and for that reason will do so in future; but as for a productive principle, it is unworthy of a philosopher to expect it, or to seek for it; or to need it, in order to account for any appearances. We have objects, variously diversified—this is all and this is enough!*"

It is hence, (so Mr. Lawrence argues,) absurd *to seek a Cause* for sensation or thought, although no efficient one is pretended to be assigned, in the union of the powers of life with organization.[12] The living nerve is an object having sensation—"*this is all and this is enough.*"—Whereas there must be causes for every thing, and sometimes a *vast multitude of objects are wanted*, before their *mutual bearings* and *mixtures* with each other operate so as to *produce* any peculiar existence. The highest, and the greatest we know of is, *sensation, and its varieties*; and although we know that life is *wanted* as a *cause* without which it cannot exist in *this world in the nervous system*; yet we have no notion of *all* the objects that may be necessary to its creation.

Of all philosophical errors, the substitution of false, partial, or insufficient causes for the production of an end or object, is the most dangerous, because so liable to escape detection; and the idleness of the mind which prosecutes with reluctance difficult researches into remote proofs; its impatience which eagerly grasps at the readiest solution of a doubt; and its pride, so prone to triumph indiscreetly at the glimpse of a discovery supposed to be complete; for ever occasion it to be guilty of that mode of sophistry scholastically termed *non causa—pro causa*.[13]

And this is *truly* the amount of Mr. Lawrence's error—for with all his denial that there are such things as *cause* and *necessary connexion*, he virtually

---

[12] [Lawrence uses 'organization' in its specifically biological or physiological sense, defined by the *Oxford English Dictionary* as "the development or coordination of parts (of the body, a body system, cell, etc.) in order to carry out vital functions; the condition of being or process of becoming organized. Also: ... the structure of an organism."]

[13] ["*Non causa pro causa*" is the fallacy of taking what is "not the cause for the cause."]

assigns a *"false cause"* for sensation, because he asserts that *all* is found that is *necessary* in order to it[14].

Now the truth is, that nature affords not experiment, or data enough to show, what are the *whole* causes necessary; i.e. *all* the objects required, whose *junction* is necessary to *sentiency as the result*.—For as the words *life*, and *nerve*, stand only for a few sensible qualities, whereby they affect us; so does it appear there is no existing definition of them, no possible experiment which can be made on their nature, sufficient to afford premises wide enough to admit the conclusion, that sentiency shall result from their conjunction only, and shall not be able to exist without them.

SECTION THE SEVENTH.[15]

If indeed the powers of matter in general, (whatever matter may be,) were sufficient to elicit sentiency when placed under *arrangement* and mixed with life, then the true causes for it are assigned, and found. But we cannot *prove* this. If on the contrary, the essential qualities of matter arranged and in motion be not thought sufficient to account for so extraordinary a difference as that between conscious and unconscious being, then there must be a *particular* cause for it: which cause must be considered an immaterial cause, that is, a *principle, power, being,* an unknown quality *denied* to exist in matter.—This must have a name, and may be called *soul*, or *spirit*. And this statement, really contains the whole argument either way. It is on this point, that not only *here*, but in an after Lecture ("on the functions of the brain,")[16] Mr. Lawrence betrays a want of philosophical precision, by denying that any cause beyond the brain is necessary to thought, on account of the impossibility of assigning the *time* of its union with the body; whereas a Cause must have originally been necessary, upon the creation of man, for the phenomenon in question; and the capacity of sensation may, as a component part of the whole animal mass, be always generated with it, yet retain its individuality, after having once been formed with each being;—analogous to the whole plan of nature, in other respects;—analogous to the physical individuality of all the millions

---

[14] Mr. Lawrence says, there is no more reason to search for a cause for sensation or life—than for attraction or electricity—yet these powers must have Causes, and philosophers have searched for them; and if they have given over the inquiry, it is because they despair of success.

[15] [There is no section entitled "SECTION THE SIXTH" in this chapter.]

[16] [The final section of Lecture IV carries the page heading "Functions of the Brain" (*Lectures* IV: 105–14).]

of mankind, each of which was formed of the general clay;—analogous to the separate, and particular properties, which wait upon the differences of vegetable life, where every various plant is expanded from similar juices.

But I must be true to my own doctrine in all its bearings; and as I have said, that in order to form the *proximate cause* of any event, a *junction or mutual mixture of all* the objects *necessary to it must take place*; so I conceive it to be impossible, but that a *distinct* and *different* action of the brain (without which organ there is no sensation in man, and all thought is but a mode of it) must be *synchronous* with whatever other powers are also necessary for that result; viz. sensation and thought with their varieties. I say, the junction must be *synchronous*—for sensation is an *effect*, and must require the union of those objects whose mixed qualities elicit it.

Now those causes *not* contained in matter, may be called mind, or soul. I have said also, that a different action of brain is wanted for *each variety of thought and sensation*; and so it must, because there must be a *separate* or different cause, for every *separate or diverse* Effect in nature, as before discussed. And thus the brain becomes the *exponent of the soul*; or is *in the same proportion in its actions*, as the actions of mind: and thus what is termed *association of ideas*, must have *corresponding unions*, in the actions of the brain.

Now Mr. Lawrence contradicts at once his own arguments for materialism, as well as nature, and fact; when he says (tauntingly) "thus we come to diseases of an immaterial being! for which suitably enough *moral* treatment has been recommended,"[17] inferring thereby the *absurdity of moral treatment*, to a *material mind*.

Now moral treatment, according to his *own notion* of *only a material* capacity for thought, might still be proper, as it would still act on that *material capacity for thought*,—and though "arguments, syllogisms, and sermons,"[18] might not reach it, of an *ordinary kind*; yet, the persuasions of friendship; the influence of beauty, and of love; the pleasures of social intercourse; the calm discussions of reason; scenes that please the imagination, or enchant the sense, will reach it, and do. Nevertheless all this is "*moral treatment*," and which yet requires the brain and nervous system. In short, to address the mind is to address the body, which *instantly* acts along and with it, not *after*

---

[17] [Shepherd is quoting with minor changes from *Lectures* IV: 111.]
[18] [Lawrence writes at *Lectures* p. 114: "Indeed they, who talk of and believe in diseases of the mind, are too wise to put their trust in mental remedies. Arguments, syllogisms, discourses, sermons, have never yet restored any patient; the moral pharmacopœia is quite inefficient, and no real benefit can be conferred without vigorous medical treatment, which is as efficacious in these affections, as in the diseases of any other organs."]

it. And to address the body is to address the mind—for *every sensation*, however popularly called *bodily*; requires *mind*, equally with thought as a cause for it, and is not merely to be considered as a simple being, or feeling, beginning and ending in itself; but as intimately *associating with those of a* LIKE KIND, *which certain* THOUGHTS *are capable of exciting, and as having, therefore, a most material agency, when first in order, by suggesting such specific thoughts.*—This mode of thinking on the subject I know not that any have sufficiently heeded, much less cultivated.

It is to be lamented that the use of pure metaphysics has not been more strictly adopted into the researches of physiology, since the just application of these sciences to each other, would tend to the advancement of both.—Nor have the talents and genius of Mr. Lawrence exempted him, in this respect, from the common failure.

For (in his Lecture on the functions of the brain,) he is guilty of a very great oversight in supposing philosophers speak of an *immaterial* being as wanted for *thought*, and *not for sensation*.—Instead of which Mr. Locke, Bishop Butler,[19] David Hartley,[20] Bishop Berkeley, all distinctly argue that matter in motion, not seeming *cause* sufficient for the most *simple sensation*, therefore *spirit* is wanted to that end; which is merely a name for the cause desired: and this mistake shows the little attention he has paid to these authors. But I consider it as impossible that any material improvement should be made in the method of applying philosophy to physiology, as long as men argue, that in every action of the senses, the *body* acts BEFORE *the mind and* UPON *it*. And *vice versa*, as I have heard it contended in argument *"that the actions of the memory, the imagination, and the reasoning powers, begin in the mind, exist entirely in the mind, act before the body, and upon it."* Nor will it advance, as long as any anxiety among materialists makes them *wish* to show *all* is body. Or, on the contrary, if whilst religious men are fearful that their dearest hopes may fail them, in case *any* thing of *body* is wanted, in order to *thought*. Whereas religion is not concerned in this matter so much as they imagine. If immortality is man's inheritance, it is not as a natural birthright. The meanest worm must *feel and think* as well as man, and yet may not be immortal—If it is his; it is a *gift*, which the Giver has power enough to make good by ways unseen to us; but not surely by conveying to man a power *so indiscerptible*,

---

[19] [The Anglican bishop Joseph Butler (1692–1752) was a leading moral philosopher.]
[20] [The English philosopher David Hartley (1705–57) played a central role in the development of psychological "associationism" based on the association of ideas, for which he sought a basis in physiology.]

indivisible, &c. that he becomes a rival to his own omnipotence and *"shall not surely die."*

SECTION THE EIGHTH.

But to return from this digression which yet was necessary, in order to represent, the whole of Mr. Lawrence's mistaken reasoning on this branch of the subject, I shall only at present further observe, that as the *nature of life* is become a question of great interest, I must reserve a few more observations upon it for another chapter, as Mr. Lawrence has given *various*, and apparently, *inconsistent* definitions of that word. Nor must it be supposed irrelevant to the present subject so to do, for I think his erroneous views in this respect arise also on account of his not supposing that a real efficient cause is necessary to be assigned for *life* any more than for *sensation*. Therefore all philosophers are reckoned absurd, who have hitherto endeavoured, or who still continue, to seek for the proximate cause of it; it being considered by him quite sufficient to look upon it as a *circumstance only concurring with organization,*—whereas "there must be a cause for every thing," *and a cause for that cause,* backwards towards an uncreated Essence.

But every step gained in the knowledge of causes, (i.e. of what objects are necessary in order to the *production* of another) is of exquisite value, and it is pity if a false philosophy should succeed in slackening the emulation of inquiring minds upon this subject, which is one of the highest moment to human health and happiness.

I shall therefore, in order to show that I do not mistake my author, take an opportunity of placing together these definitions, &c. in his own words: but in order to be brief, leave out entirely all foreign matter with which they are interspersed, and which prevent the exact noticing of the contradictions that appear to be among them.

CHAPTER THE SIXTH.

SECTION THE FIRST.

I RESUME the subject by saying, that it is difficult to controvert Mr. Lawrence's opinion of the nature of life, because his definitions bear no resemblance to each other. They are as follows:

(Lecture 1st, p. 7.) "That life then, or the assemblage of all the functions, is immediately *dependant on organization*, appears to me as clear, as that the presence of the sun causes the light of day; and to suppose that we could have light without that luminary, would not be more unreasonable than to conceive that life is independent of the animal body, in which the vital phenomena are observed."[1]

Lecture 2d, p. 61. "To talk of life as independent of an animal body, to speak of a function without reference to an appropriate organ, is physiologically absurd—it is looking for an effect without a cause."

(Lecture 3d, p. 81.) "The living muscular fibre is irritable. The living nervous fibre is sensible."—(p. 82.) "To call life a *property of organization* would be unmeaning, it would be nonsense. The primary or elementary animal structures are endowed with vital properties; their combinations compose the animal organs, in which by means of the vital properties of the component elementary structures, the animal functions are carried on."

Lecture 4th, p. 92. "The body is composed of solids and fluids;—*the component elements of which nitrogen is a principal one*, united in numbers of 3, 4, or more, easily pass into new combinations; and *are, for the most part, readily convertible into fluid or gas*."

(P. 93.) "Life presupposes organization."

(Ibid.) Again; "Living bodies exhibit a constant internal motion; whilst this motion lasts, the body is said to be alive —when it ceases, the organic structures then yield to the chemical affinities of the surrounding elements."

---

[1] [Throughout this chapter, Shepherd's citations refer to the four lectures on "physiology and zoology" contained in the first main division of *Lectures*, from which she quotes with minor changes.]

SECTION THE SECOND.

Now, surely, it is a contradiction to say, life is *"dependant on organization,"* as light is upon the sun, and yet that it is *"unmeaning"* and *nonsense*, to call life a *property of it*[2]. It is a second contradiction to say, that life is *dependant as a function*, upon an animated body[3]; when the body could not be animated without it; or that as *"assembled functions,"* it is "dependant on organization, as light is dependant on the sun[4]." When life is so far from consisting in "the *assembled functions,"* that none of the functions can take place without life,— and thus it is wanted as a quality, or *being, first in order to coalesce* and form a junction with the organs in order to their action. Accordingly, although life may never be found without organization, because life requires *its cooperation in order to a certain result*, yet life is not thence *dependant* on it, as an *effect* upon *its cause*, as light is upon the sun, which is never above the horizon without its brilliant attendant.—But many a beautiful and youthful set of organs are *perfect*, without animation.—This error arises entirely from considering that as Cause and Effect are *things that go together;* so *things that go together* are to be considered as in that relation. Whereas vast varieties of objects, have been invariably together in past time, which are not Cause and Effect; and as *past invariableness will not answer for the future*, may not in future be so found. *Joint Causes are always found together; joined qualities also from a common Cause*: and many objects have hitherto always been found together, from an arbitrary position of them, independent of the relation of Cause and Effect, as the letters of the alphabet, &c.

It is a third contradiction to say, that the elementary structures are endowed with vital properties[5], and yet to reduce them into the inorganic matters of nitrogen and gas[6].

In my opinion, the only clear and valuable definition is the latter one; viz. "life is a constant internal motion, which enables a body to assimilate new and separate old particles, and prevents it from yielding to the chemical affinities of the surrounding elements." Such a definition as this, comprehends *all the ideas* under the *term*, without begging the question of its cause, or mentioning what it is found with.

---

[2] Lect. 3. p. 82 [*Lectures* III: 82].
[3] Lect. 2. p. 61 [*Lectures* II: 61].
[4] Lect. 1. p. 7 [*Lectures* I: 7].
[5] Lect. 3. p. 82 [*Lectures* III: 82].
[6] Lect. 4. p. 92 [*Lectures* IV: 92].

It has also the merit of universal *comprehension*, as it comprehends vegetable as well as animal life—and of *exclusion*, not suiting any thing else but itself. It thence leaves free the varieties of the functions, to arise from appropriate organs; and it proves that either *all living* beings must be *sentient*, or else a *further cause* must be sought for *sensation* than *mere life*.

SECTION THE THIRD.

That "life must presuppose organization[7]," is another proposition of Mr. Lawrence's, which I must also deny; and that because life is absolutely necessary both for its formation and support. Without life in the parents, the organs could not have been formed; and without life they cannot act in their juxta-position, upon the surrounding *elements*, either before or after birth, in order to their growth and support. Yet when life is once *given*, the *use of the organs is absolutely necessary to keep it up*.

Thus combustible matters may be heaped upon each other, yet neither warmth nor light succeed; but let an "*extra cause*" kindle the pile, then the flame may be kept alive for ever, by the constant *addition* of such substances.— In like manner life as we find it, as a perpetual flame, must be kept up and transmitted, whilst the proper objects for its support are administered: but for its original *Cause*, we must go back, until some extraneous power is referred to as its first parent. It is an *Effect*; it begins to be in all we know and have known, yet it is wanted in its own turn as a cause, and as a quality already in being, to mix and unite with the gross elements of brute matter, for the formation and continuance of all animated nature.

We are told that "*God breathed into man the breath of life*,"[8] and here philosophy supports Scripture, for the organs must originally have been kindled into life by a power, equal to giving them that internal vigour and motion, capable of enabling them to act afterwards for themselves, upon the objects which surrounded them. Then the living lungs could play upon the air, the living stomach be hungry and assimilate its food, the living heart beat, and the living blood circulate through every vein, and become capable of transmitting *the principle* communicated to it, to similar natures, without any assignable termination.

---

[7] Lect. 4. p. 93 [*Lectures* IV: 93].
[8] [Shepherd is alluding to Genesis 2:7.]

My notion of life therefore agrees in this respect with that of Mr. Lawrence, viz. "That it is a peculiar inward motion of the organs."—And I consider it further, as continually propagated through the species, and mixing with the newly evolved forms of arranged matter; *and that it is kept up, as long as the organs remain sound, and they are placed in fit circumstances for their respective actions.* 184

But men and animals are all of them *Effects*, and the first of each kind *and its life could not have begun of itself*,—nor yet as *Effects*, could they go back to all eternity, for *they might as well be here in time without causes*, as in eternity; Effects, however far removed from the present date, are still Effects; are still only *new qualities* from the *junction of previous objects*; which objects (the Causes) could not have been the same with the qualities, (the Effects).

The first cause of life therefore must be "*extraneous*" to any of the bodies among which it is found. For at their first creation, and in order to act their *parts* as it were, the organs must not only have been *arranged* but have *lived*, and this life communicated to them at the same time, and probably by the same forming powers, as a joint quality with their arrangement. Thus a clock may be ever so well put together, but the different instruments will not perform their *functions*, without an "*extraneous power*" originally to put the pendulum in motion:—then afterwards the pendulum by the *natural physical laws between it and the surrounding objects*, will *continue* to beat; whilst also the motion *of the other* mechanical instruments forms a *part* of the *whole* power necessary to keep it going, though not wanted *at first* to that end. This would form such a *circle* of Cause and Effect, as would be inexplicable, except upon the principle of the original *former* and *mover* being "*extraneous*" to both. 185

In like manner, all qualities of existing objects, which now play on each other as mutual Cause and Effect, the lungs, which are necessary to the heart, and the heart to the lungs,—and both to the action of the brain, and the action of the brain to both;—life which is necessary to sensation, and the movement of the whole;—and sensation, and the movement of the whole to life, must all of them (in order to explain such phenomena) have originally had their builder, and mover, not contained in their own powers. 186

Now the proximate cause for the principle, or motion termed life, *may*, and ought to be inquired into by physiologists.

But that it is only, and *essentially*, the result, and consequence, or property or element, of the being to whose results, qualities and finest elements, it is necessary in order to give them birth; is a contradiction, inadmissible in the application of abstract demonstration to the objects of life.

SECTION THE FOURTH.

But as long as the notions of Mr. Hume shall prevail, inquiries of this nature will be instituted in vain; nor indeed is there any received doctrine upon the relation of Cause and Effect, which can be securely used, as an efficient instrument in the advancement of science.

Bishop Berkeley thought a Cause must necessarily be *active*, and so a *spirit*! And it is universally imagined that a Cause is, in its very essence, *before* its Effects.

There is also, a notion that one object is *sufficient* to an event; when many are perhaps wanted in order to produce it.

I pretend not to have found the whole nature of this relation;—But I shortly recapitulate what I have advanced.

1st.—The junction of two or more qualities or objects is wanted to every new creation of a new quality.

2dly.—That any *one* of the qualities or objects needful in order to the formation of another, may be termed a *Cause*, because *absolutely necessary*, and, when all the other needful circumstances are duly placed with which it is to unite, *efficient* to its production.

But, 3dly. The *whole* number of objects existing, which are necessary to it, may also, under one complex idea, be deemed *the one whole* cause necessary.

4thly.—The *union of these*, is the proximate Cause of, and is *one* with the Effect.

5thly.—The *objects* therefore are *before* the Effects, but the *union of them* is *in* and *with* the Effects.

This ambiguity, arising from the necessity of naming each object, wanted to an end, and all that are wanted to it, and the junction necessary to it, the *Cause* of it, is a fruitful source of error in every branch of analytical philosophy.

6thly.—When Effects or *new qualities* are once formed, they may re-act as Causes, in order to keep up the original objects, which contributed to their formation.

7thly.—Although the very word Effect implies a *change* in qualities, yet among a set of new qualities formed, *all* of them are not therefore entirely changed.

The spark first elicited from the tinder, is kept separate, as to its appearance, its warmth and light, amidst all the alteration, in which it involves the objects it approaches.

8thly.—*It is not necessary, however,* that *any* of the Effects, *should resemble any of the objects*, by whose union they are caused;—and in general, an entire mixture, junction and concussion of qualities, involves the whole original objects in ruins, whilst it strikes out a vast many new and altered ones, creating other masses, other complex objects, totally unlike those whose union was their Cause. On the other hand, it sometimes appears that nature intends to render one individual essence, the prime object intended to be preserved; and therefore in its mixture with others, ordains that they shall only administer to it, by contributing to the perpetual nourishment, support, and increase of its qualities; as in the growth of plants and animals; or the vigour, improvement, character, individuality, &c. of the sentient principle.—

SECTION THE FIFTH.

But to conclude;—Mr. Lawrence's error lies, 1st, in the adoption and application of the principle, that invariability of concurrence, is of the same nature as the relation of Cause and Effect, object and property; which is the result of an argument in a circle, and which cannot be too severely deprecated, however authorized, by the illogical definitions of Mr. Hume and Dr. Brown.

And, 2dly. In concluding that because *one or more Causes* known to be necessary to an end, are discovered, therefore *all* are discovered, which is to draw general conclusions from particular premises. Did an ignorant person, unacquainted with the method of forming a mirror, consider it as no more than polished glass;—did he only observe that it reflected images when polished, and that injuring the polish prevented their reflection, he might form a proposition very similar to that of Mr. Lawrence, and say; *polished glass reflects the images when presented to it*; polish, and glass, and reflection, always go together; and as this is the case, we need not seek for any "*extrinsic aid*," to the production of reflected images from its surface. But we know that *extrinsic aid is wanted to the whole Effect*. And indeed before a reflected image from a mirror can be attained, let the mind pause, and wonder at the great variety of objects necessary to cause it. Can we much better enumerate those that may be requisite, to the formation of the most simple modes of sensation? Do we know the qualities of matter, when we use the term? Do we know the reason of all its varieties when we name them by some feeble impressions they make on our organs? As unperceived by the senses, have we the least idea of what is in matter in general, or in the *nerve* in particular, or in the formation of animals, or in the nature of life, that we should suppose nothing more is made use of for so extraordinary a difference, as that between sentient and insentient beings, than *arrangement*, (i.e. organization,) and *motion*, (or whatever other mode of being is termed life?) Certain it is, there is no experiment can be made on animated nature, which shall prove what are *all*, and *only* those objects, which may be necessary to SENSATION; or whether the sensient principle[9] *be like*, or altogether unlike the *Effect*, SENSATION; and indeed in any experiment which destroyed the life and the nerve, if this principle should continue to exist, our senses could not descry it.

SECTION THE SIXTH.

What probable arguments may be advanced upon the matter, is foreign to the object of this Essay, and I shall not now enter upon them; but conclude by expressing my astonishment, that Mr. Hume's and Dr. Brown's definition of the relation of Cause and Effect, should have continued so long, admired, adopted, and unanswered.

The necessary connexion of Cause and Effect, and our knowledge of it, in opposition to mere *fancy or custom*, is the governing proposition in every science. In vain should we look for improvement in any, *could we run the risk of so vital* a mistake, as to suppose that objects, however frequently conjoined, were *therefore necessarily connected*, or, on the contrary, that in the necessary production of qualities, there was no more than an experienced conjunction of them, and that they might change their places by a "change in the course of nature."

I have endeavoured to show, that any one junction of bodies in fit circumstances for what is termed the experimentum crucis, may be sufficient to establish where the power lies towards the production of certain qualities,—that ordinary life affords such experiment to the mind; and that

---

[9] ['Sensient' is a rare and now-obsolete term meaning "sensation-providing."]

without it, constant conjunctions of antecedent and subsequent objects, will not prove where the Cause of an Effect is. Conjunctions, however frequent, may be separable both in fact and fancy; Cause and Effect, a changed object with its changed qualities, are inseparable in both.

Let then the following just propositions be again received—

That objects cannot begin their own existences.

That like objects, must ever have like qualities.

That like Causes, must generate like Effects. **194**

And that objects, of which we have had no experience, must resemble those of which we have had experience, for that the course of Nature continues uniformly the same.

These are the only true foundations of scientific research, of practical knowledge, and of belief in a creating and presiding Deity.

THE END.

Errata.

Page	12	*line*	16	*for*	"a," *read* "or."
	37	—	32[1]	*dele*	"by."
	51	—	25	—	"of."
	52	—	1	—	","
	57	—	7	*for*	"exists" *read* "exist."
	74	—	13	*dele*	"with."
	77	—	22	—	"else."
	90	—	22	*for*	"shew," read "shewing."
	104	—	2	—	"excited," read "elicited."

EDITOR'S CORRECTIONS MADE IN THIS EDITION

Page	5	*line*	12	insert 'very' in place of 'vsry'
	28	*line*	24	insert closing quotation mark after 'Cause of existence'
	29	*line*	7	delete opening quotation mark before 'This imagination is plausible'
	40	*line*	8	insert closing quotation mark after 'we repose in it?'
	40	*line*	11	insert closing quotation mark after 'LIKE EFFECTS?'
	49	*line*	23	insert opening quotation mark before 'Cause and Effect;'
	59	*line*	15	insert closing quotation mark after 'such *particular* effects?'
	77	*line*	13	insert closing quotation mark after 'of nature'
	78	*line*	19	insert closing quotation mark after 'secret powers'
	83	*line*	7	insert closing quotation mark after 'like effects;'
	103	*line*	11	insert period after 'existences'
	112	*line*	13	insert closing quotation mark after 'this moment,'

---

[1] [The correction is actually to line 23; there is no line 32.]

120	*line*	12	insert closing quotation mark after 'other bread'
129	*line*	2	insert 'impossible' in place of 'imposible'
130	*line*	17	delete opening quotation mark before '*which the Effects*'
132	*line*	8	insert closing quotation mark after '*the past;*'
134–35	*lines*	18–19	insert '*principle*' in place of '*principal*'
147n	*line*	9	delete opening quotation mark before '*copied*'
150	*line*	6	insert opening quotation mark before 'Power'
158	*line*	13	delete opening quotation mark before 'be utterly'
164	*line*	8	insert 'bile' in place of 'vile'
177	*line*	177	insert closing quotation mark after 'observed.' in place of apostrophe
185	*line*	18	delete extra 'to' before 'the lungs'
189	*line*	25	insert space between 'same' and 'nature'

APPENDIX I

Two Essays of 1828

1. "Observations by Lady Mary Shepherd on the 'First Lines of the Human Mind'"
2. "On the Causes of Single and Erect Vision"

624 Observations by Lady Mary Shepherd on the 'First Lines of the Human Mind.'

"Mr. Fearn's book, *First Lines of the Human Mind*, although it contains many ingenious observations, great subtilty of reasoning, and the important truth, 'that *visible figure* can only arise as the result of conscious contrasting 'colors,'—yet is radically unsound in the process of its reasoning upon the subject of EXTENSION.—The main causes of this deficiency appear to me, to be the two following:—

I. An entire absence of the knowledge of the nature of cause *and of its manner of action;* by which means it comes to pass, that he makes no distinction between the *definitions*, which ought to belong to *perceived internal qualities*, the EFFECTS of *external qualities*; and the external *aggregates of qualities* themselves, which form the *determining causes of these on the mind;* and which also possess *other* properties in relation to *other* senses, and *other* external objects;—which *properties* are always implied in the general nomenclature of *those causes*.

II. That there are no regular definitions attempted whatever, of the great objects of controversy discussed, neither previously to the reasoning, nor subsequently intended by the reasoning, as a *posterior statement of logical conclusions*.

For this reason the great doctrine, which he conceives it important to have discovered, and happy in having arrived at, namely—'that the sensations of color and of touch are themselves EXTENDED as well as the mind, in which they inhabit,' becomes merely an illogical conclusion from *ambiguous* premises; a conclusion capable of bearing out so many ludicrous corollaries, that, should Mr. Fearn ever perceive them himself, he will be the first *to laugh*, that he could ever sit down soberly to support them. Now *extension* is a word applied to that *external object, or cause*, which is capable of determining its own peculiar sensible qualities to the mind; and that not only to one mind, but to many minds. This object, capable of producing such *effects*, is also capable of admitting *motion*, (i.e. unperceived motion, whatever that quality may be, *when unperceived,*) and of determining the SENSE OF IT *to many minds also*.

It has dimensions, therefore, and which dimensions, when void, are capable of admitting the powers of solidity, and when applied to solidity, become capable of filling the dimensions of that void.

This definition will not apply to the *mere* SENSATION *of extension itself*; for this sensation will *not* admit of motion;—will *not* fill up empty place;—admits *not* of the measurement of any dimensions. Were it possible that it should do so, then THE SENSATION *of a fat man would itself be fat*. The *idea* of his being extended *'two cubic inches'*[1] every way beyond the size of another man, would render it requisite to provide two cubic inches farther of empty space, for the occupation of the ideas of the lean man, who was thinking of a fat man, or who was perceived by him, as well as for the fat man himself perceived.

Mr. Fearn admits the REALITY of the *extension of space*; and as *a reality* supposes 'a bird to move through it from London to York.'[2] Now, can a bird fly through his *idea* or *perception* of the distance between London and York? He admits the *reality* of that *empty space*, which may be filled by two solid cubic inches of what he terms *'the energies of the Deity'* under the forms of two dice. Will two cubics of such *solid energies* find room in his IDEAS *of two cubic inches* of empty space?—Or will his *ideas* of those solid energies require two cubic inches of empty space, and be efficient to the filling of them?

---

[1] See *Lines of the Human Mind*. [Fearn discusses magnitudes using an example of "two inches" in *Lines* III.iv: 352–54, although he does not refer specifically to "cubic inches."]
[2] Ibid. [Shepherd is referring to an example from *Lines* IV.ii: 511.]

Whenever words are ambiguously used, whenever objects containing different qualities are *defined* as though they were the same and similar words used for various *aggregates* of qualities—*absurd* and *contradictory* conclusions, from principles holding such, must be the result.

External objects, (or certain aggregates of external qualities,) are named by certain names, not only on account of the sensible perceptions they can determine on the mind, by *one* or even more senses, but by their *properties*, when meeting with other objects in nature, of which also we can judge by the *effects* determined upon the mind by those further MIXTURES. *Wind*, for instance, is not *merely* the sensation of wind, by means of its sound, or its coldness, etc., but by its *effects* on those other objects called trees, ships, the ocean, etc.; for which reason it would be very absurd and contradictory to consider the sensations of wind, as being themselves *windy*. The properties of wind belong not to their definitions. The noise and coldness of wind, are but *effects* of an EXTERNAL CAUSE, capable of producing many other effects and perceptions, which themselves cannot perform:— the same reasoning applies to every other quality determined by the organs of sense. In as much as the sensation of wind, therefore, is itself not windy, because it cannot swell the sails of a ship, or raise the waves of the ocean; no more is *the idea of heat*, in a man's mind, an object, which is *hot*, for it cannot *warm another's sensations*; the feeling of the sharp edge of a razor, is not in its own nature *the sharp edge of a razor*, it not being possible for it to perform the office of that instrument. The *mere sensation* of *blue* in one man, will not enable another to take notice of it. Nor can the comprehension of all the colors of the prism, which any single individual may perceive, and understand the nature of, render the ideas themselves such, as will reveal the objects of his thoughts to the knowledge of the keenest observer. *My sense* of the song of the nightingale, will not be heard or responded to by *another warbler*; its *ideas* of those sweet sounds are not themselves so *clear* and *loud*, as to be heard by him;—In like manner, *my notion* of a high mountain will inspire no fear, nor can any man climb up its *barren and rugged sides:*—Whatever *size* may be the perception of the extended ocean, no ship could sail thereon, or *find sufficient depth in its ideas of it*.

The conception of the distance between these and the Indian shores will occupy no time to travel through, nor will *my dream of a palace*, make the *idea* SWELL until the cottage is too small to hold me.

Thus the *sensation of extension* is on the same footing, as all the others, which are yielded to the mind by means of the organs of sense;—a certain definition belongs to the external cause, which determines the effect in question;—and this definition is according to *the* WHOLE known properties, *general* and *particular*, belonging to it. The esteemed *cause* for the sensations by touch and color, admits of measurement, and of *motion;*—if empty, of receiving solidity;—if solid, of filling the vacancy. Whilst the *ideas* and sensations of extension, of whatever *large* things they may relate to, require no *empty space* for their habitations, nor however empty *ideas may be*, will they give place to more solid materials. M. S."

LXIII. *On the Causes of Single and Erect Vision*[1]. *By* L*** M*** S*******.[2]

IN order to understand aright the reason of single and erect vision, it is necessary first of all to perceive the truth of certain metaphysical positions in relation to vision, without the establishment of which, confused ideas, hypothetical assumptions, and inconclusive reasonings on optical experiments and facts are presented to the mind, and tend to embarrass the simplicity of that truth which might otherwise be immediately revealed.

First,—Vision is a consciousness in the mind, and its next proximate cause must be a power equal to its production, and which unites it to the material world.

Secondly,—Vision of *one colour only* can never yield the vision of figure, because the proximate cause of the vision of figure is a line of demarcation formed by the sensation of the junction of *two colours*.

Thirdly,—The physical impulse producing such consciousness of colouring, is an equal proportional variety upon the retina of an eye; one eye alone being first supposed, as it is truly efficient to yield the idea of figure.

Fourthly,—An object cannot be in two places at the same time.

Fifthly,—An object cannot exist and put forth its action *where it is not*.

These premises being supposed to be granted, let the question be asked, Why with two eyes given, two objects are not seen, although there be but one object given externally?

The answer (when supported by the foregoing premises, and conjoined with certain optical facts with which all who are conversant with the subject, are acquainted) will be, *because there is not presented to the mind that variety of colouring which is necessary and alone efficient as the next proximate cause of vision; that is, there are not two lines of separate demarcation between two objects, but one line of demarcation only is presented, as in* ONE *eye supposed*. Should it be asked, whence is it that such a proportional variety is not presented to the mind? The answer which the premises and optical experiments equally support, is, *because the impulse upon each eye (when the axes of both are directed to the same point or object,) being precisely alike, there is no variety of colouring painted upon either eye, equal to the production of that variety of perception, necessary to yield the ideas of two objects separated from each other, between their interior and horizontal edges*.

Let the letter A, for instance, be painted upon *one* eye, and the perception of its figure arises in the mind, from the points of distinction between the black letter and the white around it: there is a sense of difference created. Place it on similar points of two retinæ, and each point of the figure painted on each retina will yield to the mind but *one* point of conscious black against *one* point of conscious white; and not *two* points of black against *two* points of white, because there is no intervening white painted on either retina, which can yield a consciousness of the separation of the two A's to a distance from each other, thus, A—A.

The white space between the two A's is not painted on either retina. How then can any idea of it arise in the mind?

If, in order to render these ideas more intelligible, we analyse with still greater nicety the question, why we see duplicates of similar figures with *one* eye only supposed, it will at once appear obvious why we can perceive but *duplicates* of such figures, instead of *quadruplicates*, when *two* eyes are used.

---

[1] Communicated by a friend of the Author.
[2] Author of "An Essay on the Relation of Cause and Effect;" [ERCE] and of "Essays on the Perception of an External Universe," &c. [EPEU]

Now if *one* eye should see but one colour only, it is supposed to be granted that there could be no sense of any defined figure whatever: one impulse therefore yields not figure.

If one and the same colour should be seen by two eyes, it must still be acknowledged there would be no figure: two *similar* impulses therefore cannot give the sense of figure to the mind. Now upon *one colour* (say a purple ground) painted upon one retina, mark a scarlet circle O; a sense of one figure will immediately arise from two varieties of colour being carried to the mind, viz. a line of demarcation to the purple ground by the scarlet circle: *two* impulses, or *two* varieties of colouring, are therefore necessary to the perception of *one* figure. Again, if with *one* eye given, I wish to see *two* scarlet circles upon the purple ground, what must I do? Will *four* impulses yield *two* similar figures? I answer, No. There must be *five* impulses in order to convey to the mind the sense of *two* figures: there must be $\overset{2}{\underset{\underset{5}{\ominus}}{\ominus}}\overset{4}{\ominus}$; that is, the impression of the purple ground must be repeated in *two* different parts of the sentient retina; *two* scarlet lines must be thence impelled, and these made obvious by *the intervening horizontal impulse between the circles*; for could the intervening space be absorbed, and each point of scarlet coalesce with each point of scarlet, and purple with purple, there would then be but *four* impulsions of colouring, but *four* varieties, which would be inefficient to the observation of *two* figures. A coalescence of similar points of colour may perhaps produce a superposition or increment of colour, so as to create a superior brilliancy in the appearance of the object; but a *coalescence of points* cannot give a sense of *the separation of points*. Therefore for the mind to have a sense of *one* figure, there must be two consciousnesses of colour; and to have a sense of *two* figures, there must be *five* distinguishable consciousnesses of colour. However often *one* colour only be repeated, there will be no figure; however often *two* similar colours be repeated, (no intervening one being supposed,) but *one* figure will arise; whilst to entertain a sense of *two* figures, *five* impulsions are necessary. I hold it therefore as an axiom in the laws of vision, *that the repetition of similar impulsions of colour will not yield a number of figures equal to the number of such impulsions; but that the number of figures perceived, arises from those proportional intervals of the impulsions of colour, which must vary in a certain ratio to the number of figures impelled*.

However, therefore, the number of eyes may be multiplied, the mind can have no consciousness of any additional number of figures, whilst only similar impulsions of colour are yielded to it.

Let us enter into some further detail. If *one* scarlet circle on the purple ground be painted on the corresponding points of *two* retinæ, and thence impelled to the mind, there can still only arise the sense of *one* scarlet circle; for there have existed but *four* physical varieties on the retinæ, and but *four* varieties have been impelled to the mind: and it has been proved that *five* physical varieties are necessary to exist upon a retina, or upon retinæ however numerous, in order to impel corresponding consciousnesses to the mind, and which would be necessary for the mental apprehension of *two* figures. Let the figures without an intervening horizontal colour be supposed to be marked thus, $\overset{2}{\underset{\underset{0}{\ominus}}{\ominus}}\overset{0}{\ominus}\overset{4}{\ominus}$. The intervening horizontal colouring necessary to separate the painting of *two* figures on the retinæ, is not painted on either retina; *it does not exist;* and therefore no conscious separation of *two* figures can possibly arise to the mind. There exists indeed a certain space between the two eyes outwardly on the face, but the colouring of this intervening space is not painted on either retina, and therefore cannot be noticed by the mind; nor is there any intervening horizontal purple presented to the mind: Each point of scarlet does but coalesce with each point of scarlet, and each point of purple on *one* retina, with each point of the similar purple on the *other* retina; there is no surplus intervening purple on either retina, and it has been shown that "repetitions of similar impressions of colour do not yield to the mind the sense of an equal number of figures."

But should the scarlet circle be painted on points of the retinæ which do *not* correspond, then there will necessarily arise the sense of *two* figures; because in that case dissimilar impulsions of colour are carried forward to the mind, and yield that proportional variety which determines the observation of conscious duplicates: for the pictures are then immediately painted upon different parts of their respective retinæ, and the distance between two objects "will be proportional to the arch of either retina, which lies between the picture on that retina, and the point corresponding to that of the picture on the other retina[3]." On this intervening arch a surplus quantity of purple would be interiorly and horizontally painted, and would thence separate the two scarlet figures: *five* impulsions would carry *five* conscious colours to the mind, and *two* separated figures would immediately be observed.

An illustration of these ideas, and especially of this last statement of Dr. Reid's, might very easily be imagined, by conceiving two small terrestrial globes to be painted with precisely similar colours: Let them be rectified to the same degree of latitude and longitude, and similar colours only will appear on the visible surfaces of each; turn them both so many degrees to the east or west, still only similar colours will present themselves; but let one of the globes remain at rest, and turn the other any number of degrees of longitude to the west, a new country will arise to the east on the globe so moved, whose *variety* of colouring must necessarily prevent the notice of *a mere uniformity of colouring* on the two globes, and which variety will separate the appearance of any given country on them, "*proportionally to the number of degrees marked on the arch of the horizon*," through which the globe so moved had passed. Inspire the colouring on their surfaces with a simultaneous single sensibility, and it will immediately be perceived, that no consciousness of the existence of any two similar countries could arise, so long as the surfaces were regulated to the same degree of latitude and longitude; but the moment they were separated by an alteration of the longitude of either, or both, the sense of that newly arisen continent, or sea, would divide the sense of the remainder.

The following passage is extracted from the Encyclopedia Britannica, and is a quotation from Dr. Wells's Essay on Single Vision. "If the question be concerning an object at the concourse of the optic axes, it is seen single; because its two similar appearances in regard to shape, size, and colour, coincide with each other through the whole of their extent."[4]

This opinion thus expressed, comes nearer to my meaning than any other with which I am acquainted; nevertheless Dr. Wells's argument on the subject (and which is too long to insert here,) is as fallacious as that of any of his predecessors; inasmuch as it assumes *an hypothetical law of vision,* in order to establish that *coincidence of shape, size, and colour* upon which he perceived single vision did necessarily depend.

This laborious argument of his, is as entirely needless as it is futile; because it proceeds upon the supposition that objects are *seen by the mind, beyond the mind,* at the angle formed by the axes of the eyes, in their direction to the same point of distance.

Now when, on the one hand, colour (conscious visible colour) is admitted to be *in* the mind, and never to proceed again *out* of it, in any line, or at any angle to form an object;

---

[3] See Dr. Reid's Inquiry, ch. vi. sec. 13 [*Inquiry* 6.13]. [The section is entitled, "Of seeing objects single with two eyes." Shepherd is quoting, with some paraphrase, from *Inquiry* 6.13: 136.]

[4] [Shepherd's source for the quotation, which she alters only slightly, is the discussion of William Charles Wells on pp. 225–26 of the article "Optics" in the 1823 sixth edition of the *Encyclopaedia Britannica*, vol. 15: 171–295. The article quotes (on p. 226), from Wells 1818: 45.]

and on the other hand, by those demonstrable laws of optics established by Sir I. Newton and others, "that when the axes of the eyes are directed to a given point or figure, the said figure is painted on corresponding points of the retinæ,"[5]—then the *coincidence* which Dr. Wells speaks of, must of necessity take place; and such coincidence can only determine a consciousness of single vision to the mind; or in other words, can only determine those similar appearances of colour, on which visible size and figure ultimately and alone depend: for the centres coincide with the centres, and the edges with the edges, of the figures; without any variety, or interval of colouring between the interior and horizontal edges,—the conscious sense of which is absolutely necessary in order to induce a *sense* of *variety* or plurality of figure. When the figure is painted upon points of the retinæ which do not correspond, then there must necessarily arise a *sense of two figures;* because the centres *not coinciding* with the centres, nor the edges with the edges, *there exists a surplus colour* in one eye which divides the interior and horizontal edges of the two figures. This surplus colouring is determined to the retina by some exterior object, which by the shifting of the axis finds a place on which to paint its rays, "and is equal to the arch between the picture of the given figure on that retina, and the point corresponding to that of the picture on the other retina;" and which surplus colouring must determine a proportional consciousness to the mind, observing thereby the same rule which determines the "notice of two similar figures, when one eye only is used; ... *when the apparent distance of two objects seen with one eye is proportional to the arch of the retina which lies between their pictures,*" and on which an interval of colouring is necessarily painted, *but which circumstance Dr. Reid did not consider it material to notice*[6].

The optical facts to which I have alluded are very shortly and very well expressed in Dr. Reid's "Inquiry[7]:" The passages in the chapter from which I have partially quoted, and which it may be as well to give entire, are the following; and I repose on them as stated facts, not containing either hypothesis, opinion, or reasoning.

"First,—When the axes of both eyes are directed to one point, an object is seen single; and in this case the two pictures which show the objects single, are in the centres of the retinæ. Now in this phænomenon it is evident that the two centres of the retinæ are on corresponding points.

"Secondly,—Pictures of objects seen double, do not fall upon points of the retinæ similarly situate with respect to the centres of the retinæ.

"Thirdly,—The apparent distance of two objects seen with one eye, is proportioned to the arch of the retina which lies between their pictures: in like manner the apparent distance of two appearances seen with two eyes, is proportioned to the arch of either retina, which lies between the picture on that retina and the point corresponding to that of the picture on the other retina."[8]

These facts are valuable for many reasons; but on no account more so, than because they serve to explain the manner by which nature yields the knowledge of external tangible figure, and the proportional motion which is in relation to it, by means of corresponding varieties of colour.

---

[5] [I have not found this precise phrasing in the writings of Isaac Newton or others, but it expresses a thesis that was widely shared (including by Reid).]
[6] See Dr. Reid's Inquiry, ch. vi. sec. 13. [The quoted material is drawn from *Inquiry* 6.13: 136.]
[7] Ibid. [*Inquiry* 6.13]
[8] [Shepherd is summarizing three of the nine numbered "phænomena" that Reid describes in *Inquiry* 6.13. These are, respectively, numbers 1, 3, and 7 (*Inquiry* 6.13: 133, 134, 136).]

Dr. Reid's *arguments* (although he was in possession of these facts, which might have afforded premises for better reasoning) are altogether inconclusive, not to say puerile; and that on account of his steady adherence to the main object with which he set out upon his "Inquiry," namely, to show upon the principles of *common sense* whence comes the knowledge we have of the existence of an external universe: Following up these principles, he placed *visible* figure beyond the body, at a distance from the perceiving mind, denying it to consist either in a sensation, impression, or idea,—and as possible to be *seen* without the intervention of colour[9].

It appears to me strange, when contradiction is stamped upon the very expressions which convey these ideas, that Dr. Reid's notions should seem to be the data for the reasonings of the author of the "*Explanation of Erect and Single Vision,*" published in the "Library of Useful Knowledge."[10]

I must however, in common honesty, here take notice of an objection which I have known to be made to the views I entertain on this subject: it is, "that we see objects in different directions by either eye, when the other is alternately opened or closed." This objection appears to me perfectly nugatory, when it is considered, that both eyes being opened together, they are allowed by the condition of the question to be *directed to one point*; in which case *neither* of them can be directed *to any point beyond that point*; it would be a contradiction in terms to admit it. The axes cannot *cross* each other, and look *at points beyond the given point,* and that with a separate consciousness in the mind of so doing; for then these would not be merely *one* given point, but *three* given points; and the figure, the cause of whose single vision is in question, would be supposed to be placed, and at the same time supposed *not* to be placed, at the junction of the axes.

For instance, when two eyes are directed to A, the left eye cannot be turned to B, look by itself at B, and the right eye at the same time be made to look by itself at C. Experience shows this to be an impossibility; but when either eye is shut, the other may be moved in any direction we please. However, were I in error in this statement, the argument of my objector would by no means be conclusive against my doctrine of single vision, provided only that A be placed at the junction of the axes; for the utmost which could happen would be, that A plus B, plus C would appear to the mind; but *not* two A's (two B's and two C's), because there would still be only a superposition, or increment of the colouring of A.

The central point of the colour of A would coincide on each retina; the whole of the rest of the colouring in relation to it would be painted on corresponding points, and coincide on their respective retinæ; and there could in no wise arise that proportional variety of

---

[9] See Dr. Reid's "Inquiry," ch. vi. sect. 12. p. 135. 12mo. [The version of this note printed in *The Kaleidoscope* changes 'sect. 12' to 'sect. 13'. In fact, however, *both* section references are in error. The statements of Reid to which Shepherd refers do indeed occur, as she indicates, on p. 135 of the duodecimo ("12mo") edition of his *Inquiry* (which is the 1764 first edition), but the correct chapter and section reference would have been 'ch. vi. sect. viii'. The correct modern reference is *Inquiry* 6.8: 101.]

[10] [This author is David Brewster (1781–1868). Shepherd is referring to *Optics* XVII.2: 42 ("*Cause of erect vision.*") and *Optics* XVII.9: 45 ("*Causes of single vision with two eyes.*").]

colour, painted between the interior horizontal edges of the two A's, which is necessary to yield the ideas of their separate figures.

But to return "to the explanation of the Cause of Erect and Single Vision, published by the Society for the Diffusion of Useful Knowledge[11];"—it appears to me to be as much at variance with a sound, metaphysical, demonstrable conclusion concerning the nature of the perception of visible figure by the mind, as are the authors to whom I have alluded; and as much so with an acknowledged law,—with a proved physical fact, in respect to the *time* required for the motion of light.

The author of the "Explanation of the Cause of Erect and Single Vision," says[12]: "As the lines of *visible direction* cross each other at the *centre* of visible direction, an erect object is the necessary result of an inverted image;" but this is not the same thing with THE PERCEPTION *of an erect object*. If it be said the word *perception* is understood though not expressed, then the mind is supposed to see the very erect object, out of itself, at a distance from itself; that is, the mind feels colour, perceives visible figure (its result), *there, where it is not*, which is impossible.

Again, it is a known fact, that the light emitted from the sun, employs about eight minutes in its journey to the earth. Now let an object be seen at that distance in an erect position, but the moment after its light is effused, let it be obliterated: the mind will still see it erect, eight minutes after its annihilation, how then shall it signify the drawing of any rays back through a centre, towards the place of an obliterated object, which *once* stood there erect? The author's explanation is little more than the very circumstance in question, re-stated by an inversion of words. "An erect object (at a distance) is the result of an inverted image on the retina by the crossing of rays at a centre;" is merely saying over again, *that an inverted image on the retina is the result of an erect object at a distance*, when rays cross at a centre.

The question still remains untouched and unexplained; namely, why does the mind perceive an erect image, the result of an inverted image, which inverted image is the proximate cause of vision, and not the erect object which might be obliterated without affecting the mental consciousness of it? The only answer appears to me to be that, which I have formerly stated in my "Essay on Single and Erect Vision;" viz. "*Inversion of figure is merely a* RELATIVE *quality: when all rays from every object within the sphere of vision become inverted on the retina, there truly can be no mental consciousness of any inversion whatever: for there is no relative variety by comparison with any other set of similar images; and they will necessarily bear a given relative proportion to the ideas of motion and tangibility; and which ideas, taken collectively, include all the* ELEMENTS *we have of the knowledge of the position, figure, and colour of objects*[13]."

No doubt the relations of these in indefinite modifications are perceived by the judgement, as well as innumerable associations of them by the imagination; and thence the large use of vision in the world; thence the warm affections which are approved of by the understanding, or delighted in by the fancy.

But instead of taking this simple and easy mode of viewing the subject, philosophers, when they discuss the reason of erect vision, really suppose (although they may not be willing to allow it in so many words), that mental vision arises from, and is occupied

---

[11] Optics, part ii. "Library of Useful Knowledge" [*Optics* XVII.2: 42].
[12] Ibid. [Shepherd is quoting, with some omission, from *Optics* XVII.2: 42.]
[13] See "Essays on the Perception of an External Universe," &c. by Lady Mary Shepherd. 1827. Essay, xiv. p. 408 [*EPEU* 198/408 (in *EPEU* II.XIV)].

about, *two* sets of objects at the same time; viz. the *external objects in nature,* and the *inverted images of them on the retina:* whereas the external object becomes virtually null and void immediately upon the rays of light being emitted from it.

The idea of inversion is the result of the comparison of the line of demarcation of one object with that of another of a similar kind placed in a contrary direction to it. But as in the picture on the retina, the line of demarcation of each particular image touches the line of demarcation of the rest, in the same manner and after the same proportion as their corresponding objects do in external nature; so no such comparison can take place: for *one* set of images only is painted, and these in precisely the same relative positions to each other as are their counterparts. The mind therefore necessarily perceives the same positions with respect to each other; for no *two* objects of a kind present themselves, by which a comparison can take place.

Philosophers, therefore, when they compare the image on the eye of an ox, for instance, with the object in external nature of which such image is the reflection, forget that both together make but one picture on their own eyes: For any given object forms on the human eye an inverted image, and the mind sees it erect; but the image on the eye of the ox (which is already inverted) makes on the eye of the person who observes it, an image again inverted that is erect, and the mind perceives it *inverted.*

415 *In this latter case there is a comparison of the line of demarcation of one object with that of another of a similar kind, placed in a contrary direction to it.* In the former case, *two* objects do not present themselves, but only *one* of a kind, and that surrounded by each and every line of demarcation, precisely in the same relations to each other as are those of external nature. The same observation holds good when drawings are used with two images on them, placed contrariwise to each other; as an arrow without the retina, and an arrow within the retina. Did the arrow within the retina *feel* along with the surrounding lines of colouring, there could be no *sense* of an inverted arrow; for there would exist no reference to another arrow, which reference is only made by the observer, who is looking on *two* arrows.

Observations analogous to these must be made on the attempted explanation "of the cause of single vision," by the same author, who says[14], "Because the lines of visible direction from similar points of the image (on *one retina*) meet the lines of visible direction from similar points of the other *image* upon the *other retina,* each pair of similar points must be seen as *one* point." How so, when the mind sees not *out* of itself *at the junction of the points,* and when if the object which sent forth the rays were annihilated, there would still result a *single vision from separated points of colour painted on* SEPARATED RETINÆ *at a distance from each other;* such duplicate separate figures on the retinæ being the proximate cause of the single vision of the object, and *not the junction of similar points,* when rays are drawn *back* again from the retinæ to such points of junction.

The question still recurs, and is still untouched and unexplained; *Why are pairs of points perceived by the mind as single points?* No doubt the determination of rays upon the retinæ in such a manner that when drawn back again they will meet at a central point, is a property closely connected with the method of vision; but it is rather *a corollary or consequence of the manner of the entry of the rays at the pupil of the eye* by which equal arches are subtended upon the retina, than the efficient cause of either *single* or *erect* vision. I again ask, Why are *two* objects on the retinæ perceived as only *one* object by the mind? For it

---

[14] Optics, part ii. "Library of Useful Knowledge." [Shepherd is quoting from *Optics* XVII.9:45, adding emphasis and the references to the retinas.]

is *not* a junction of *external* points which is perceived, but *two* sentient retinæ determine two separate images (equally perfect in their form, equally brilliant in their colouring), as but *one* image to the mental capacity of perception. Is not the answer, *Because there are no points of colouring painted on either retina, by which the separation of their forms can be distinguished?*

Press the axis of either eye sufficiently to the right or left, a larger quantity of colouring will immediately be painted upon one retina than upon the other, which will separate their interior and horizontal edges, and *two* images will thence immediately and necessarily arise upon the perception of the mind.

I feel convinced that the more these ideas are contemplated, and the more clearly they are apprehended, the better will they serve to elicit the reason of several other phænomena concerning vision, which it has hitherto been considered difficult to explain; and what is of still greater importance, they may throw some light upon those which belong to every analogous operation of the human senses and intellect.

APPENDIX II

Letters

Letters to Charles Babbage (Letters 1–8)
Letters to William Whewell (Letters 9–11)
Letter to Robert Blakey (Letter 12)

Letter 1: Mary Shepherd to Charles Babbage
(October 8, 1824[?])

Argyl St.
Friday 8*th*

My dear Sir[1]

I hope I do not betray an unpardonable vanity in requesting your acceptance of this little volume — I do assure you my motive for offering it to you is not merely that I may thereby chance to gain you as my Convert by affording to you a *ready* reference, to some arguments which favor my notions of *Induction*, Causation &c, but chiefly as a small testimonial of the high gratification I felt in being permitted to peruse & observe upon your Papers, & in being considered as in any degree qualified by you to apply the Doctrine of this little Volume to such abstruse enquiries, where to say truth they come into play more as I conceive than yourself as well as the generality of philosophers at present suppose. I have ventured to open the leaves in order to come on the Passage — page 85 — (* see also Pp. 77 91) as an instance of that latent *reasoning* used in *Experiment* by which it comes to be an *Example* of all *future*, or *other* instances of a *like* kind; & in which point of view an exact Experiment in Physics (supposed) becomes precisely analogous, to any *Example* used in for proportions in Mathematics or for results in Algebra. —

I shall hope to see you tomorrow, when however we must be a little diverted from the *Grave* to *Gay*.

till when I remain
very sincerely y^{rs}
MS —

Charles Babbage Esq
No. 5 Devonshire St

---

[1] [British Library Add MS 37183 (1823-27) ff. 204–16. The "little volume" is clearly *ERCE*, so this letter cannot be earlier than 1824, and it is plausible that Shepherd would send a copy soon after its publication. On the assumption that the heading of "Friday 8*th*" is correct, the only possible date in 1824 would be October 8; the possible dates in 1825 are April 8 and July 8. If Shepherd has already received the "Papers" to which she refers in this letter *and* they are the same "papers" discussed in Letter 2 (received in November 1825), then the earliest possible dates for this letter would be September 8, 1826 and December 8, 1826. However, Letter 2 contains page references to *ERCE*, implying that Babbage already had a copy of the book in November 1825.]

Letter 2: Mary Shepherd to Charles Babbage
(November 18, 1825)

A.¹ S^t
Friday November 18.
1825

My dear Sir[1]

The pressure of a recent & heavy affliction must excuse my being so explicit as otherwise I should have Endeavoured to be, in the observations you flattered me so far as to request me to make on the interesting papers you entrusted to my perusal on Sunday last.[2] My capacity & acquirements are quite inferior to the comprehension of the greater part of the mathematical & algebraic illustrations which form much of the subject matter of these Essays, & therefore I should only betray my own ignorance by making any comment upon their nature: — Nevertheless I know sufficiently both mathematical & algebraic science, (especially of the foundations & method of reasoning employed in their analysis,) to feel myself fully capable of understanding every general appeal made to their powers, as well as competent to compare their modes of *induction* w^t those employed on other subjects. —

In this point of view I hope you will bear with me if I allow myself freely to make some remarks upon the general & metaphysical observations I find in these short, but useful treatises: — They will be expressed under the 3 following heads. —

First; — The objections I would make to the expression of two short paragraphs, the one on the *difference* between mathematical & physical induction; — the other on the *difference* supposed to exist between geometrical & algebraic *signs*. —

Second; The satisfaction I feel in the author hitting in several *passages* (in the Essay on *Induction*) upon the reason whence there is a *logical* method of the mind in forming *general* inferences from particular premises, altho' these explanations be too short; altho' he seem hardly aware of their compass & importance, & does not as I think perceive that the same are also applicable to the Objects of Physical Science.

Third — The importance of, & feasibility of applying the strictest order of metaphysical reasoning to the process of the mind in its attention to every branch of mathematical & algebraic analysis. —

First. Mr Dugald Stewart has the same sentiment as our author, — when he expresses himself thus. — "The term *Induction* when employed in mathematics is not to be understood in precisely the same acceptation, as it is used by the followers of Bacon in enquiries of natural philosophy."[3] —

---

[1] [British Library Add MS 37201 (undated) f. 433.]

[2] [These "papers" are, or include, two essays—"On the Influence of Signs in Mathematical Reasoning" and "Of Induction"—written by Babbage himself (despite Shepherd's reference to their author as "your friend"). He intended them to be part of a collection of eleven essays to be entitled *Essays on the Philosophy of Analysis* (see Dubbey 2011 for details). The former essay was read to the Cambridge Philosophical Society on December 16, 1821 and subsequently published as *On the Influence of Signs in Mathematical Reasoning From the Transactions of the Cambridge Philosophical Society* (Babbage 1826). None of the other essays was published, but a manuscript draft version of the projected collection, excluding "On the Influence of Signs in Mathematical Reasoning," is held in the British Library (Add MS 37202; dated by watermarks to 1812–20). A recent draft transcription of "Of Induction" is available online (Babbage 2013).]

[3] [This is a direct quotation from "Of Induction" (Babbage Unpublished: 56; Babbage 2013: 2).]

I consider this notion to arise from an erroneous view of the nature of physical Cause, as tho' it were not *necessarily* connected with its Effects; — in opposition to the perception there is that in all mathematical & algebraic conclusions, the results are *necessarily* included in the relations of the stated quantities, if the operations on them be supposed correctly formed. This error is I think prevalent on account of Mr Hume's introducing a confusion between, the *detection* of the presence of *Like Cause*, & the *necessity* of its Connection with its Effects, when *supposed* & *allowed* to be present — (See - Essay on C. & E. p. - 60 & note on it.)[4] The method in which Bacon used the word "*Induction*", was in opposition to "*hypothesis*," as the method by which conclusively to find the true operations of nature.— He ordered the mind to be "*induced*" to its conclusions, by reasoning from facts brought under experimental observation. —[5]

In like manner it were in vain *previous to trial*, to predicate the results of the involvements of quantities; — But when *tried*, the mind holds them as *universals* in similar cases. —

The *reason* whence the conclusions are thus "*induced*" from *particulars* to *generals*, is the same (as it appears to me) in both Cases; & the difficult part of the Question recurs equally in each; namely; "What is that reason which can render so apparently an *illogical* procedure of intellect, to possess a *logical* & *demonstrative* force of conclusive evidence." —

To explain this has[6] the object of my "Essay," & indeed it requires one apart to itself in order to execute the solution of the problem after a proper manner. — To be brief is to be obscure. Yet it is all I can be at present[7] —

'The mind by the faculty of *abstraction* perceives that *individual* qualities *repeated* are not altered in their nature by the accidents of time, place &c &c &c. — By *one* example we may know by the sense that 1 Equal added to another Equal, in 2 separate parcels, the wholes will be equal; — by *reason* we discern, that no accident, can *ever* prevent *Equals* when *Equals* are *supposed* to be present, from being thus affected by their mutual addition. — Then is a perception of the *general* nature of a quality, by *one* example of universal similarity.'

'There is thus an experiment (or experience) of *one* quality to see *what it is*; & there is then a *reasoning* on the experiment to this effect namely; "That *whatever* it be, it will be an *universal* not affected by such accidents as *interfere not* with it."'

'So also in Physics; — Very nice experiments are needful, in order to *find* what qualities will arise, under the *interactions* of certain bodies; — but when *found once*, they are found *for ever*; i.e. when the *same* bodies *only* are *supposed* to interact; for they are to all intents & purposes merely the *same* things *repeated*, — & must *necessarily* therefore be similar & not different; be objects of *necessary* qualities & Effects, not of contingent qualities & Effects. —[8] —

---

[4] [*ERCE* 57/60.]

[5] [Francis Bacon characterizes *induction* as "the form of demonstration which respects the senses, stay close to nature, fosters results and is almost involved in them itself," and he proposes "a form of induction which takes experience apart and analyses it, and forms necessary conclusions on the basis of appropriate exclusions and rejections" (Bacon 2004: 3–4).]

[6] [Presumably Shepherd meant to write 'has been'.]

[7] [The discussion that follows broadly anticipates *EPEU* 149–51/291–94.]

[8] [At this point, a phrase has been struck out. It appears to read: "The ineluctability of affected qualities, not subsequences to antecedences." Presumably there should be a closing single quotation mark to end this paragraph.]

I grant that the *detection* of the presence of like qualities, is much easier in those of *arbitrary* quantities, than in any other subject, because we ourselves *form* them, & name them. — Every thing is what it is by its formation, & however nicely we observe nature it is true, "her secrets are beyond our grasp";[9]— Still, this is another part of the Question, — and I shall not enter upon it here; — Suffice it to say that the authors who object to *induction* in Physics being of the same force in its conclusions as those of a mathematical nature, always consider Fire as fire — Water as water — Man as man — & the mistaken views arise from an ignorance rather of the nature & manner of Cause as a *productive* principle, & as *necessarily* in, & with its Effect; not from any supposed inability in the use of the senses to *detect* the presence of like *Cause*; when, to my mind, a rational scepticism alone arises. — Upon this part of the Question I have a *separate* chapter in the Essay, but it is too short, hasty, & inadequate — at P. 99.[10] Mr Talford[11] has a little diagram representing the inference of the mind from sensible qualities (the Effects) to exterior Causes, with remarks to shew its latent process of reasoning in order to detect like Objects present or the contrary which, tho' *perhaps* puerile, is an "*artifice*" for explanation which your friend might not wholly despise — But this part embraces the whole of the Berklean theory — & has nothing to do with the demonstrative evidence for *universal* & *future* conclusions, from *particular experiments* on bodies, when made to interact on each other, as *examples* for the *qualities*, & *Effects* of such bodies when again <u>supposed</u> present. In mathematics & physics *equally*, unless a *reasoning* occurs on *experiment* which shows nothing can arise to *interfere* with the Qualities or quantities, the *inductive* reasoning is *not* demonstrative — Perpetual recurrence merely does not amount to *proof*. It only amounts to a proof there is a *Cause* as general & frequent as that recurring Effect; & that as there must be a *reason* or Cause for such *frequency* of recurrence so it *may* have a still further range. —

But here physical analogies have the advantage over those which relate to quantities — because the slightest unexpected alteration in the involvement of any quantity will serve to spoil the analogy, & all its results. — But in the grand operations of nature, her *intentions* & *ends* are ever taken into the account, & bread is supposed to be truly bread when *formed* by *apparently* similar materials (& hence fitted to nourish")[12] not because of the impossibility of imperceptibly injurious particles creeping in, but because nature's *regular* kindness in ordering it otherwise *must* have as *regular* a Cause, & that *Cause* appears her *designing* care for us in which she cannot be supposed to intend to fail.

Saturday

The next passage I would allude to is the following "The reasonings employed in geometry and algebra are both of them *general*, but the *signs* which we use in the former are of an *individual* nature, whilst *those* which we employ in the latter, are as *abstract* as any of the Terms in which the reasoning is expressed."[13]

---

[9] [Locke (*Essay* 3.6.11) and Hume (*Enquiry* 4.16) each refer to nature as having unknown "secrets." Shepherd cites Locke at *ERCE* 79/115 and Hume at *ERCE* 40/19, 67/86, and 70/94; see also *ERCE* 90/140.]

[10] [Chapter 3 of *ERCE* begins on p. 99 of the 1824 original edition.]

[11] [The reference may be to Sir Thomas Noon Talfourd (1795–1854), described by Shepherd's daughter as a "Judge, Poet, and Christian Philosopher" who was a frequent dinner guest of her parents and a close friend of her father (Brandreth 1886: 42).]

[12] [Shepherd likely intended to place the words 'fitted to nourish' in quotation marks; see *ERCE* 82/122.]

[13] [This is a very nearly exact quotation from "On the Influence of Signs in Mathematical Reasoning" (Babbage 1826: 14).]

Now I hardly accede to this distinction between algebraic & geometrical signs; I think they must *both* of them be considered as *abstract* signs, or *neither* of them be so considered. — For my own part I conceive it a *contradiction* to suppose any *"sign"* whatever can possibly have the quality of *abstraction* predicated of it; because *by its very nature* it is an *individual*. *That* only can be an *abstracted* quality which has formed or can form part of a *complete* Object; — Therefore a *sign* is but an individual example, a substitute for a quality which may be more or less a *general* quality.

There appears to me to be this difference between the sign used in algebra, & that in geometry; viz. that the sign used in algebra being *un*like the thing signified, (& therefore open to any arbitrary definition;) may represent an idea the most universal & abstracted; whereas a geometrical sign being a resemblance of the thing signified, (that is of the individual of any given specie,) can represent no idea more abstract than the common qualities of a species. —

I would conclude therefore that

The geometrical sign is a *particular* sign of general similarities to it; —

The algebraic sign, is a *particular* sign of *any quality* whatever; — therefore that

The Conception of the geometrical universal, to which the sign relates, is more limited than the algebraic universal to which its sign relates, but not the sign itself more limited in the former case, than in the latter; — the *signs* in each being equally *individuals*; & in each, are the *examples* of all imaginable similarities *signified* by either.

Sunday Nov 20.

Second — The remark Page 17 "On Induction," contains in my opinion the true, the only reason which ought ever to make the mind draw a larger Conclusion than that contained in the Premises — "The reason which compels our assent" (to an universal Induction from a certain number of recurrences) "appears to be that we *cannot discover any new Cause*, which may come to play in the higher powers, which shall disturb that regularity that is apparent in the lower ones" — This observation is I consider of exquisite nature, & would in my humble opinion, if received in all its bearings, & allowed its utmost latitude of consequence, considerably alter the whole metaphysical & physical reasonings of modern Philosophers. — Excuse me if I say, that I do not think your friend himself perceives its full force for he goes on "Had the experiment been restricted to prime numbers, so *small* a number of coincidences would hardly have satisfied the most careless enquirer" — I consider that ever so frequently recurring co-incidences would not satisfy a *logical* much less a *sceptical* enquirer, if the *relations* of the quantities so recurring did not evince that the *reason* of the appearance was such, that it must *necessarily* arise among other Powers supposed; the *difference* of their qualities being such as could <u>not</u> interfere with the Phenomenon in question; — When such a *reasoning* can occur, *one* example is enough: when it cannot, it does not appear to me that a million of co-incidences can *positively* answer for more than *themselves*. Of the value of such reasoning to a certain degree your friend must however be aware, because he applies it in all its vigor at Page 8 & 9 — After showing the *reason*, why a certain phenomenon takes place in a given column of figures, he applies it universally. "This reasoning (says he) may easily be applied to all the succeeding vertical columns, & hence we deduce this conclusion; That if any given combination of figures occur in the first period they will be repeated *indefinitely* at stated intervals;" &c

Yet of the *full* importance of such reasoning & such application of it, he hardly seems to be acquainted, because he himself allows (P. 7) that "To state with precision the reasons which influence our judgments of these degrees" (of probability) "would greatly add to the value of this instrument of investigation" — (i.e. — *Induction* from particular facts); "*but the difficulty of accomplishing this is great*" — Now it appears something presumptuous in an unlearned Person, to suppose the difficulty *less* than that which the profound mathematician I cope with supposes; yet I cannot avoid suggesting a hint on the subject.

1*st* Frequent occurrence of similar Phenomena influences our judgement to expect similar Phenomena without a *full proof* of its necessity to arise, because there must be *some* reason for such a recurrence, & among the *differences* of the future qualities supposed, if no circumstance occur to the mind as *probable* to *interfere* with the *Cause* for the given Phenomenon, in like degree will the Judgement be influenced in its expectation — The more frequent the recurrence of *one* particular circumstance amidst qualities *changing* in other respects, the higher also will the probability become of the same occurring amidst other *analogous* changes, because it is thereby shown *such* do not affect the *Cause* for it — and when any changes do *not* appear analogous, yet if the mind thinks she perceives they cannot affect the Cause, so will be its expectation but

2*dly* This method of the mind only amounts to full proof, when the *Cause* of a particular Phenomenon is distinctly discerned, & when it *perceives* that no *other* changes of Qualities supposed, amidst *those* which remain the same can affect their relations, & their results in consequence: — Thus, if by *trying* in the multiplication Table I find — 1 times 2 = 2. and 2 times 1 = 2; & so on with the multiples of 2. — I could not have *much* data for concluding from 12 co-incidences, that 144 would take place of a similar nature, with respect to the multiples of 12 Digits; — Yet there must be a *reason* for these 12 co-incidences — and as each operation upon every subsequent digit, was similar in its bearings, so the reason (altho supposed undiscernable) would, by appearing *not* to be affected by the *nature* of the digit, become of a larger application. — Still, there would never arise an *entire proof* for the succeeding digit, as it might be impossible to discover, whether some alteration of the qualities occurring, would not *interfere* with its application, altho' the probability for the number 12, would be 12 times higher than for the number 2; — whilst the intervening numbers would be under a *probability after the same proportion* — But when the *reason* for the Phenomenon alluded to be either *known*, in one example *or* it be perceived that *whatever* it may be (if supposed unknown) no qualities among the remaining numbers can interfere with it, — then demonstrative proof arises; — For demonstration is nothing more than a clear perception of an universal relation.

Third — Of the use of finding the metaphysics of mathematical & algebraic science, it is impossible not to perceive your friend is fully aware, & not to be filled with admiration at the undertaking. — If the process of the mind is discovered in its reasonings & conclusions, & probable judgements &c, in these sciences, it will afford I trust an *example* whence *may be induced* better rules & methods than we possess for the advancement of every other. — Tho' I cannot understand the illustrations yet I perceive their drift & bearings; — the subject appears to me equally *novel*, & interesting. — With respect to its application to physics, you know my opinion; & I can truly say that from a very early age, I have examined my thoughts as to its manner of reasoning in numbers; & from time to time have applied such notions to other reasonings, either for amusement or improvement; — indeed chiefly in order to chastise the vague, illusory, illogical method of reasoning admitted into every part of discourse, whether gay, or serious, & into each department of literature however important its object.

I am very sincerely yours
M Shepherd

Letter 3: Mary Shepherd to Charles Babbage (1831 or later)

My dear Sir[1]

Professor Leslie says that Biot and Humboldt assign for both magnetic poles the opposite latitudes of 79° 1' the longitude of the northern being 27° 37', and that of the southern 205° 12' west from Greenwich.[2] The plane perpendicular to the magnetic axis he says intersects the Equator at an angle of 10° 59' and in west longitudes 117° 37' and 300° 27' But it appears that in 1824 Captain Lyon found the magnetic pole was in latitude 63° 26' 51" and in 80° 51' 25" west long.[3] pray what is the true faith?

yrs truly M.S.
Lady Mary Shepherd

Charles Babbage Esq'.

---

[1] [British Library Add MS 37201 (undated) f. 432. The signature after the initials 'M.S' is in Shepherd's own hand, but the rest of this letter appears to be in the hand of her husband. The dating is based on the fact that the statement by Leslie to which Shepherd refers first appeared in print in Leslie 1831.]

[2] ["Dissertation Fourth: Exhibiting a General View of the Progress of Mathematical and Physical Science, Chiefly During the Eighteenth Century," in *Encyclopedia Britannica*, Sixth Edition, Supplementary Volume (Leslie 1831). Leslie's report refers to Jean-Baptiste Biot (1774–1862) and Alexander von Humboldt (1769–1859), who collaborated on investigations of magnetism; Leslie does not provide a reference.]

[3] [*The Private Journal of Captain G. F. Lyon of H.M.S. Hecla, During the Recent Voyage of Discovery under Captain Parry* (Lyon 1824).]

Letter 4: Mary Shepherd to Charles Babbage (1833)

Lady Mary Shepherd

Dear Sir,[1]

I am delighted that Ladies are allowed to subscribe — I shall be too happy to do so. Unluckily I am engaged next Tuesday I fear till past 2 o'clock: but that need not hinder the subscription. I accept with gratitude your offer of managing the *detail* — Beg pray do so for me — and I will refund the money — *I will call on you to pay it.* I have studied so much in Mr. Lyell's Book,[2] that all he said was quite familiar to me & easy to be understood as consistant with his principles — The maps were beautifully illustrative of the whole. — Yet I cannot beleive upon any evidence less than demonstrative, that there could be such an *uniformity* not merely of the *laws*, but of the *facts* or *events* in nature, that there being supposed sufficient land &c, which man might occupy, that no man occupied the same; — & that for ages: — Shew me the world in *impressure* & not under *analogous* change merely, & then "I might beleive," however long & various might have been the changes our planet might have undergone: — Also, I do *not* see, why the tertiary rocks should not hold as much granite as the secondary —

In haste
Mary S.

---

[1] [British Library Add MS 37188 (July 1833–Dec. 1834) ff. 121–22. Although Shepherd did not date this letter herself, is it contained in the volume of Babbage's correspondence dated "Jul 1833–Dec 1834," and it contains an editorial pencil annotation "1832 or 3." Charles Lyell gave a celebrated series of lectures on geology at King's College in London in the summer of 1832 and then again in 1833; this is perhaps the basis for the annotation.]

[2] [The book to which Shepherd refers is *Principles of Geology, Being an Attempt to Explain the Former Changes of the Earth's Surface, by Reference to Causes Now in Operation* (Lyell 1830–33). The first volume appeared in 1830, the second in 1832, and the third in 1833.]

APPENDIX II

Letter 5: Mary Shepherd to Charles Babbage (February 8, 1836)

		49	---- 7
		240	
		289	---- 17
+ diff 200)		440	
		729	---- 27
2d diff 200)		640	
		1369	---- 37
3rd diff 200)		840	
		2209	---- 47
4th diff 200)		1040	
		3249	---- 57
5th diff 200)		1240	
		4489	---- 67
6th diff 200)		1440	
		5929	---- 77
7th diff. 200)		1640	
		7569	---- 87
8th diff 200)		1840	
		9409	---- 97
9th diff. 200)		2040	
		11449	----107

Dear Mr. Babbage[1]

I want to know if your machine could work out the *sums* of the square numbers following the law as given above — viz — Every square number ending after the square of 7 in the units is = + 240 + 200 for every ad^l *ten* in the root — + 49 — ad infinitum — I am very desirous to know, because I think it was by the knowledge of this law mixed with the observation that every square obeys a corresponding change & regular order in the place of the tens, as — 4, 8, 2, 6, with analogous laws in every other sq^r number which was the secret of the American process being said, to know roots by *inspection* —

Yours always M Shepherd

Henrietta S^t. Cav. Sq^r
Monday — Feb. 8. 1836

C Babbage Esqr
With Lady Mary Shepherd's Com^{pts}

---

[1] [British Library Add MS 37189 (1835–1836) ff. 296–97.]

Letter 6: Mary Shepherd to Charles Babbage (July 18, 1836)

>Tunbridge Wells
>~~Thursday~~ Monday
>July 18th
>1836

My dear Sir[1]

I have got a Sweet House "Durham House", with a spare Bed, & little boudoir you may have to yourself, if either you & Mrs Babbage together, or yourself will come down Saturday or Sunday next & stay a few days or a week, or as long as she or you likes. — Pray say you will — It will do you both good. — I do not ask M^{rs} B__ out of mere compliment; I know that *I shall talk* philosophy with *you a good deal* but we shall have the fancy chaise, & a piano forte — and Tea in the parlor, & then we should amuse & please you with Mary's[2] assistance —

We are *all* busy in algebra — I have begun to do it *regularly* — The more I have considered the last view I took of the roots of — Quantities, the more I am convinced of its being the correct one —

In that manner it is fraught with meaning & instruction concerning the *proportional error* in the data contained in the Question; — whilst also it keeps to the analogy expressed by the roots of other algebraic quantities, as well as that *in like manner with them* they can be *first translated* into arithmetical language, & 2dly *applied* to concrete things — without which *perception* of ideas under the terms of calculation, there could not be any security in their results. Pray *come & pay me a visit* &

>believe me y^{rs} most truly,
>M Shepherd

C. Babbage Esq
No. 5 Devonshire St
Portland Place

---

[1] [British Library Add MS 37189 (1835–1836) ff. 383–84.]

[2] [This reference is likely to Shepherd's daughter Mary Elizabeth (who married Henry Rowland Brandreth in the year following).]

Letter 7: Mary Shepherd to Charles Babbage
(February 1839[?])

Henrietta St.
Feb —

Dear Mr Babbage[1] —

I am almost afraid that you should think me either ungrateful, or indifferent to your kindness in inviting me to two of your agreeable soirées; whereas truly, I am neither one or the other; on the contrary, altho', the serious affliction[2] lately experienced, something indisposes me, to receiving the same pleasure, I had used to do in general society, yet I know not any house, where I should have sooner liked to have diverted my mind from something of its habitual seriousness than at yours — But having suffered this severe season, frequent returns of cough, I felt afraid of venturing out into the very cold wind of yesterday evening, after the warmth of a large fire in the D. room. Mr Shepherd was suffering severely from a cough, or would have gone to you with great pleasure.

I remain very faithfully yours
M Shepherd

To
C. Babbage Esq[r]
1 Dorset Street

---

[1] [British Library Add MS 37201 (undated) ff. 435–36. The upper right corner of the paper has been damaged, obliterating the date after "Feb." McRobert (2005) indicates the year as 1839, but I have not discovered the basis for this dating. Babbage lived at 1 Dorset Street from 1828 or 1829 until his death.]

[2] [The same paper damage to the upper left corner of the reverse has obliterated one or two words here, probably 'I have'.]

Letter 8: Mary Shepherd to Charles Babbage (1839 or 1840)

Dear Mr Babbage[1]
I fear that you must think me very unpolite in not having apologized ere this for my absence & Mr Shepherd's at your intellectual Banquet on Saturday last — The truth is that my spirits & time have been much engrossed by the sudden illness of Sir Sam Shepherd. I was too depressed on Saturday to enjoy the thoughts of going to you — Sir Sam is now thank God, I beleive & hope out of danger — but Mr Shepherd went off immediately on hearing the news, & is still in Berks.[2]
I read a great deal on Sunday in your Bridgewater Ninth Treatise[3] w. a new & increased delight — The chapter on miracles appears to me as beautiful, as the mechanical instrument which serves as its illustration; that on the Mosaic History, is to my faculties somewhat obscure — I read it twice over, & am not sure that I yet quite catch the full meaning of some of the reasoning. How I should enjoy a talk on it —w^t you.

> Y^{rs}. ever faithfully
> M Shepherd

To Charles Babbage Esq
    Dorset S^t.
    Manchester S^{qr}.
N°. 1

---

[1] [British Library Add MS 37201 (undated) ff. 437–38. Shepherd did not date this letter, but it contains a later editorial annotation in pencil of "1839–40." Her father-in-law Sir Samuel Shepherd died in November 1840.]
[2] [Samuel Shepherd's home in retirement was at Streatley in Berkshire.]
[3] [Shepherd's reference is to *The Ninth Bridgewater Treatise: A Fragment* (Babbage 1837). The *Bridgewater Treatises* were eight books commissioned through the Royal Society from leading scientists concerning the bearing of science on religion; William Whewell wrote the third. Babbage published a "ninth" *Bridgewater Treatise* independently of the commission. In its sections on miracles and elsewhere, he used the idea of a "calculating engine" corresponding to his own planned Analytical Engine in the course of his arguments.]

Letter 9: Mary Shepherd to William Whewell
(May 16 or 17, 1837)

A. S^t
May 17.

My dear Sir[1]

I put off thanking you for your delightful book,[2] until I read the part which was sure to interest me on Induction &c — I humbly think that if you pursue the views you have entered upon, you will open a most useful & new area in the mode of philosophical enquiry, & may thence prevent error to begin before truth, which to *explode* afterward wastes centuries & the abilities of the greatest geniuses — If proper ideas were entertained as to what the inductive process of thought really is, & what it ought to be in order to lead to certain conclusions, I do not think, that sentence on Induction would stand as it does at the head of Mrs. Somervilles last book.[3] Pardon me, if I say, I think you might put clearer *what* the nature of that step is, which the mind takes in "*reasoning* upon experiment," in order to erect inductive axioms — But I rejoice to see you boldly hold Stewart & Reid in the wrong — Reid w^t. his ultimate laws of beleif &c &c — makes out a sort of metaphysical witchcraft. I think however the phrase of laws of Nature, is neither understood nor used properly by any-body — it is used vaguely — Will you write a little essay & say what is nature, & what do *Laws of* (that is, Laws belonging to) Nature mean? — I spoke to Mrs. Somerville as to the mistaken view I thought she had followed in so remarkable a sentence. I have ventured to enclose my letter to her,[4] as she flattered me so far as to ask my opinion & I should like yours upon my views —

---

[1] [Trinity College, Cambridge University Add Ms a.212.66. The letter is stamped "FREE MY 16 1837" and "Cambridge MY 17 1837."]

[2] [The book is evidently Whewell's three-volume *History of the Inductive Sciences* (Whewell 1837), which was published in or around March 1837. The "part . . . on Induction" is likely to have been or included the Introduction to Volume 1 (pp. 3–20). The work employs the notion of inductive generalizations that become "axioms." Any rejection of the views of Dugald Stewart and Thomas Reid in connection with "ultimate laws of belief" is only implicit; Reid is not even mentioned in the work, and Stewart is mentioned only briefly in connection with God's role in causation.]

[3] [In 1837, Mary Somerville's "last book" was *On the Connexion of the Physical Sciences*, which had been published in 1834 (Somerville 1834), with a second edition appearing in 1835. However, Shepherd clearly intends to refer to Somerville's *A Preliminary Dissertation on the Mechanism of the Heavens*, which first appeared as a lengthy introductory essay to her *Mechanism of the Heavens* (Somerville 1831) and was then published separately in the following year (Somerville 1832). After a one-sentence introductory paragraph, the *Dissertation* begins: "All the knowledge we possess of external objects is founded upon experience, which furnishes a knowledge of facts, and the comparison of these facts establishes relations, from which, induction, the intuitive belief that like causes will produce like effects, leads us to general laws." Shepherd strongly rejects any characterization of induction as based on an "intuitive belief" (see especially *ERCE* 89/137–38).]

[4] [This letter has not been found.]

I must now, thank you w^t a feeling I cannot express, because I feel too much vanity mixes w^t my gratitude, for your considering me in any way able to appreciate your reasonings. I am writing in great haste not to lose my frank. Thank you again & again

I am y^{rs} truly
M Shepherd

The Revd W. Whewell
University Club
Suffolk St
London

Letter 10: Mary Shepherd to William Whewell (January 18, 1838)

Marine Parade
Brighton
Jan 18th

My dear Sir[1]

I can no longer delay thanking you for your flattering present, of your 4 Sermons, on "the Principles of Morals;"[2] not but that I wished to have read them all first; but having ¼ of an hour to spare, & having laid down the Book at the conclusion of the 2^d Discourse, I feel it a relief to the excitement of my admiration, I feel it a gratification to the "hunger & thirst of Righteousness," it has stimulated, to express to you those sentiments forthwith. If many feel as I do, at this moment, satisfied in their understandings of what is good, glowing at their hearts with the delight of their Perceptions, & elevated in their apprehensions & hopes of the attainment of the same, the seed you have sown will not return barren. — Yours is the spirit we want at this day, subtle & yet clear, enlarged on all hands, yet as deep, as it is high & wide: — we want the union of a *true* Philosophy, with religion. How I covet the conversation of one who might set forth a similar clearness of reasoning upon many subjects of contemplation, of important enquiries on which I am — constantly cogitating, I need not say: I still live in hopes of occasionally benefitting by it —

I left Town very ill, & came here for my health a few days after I saw you in London, so I could not make any attempt towards fulfilling my desire of your society: I doubt not however that from what I let drop on the Newtonian Theory, you *guess* you would have an untractable & perhaps a foolish spirit to deal with; — Be that as it may, I do here acknowledge that it is the same spirit which is inwardly glorying at each succeeding proposition as it comes under my view throughout your 2 Sermons, (from its delight in the beauty of truth,) which does *consider* your objection to the *ancient Doctrine* of the "*abhorrence* of Nature to a vacuum" to be *equally* valid *against*,— *The innate attraction of every particle of matter towards every other particle.* There is the application of sentiency to *in*-sentiency, there is the *constancy* of Phenomena as far as it is constant, mistaken for necessary *causal* action; & whilst no limit ought to be supposed possible to such a necessity, yet repulsion is such a limit; —& *Heat* is either a counter-action, or a *sort* of *matter* which *expands from* a *centre;* — & *Elasticity* does not seem to me to be accounted for in any way: — *God* is thus put in the particles, collectively, *without being God*; — So much is this inference obvious that the atheistical Book, called "Système de la nature"[3] derives its whole power from the Newtonian Theory — Your "Inductive Sciences"[4] I am still going on with, slowly but carefully; — am delighted, with all but the approbation of that Theory in the strict sense in which you entertain it.

---

[1] [Trinity College, Cambridge University Add Ms a.212.67. The letter is stamped "Brighton JA 19 1838" and "Cambridge JA 21 1838."]

[2] [These sermons were published as *On the Foundations of Morals: Four Sermons Preached Before the University of Cambridge, November 1837* (Whewell 1838).]

[3] [*Système de la nature* (Holbach 1770) was notorious for its materialism, atheism, and critique of religion.]

[4] [*History of the Inductive Sciences, three volumes* (Whewell 1837).]

The chapters on geology,[5] compared with those things other men write, appears as far as my judgement dares to premiss is of the highest order of human intellect. But my suffrage is small only that of a woman too ignorant, & self educated to say more or other than that. I am

M Shepherd

To the Rev[d]
W. Whewell
Professor Sedgwick
The Close
Norwich

---

[5] [Whewell 1837, Volume III, Part XVIII, "History of Geology" (eight chapters).]

Letter 11: Mary Shepherd to William Whewell (November 19, 1840)

Streatley near
Reading Berks
Nov. 19 — 1840

My dear Sir,[1]

I doubt you will be much surprised at receiving this from me, inasmuch as since I last saw you, you had paid me the high compliment of sending me one of your pamphlets[2] which I never I fear acknowledged, greatly as I prized the contents, as well as the honor done in your conceiving me worthy the perusal of them. —

Many things prevented my writing, — I came here to attend poor Sir Sam Shepherd in his sick bed, whom we have lately lost — Your pamphlet did not come to my hands here for a long time — Then when I read it, I did not feel satisfied as to the views of single & erect Vision, a right doctrine concerning which is so intimately connected with the whole laws & faculties of the human Mind —

I did not *dare* to *say this*, so *hesitated* — Then there were a few of the aphorisms that appeared to me so shrewd & beautiful, & of so important a nature, that I again feared lest I might appear to think "too highly of myself," in venturing to speak of their merit. I allude especially to *that* concerning *Instinct*,[3] & that concerning an "Uniformity, which includes Catastrophe in its expression"[4]; —

Besides this, my heart & mind were too fully occupied here, to give my usual attention to subjects of this nature — I trust you will beleive that I speak sincerely, & that nothing but your company & the ease of a colloquy, can give me more pleasure than your books.

I am almost immd^{tely} going to Town. I shall be too happy to see you there —

Now the immediate purport of this epistle, is to do a kindness by my Son-in law Cap^n Brandreth (whom I think you know) of the Royal Engineers, who has been proposed as a

---

[1] [Trinity College, Cambridge University Add MS a212.68.]

[2] [*Aphorisms concerning Ideas, Science, and the Language of Science* (Whewell 1840a). The work begins with a note: "The views presented in the following Aphorisms are further developed in the *Philosophy of the Inductive Sciences*." *Aphorisms* was included in its entirety as the first element in volume 1 of *Philosophy of the Inductive Sciences, Founded upon their History* (Whewell 1840b).]

[3] [Aphorism §CIV reads: "In *voluntary* motions, Sensations produce Actions, and the connexion is made by means of Ideas: in *reflected* motions, the connexion neither seems to be nor is made by means of Ideas: in *instinctive* motions, the connexion is such as requires Ideas, but we cannot believe the Ideas to exist" (Whewell 1840a and 1840b).]

[4] [Aphorism §CIX reads: "There are, in the Palætiological Sciences, two antagonist doctrines: *Catastrophes* and *Uniformity*. The doctrine of a *uniform course of nature* is tenable only when we extend the notion of uniformity so far that it shall include catastrophes" (Whewell 1840a and 1840b). The term 'palætiological' was originally coined by Whewell in his *History of the Inductive Sciences* (1837 III: 481–89) to designate "those researches in which the object is to ascend from the present state of things to a more ancient condition, from which the present is derived by intelligible causes." He presents Geology (insofar as it is concerned with the causes of past changes to the earth) as the "representative" such science, but he also applies the term to the development of plant and animal life, of the solar system, and of the productions of human beings. *Philosophy of the Inductive Sciences* lists "Geology, Glossology or Comparative Philology, and Comparative Archæology" as such sciences (Whewell 1840b II: 95).]

APPENDIX II 147

Candidate for the Royal Society, on account of his *professional attainments* and the works & improvements he has introduced into the engineering & architectural department of the Navy — If you feel you can conscientiously support him with your vote & interest, I shall feel myself greatly & personally obliged to you myself, & I am sure he will feel proud and grateful for such support, which must be of great influence coming from you —[5]

I will thank you to address me, at my house in Town, & I remain

    y^{rs} ever most faithfully & obliged,

        Mary Shepherd

[5] [Captain Henry Rowland Brandreth was elected to the Royal Society in January 1841.]

Letter 12: Mary Shepherd to Robert Blakey (May 26, 1843)

Cromsley Park, Henley-on-Thames,
May 26, 1843.

DEAR SIR,—[1]

I feel very much flattered by your letter containing a prospectus of your interesting forthcoming work;[2] but through weakness and indisposition I could not find energy enough to answer it as I could wish. Nor do I feel very well able to do so now.

The Essay on "Cause and Effect" is now entirely out of print; insomuch that Dr. Forster[3] returned me his copy for a reprint. The ideas there advanced are the foundation of all sound philosophy. This copy I lent to a gentleman, who, I understand, has returned it to Mr. Shepherd, in Hyde Park Terrace. I have requested him to have it made into a parcel and sent to you.

This "Essay" and that on "Final Causes," together with that on "Single and Double Vision,"[4] are the three whose secret principle, I think, you will not find in any other authors named in your prospectus. They confute modern Atheism, founded, as it is, upon fallacious inferences, from Locke, Newton, Hume, and Berkeley. For unless there be a *cause*, there exists no first, essential, or necessary *cause*. Unless *final causes* are *physical efficients*, they could not operate, unless upon every theory of the mind. The fact of single and double vision cannot be explained consistently with any theory, and as being deducible from the general laws of causation. Such a theory is *null*, for two reasons; therefore, I encourage myself to hope for the future success and prevalence of my own notions. Firstly, for truth's sake, which is the Word of God; secondly, for God's sake, because Atheists, more than all others, are feeling after Him, but cannot find Him, as ever existing, though invisible. To do this must be an honourable calling, and one which may prove successful whether I know it or not.

I should wish, therefore, my name were mentioned in your prospectus. I conceive there can be little doubt but that the Essay on "Cause and Effect" made a decided impression on the Edinburgh School. When I first married, about thirty years ago, every ambitious student piqued himself on maintaining there was no such thing as Cause and Effect. It was one of that school—but one wiser and better informed—that, on reading my Essay, was startled by the discovery, he was pleased to say, I had made, as to the reality and attributes of *Causation*. But through indisposition, I am scarcely able to discuss this greatest of all subjects which can occupy the spirit of man.

I am, yours respectfully,
MARY SHEPHERD.

R. Blakey, Esq.

---

[1] [Blakey 1876: 160–62. This is Blakey's transcription; the original has not been found.]

[2] [The reference is to the four-volume *History of the Philosophy of Mind: Embracing the Opinions of All Writers on Mental Science from the Earliest Period to the Present Time* (Blakey 1848).]

[3] [The reference is to Shepherd's friend and correspondent Thomas Ignatius Maria Forster (1789–1860), an English astronomer, physician, naturalist, and philosopher. See Brandreth 1886: 114–15.]

[4] [The references are to *ERCE*, *EPEU* II Essay IX, and *EPEU* II Essay XIV.]

References

Mary Shepherd's Writings

Shepherd, Mary, 1824. *An Essay upon the Relation of Cause and Effect, controverting the Doctrine of Mr. Hume, concerning the Nature of that Relation; with Observations upon the Opinions of Dr. Brown and Mr. Lawrence, connected with the same subject.* London: Printed for T. Hookham.

Shepherd, Mary, 1827. *Essays on the Perception of an External Universe, and Other Subjects Connected with the Doctrine of Causation.* London: John Hatchard and Son.

Shepherd, Mary, 1828a. "Observations by Lady Mary Shepherd on the 'First Lines of the Human Mind,'" in *Parriana: or Notices of the Rev. Samuel Parr, LL.D. Collected from Various Sources, Print and Manuscript, and in Part Written by E. H. Barker, Esq. of Thetford Norfolk*, vol. 1. London: Henry Colburn: 624–27.

Shepherd, Mary, 1828b. "On the Causes of Single and Erect Vision." *The Philosophical Magazine*, June 1828: 406–16.

Shepherd, Mary, 1828c. "On the Causes of Single and Erect Vision." *The Kaleidoscope, or Literary and Scientific Mirror*, vol. 9, no. 420 (July 15, 1828): 13; and vol. 9, no. 421 (July 22, 1828): 22–23. [reprint, with minor typographical changes, of Shepherd 1828b]

Shepherd, Mary, 1832. "Lady Mary Shepherd's Metaphysics." *Fraser's Magazine for Town and Country*, vol. 5, no. 30: 697–708.

Shepherd, Mary, 2000. *Philosophical Works of Lady Mary Shepherd* (facsimile reproductions), 2 vols. Edited with introduction by Jennifer McRobert. Bristol: Thoemmes Press.

Shepherd, Mary, 2018. *Lady Mary Shepherd: Selected Writings*. Edited with introduction by Deborah Boyle. Library of Scottish Philosophy. Exeter: Imprint Academic.

Shepherd, Mary, 2020. *Lady Mary Shepherd's Essays on the Perception of an External Universe*. Edited with introduction by Antonia LoLordo. Oxford: Oxford University Press. [Oxford New Histories of Philosophy]

Other Primary Sources

Abernethy, John, 1817. *Physiological Lectures, Exhibiting a General View of Mr. Hunter's Physiology, and of his Researches in Comparative Anatomy*. London: Longman, Hurst, Rees, Orme, and Brown.

Babbage, Charles, Unpublished. *Essays on the Philosophy of Analysis*. Manuscript dated 1812–20: British Library Add MS 37202.

Babbage, Charles, 1826. *On the Influence of Signs in Mathematical Reasoning From the Transactions of the Cambridge Philosophical Society*. Cambridge: Printed by J. Smith. [also included in Babbage Unpublished]

Babbage, Charles, 1837. *The Ninth Bridgewater Treatise: A Fragment*. London: John Murray.

Babbage, Charles, 2013. "Of Induction," https://martinfjohansen.com/ofinduction/. [Draft transcription from Babbage Unpublished]

Bacon, Francis, 2004. *The New Organon*. Edited by Lisa Jardine and Michael Silverthorne. Cambridge: Cambridge University Press. [first edition published (in Latin) in 1620]

Barker, E. H., ed., 1828. *Parriana: Or Notices of the Rev. Samuel Parr, LL.D. Collected from Various Sources, Print and Manuscript, and in Part Written by E. H. Barker, Esq. of Thetford Norfolk*, vol. 1. London: Henry Colburn.

Blakey, Robert, 1848. *History of the Philosophy of Mind: Embracing the Opinions of All Writers on Mental Science from the Earliest Period to the Present Time*. 4 vols. London: Trelawney Wm Saunders, 6 Charing Cross.

Blakey, Robert, 1879. *Memoirs of Dr. Robert Blakey*. Edited by Henry Miller. London: Trübner & Co.

Brandreth, Mary Elizabeth Shepherd, 1886. *Some Family and Friendly Recollections of 70 Years of Mary Elizabeth Brandreth, Widow of Henry Rowland Brandreth, and Daughter of Henry John Shepherd, Q.C., and Lady Mary Shepherd*. London: C. Hooker.

Brewster, David, 1806. *An Examination of the Letter Addressed to Principal Hill, on the case of Mr. Leslie, in a letter to its anonymous author. With remarks on Mr. Stewart's postscript, and Mr. Playfair's pamphlet*. Edinburgh: Mundell. [published anonymously]

Brewster, David, 1829. "Optics," in *Library of Useful Knowledge. Natural Philosophy*, vol. I, London: Baldwin and Craddock, for the Society for the Diffusion of Useful Knowledge: Treatise IX: 1–64. [first published in 1827–28 as an instalment in the Society's biweekly series of pamphlets]

Brown, Thomas, 1798. *On the Zoonomia of Erasmus Darwin, M.D.* Edinburgh: Mundell & Son.

Brown, Thomas, 1805. *Observations on the Nature and Tendency of the Doctrine of Mr. Hume, concerning the Relation of Cause and Effect*. Edinburgh: Printed by and for Mundell & Son.

Brown, Thomas, 1806. *Observations on the Nature and Tendency of the Doctrine of Mr. Hume, concerning the Relation of Cause and Effect*, second edition, enlarged. Edinburgh: Mundell & Son.

Brown, Thomas, 1818. *Inquiry into the Relation of Cause and Effect*. Edinburgh: Archibald Constable.

Clarke, Samuel, 1998. *A Demonstration of the Being and Attributes of God*. Edited by Ezio Vailati. Cambridge: Cambridge University Press. [first edition published in 1705]

Encyclopaedia Britannica; or, a Dictionary of Arts, Sciences and Miscellaneous Literature, Enlarged and Improved. The Sixth Edition, 1823. 20 vols. Edinburgh: Printed for Archibald Constable and Company.

Fearn, John, 1820. *First Lines of the Human Mind*. London: Printed by A. J. Valpy, Red Lion Court, Fleet Street, and sold by Longham, Hurst, Rees, Orme, and Brown, Paternoster Row; Black, Kingsbury, Parbury, and Allen, Leadenhall Street; and Roland Hunter, St. Paul's Churchyard.

Fearn, John, 1828. "Reply to the Criticisms of Lady Mary Shepherd on the 'First Lines:'—With Observations on her Ladyship's Views with regard to the Nature of Extension, as contained in her 'Essays on the Perception of an External Universe,'" in *Parriana: or Notices of the Rev. Samuel Parr, LL.D., Collected from Various Sources, Print and Manuscript, and in Part Written by E. H. Barker, Esq. of Thetford Norfolk*, vol. 1. London: Henry Colburn: 628–50.

Holbach, Paul-Henri Thiry, Baron d' (under the pseudonym M. Mirabaud), 1770. *Système de la nature*, 2 vols. London. [no publisher given]

Hume, David, 1777. *Essays and Treatises on Several Subjects*, 2 vols. London: Printed for T. Cadell; and Edinburgh, A. Donaldson, and W. Creech.

Hume, David, 1800. *Essays and Treatises on Several Subjects*, 2 vols., new edition. Edinburgh: Bell & Bradfute; London: Cadell & Davies. Printed for A. Millar in the Strand, and A. Kinkaid and A. Donaldson at Edinburgh.

Hume, David, 1817. *A Treatise of Human Nature*, 2 vols. London: Thomas and Joseph Allman. [first edition published in 1739–40]

Hume, David, 1987. *David Hume: Essays, Moral, Political, and Literary*. Edited by Eugene F. Miller. Indianapolis, IN: Liberty*Classics*.

Hume, David, 2000. *An Enquiry concerning Human Understanding*. Edited with introduction by Tom L. Beauchamp. Oxford: Clarendon Press.

Hume, David, 2007. *A Treatise of Human Nature*. Edited with introduction by David Fate Norton and Mary J. Norton. Oxford: Clarendon Press.

Landy, David, 2023. "Shepherd on Reason." *British Journal for the History of Philosophy*, vol. 32, no. 1: 79–99.

Lawrence, William, 1816. *An Introduction to Comparative Anatomy and Physiology*. London: J. Callow Medical Bookseller.

Lawrence, William, 1819. *Lectures on Physiology, Zoology, and the Natural History of Man*. London: J. Callow Medical Bookseller.

Leslie, John, 1804. *An Experimental Enquiry into the Nature and Propagation of Heat*. London: Printed for J. Mawman, no. 22 Poultry; sold also by Bell and Bradfute, Edinburgh. T. Gillet Printer, Salisbury Square.

Leslie, John, 1831. "Dissertation Fourth: Exhibiting a General View of the Progress of Mathematical and Physical Science, Chiefly During the Eighteenth Century," in *Encyclopedia Britannica, Seventh Edition*. Supplementary vol. 1. Edited by MacVey Napier. Edinburgh: Adam and Charles Black: 575–677.

Locke, John, 1975. *An Essay Concerning Human Understanding*. Edited with introduction by Peter H. Nidditch. Oxford: Clarendon Press. [first edition published in 1689]

Lyell, Charles, 1830–33. *Principles of Geology, Being an Attempt to Explain the Former Changes of the Earth's Surface, by Reference to Causes Now in Operation*, 3 vols. London: John Murray.

Lyon, G. F. 1824. *The Private Journal of Captain G. F. Lyon of H.M.S. Hecla, During the Recent Voyage of Discovery under Captain Parry*. London: John Murray.

Milne, James, 1819. *Enquiry Respecting the Relation of Cause and Effect; in which the Theories of Professors Brown, and Mr Hume, are Examined; with a Statement of Such Observations as are Calculated to Shew the Inconsistency of these Theories; and from which a New Theory is Deduced, More Consonant to Facts and Experience. Also a New Theory of the Earth, Deduced from Geological Observations*. Edinburgh: James Ballantyne. [published anonymously]

Newton, Isaac, 1730. *Opticks: or, a Treatise on the Reflections, Refractions, Inflections and Colours of Light*, fourth edition corrected. London: Printed for William Innys.

Reid, Thomas, 1764. *An Inquiry into the Human Mind on the Principles of Common Sense*. Edinburgh: Printed for A. Millar, London, and A. Kinkaid & J. Bell, Edinburgh; and Dublin: Printed for A. Ewing.

Reid, Thomas, 1997. *An Inquiry into the Human Mind on the Principles of Common Sense*. Edited by Derek R. Brookes. Edinburgh: Edinburgh University Press.

Somerville, Mary, 1831. *Mechanism of the Heavens*. London: John Murray.
Somerville, Mary, 1832. *A Preliminary Dissertation on the Mechanism of the Heavens*. Philadelphia: Carey & Lea.
Somerville, Mary, 1834. *On the Connexion of the Physical Sciences*. London: John Murray.
Stewart, Dugald, 1805. *A Short Statement of Some Important Facts, Relative to the Late Election of a Mathematical Professor in the University of Edinburgh; Accompanied with Original Papers, and Critical Remarks*. Edinburgh: Printed by Murray and Cochrane, and Sold by William Creech, and Arch. Constable & Co.
Thorne, R. G., 1886. *The History of Parliament: Commons 1790–1920*. London: Boydell and Brewer. [see also https://www.historyofparliamentonline.org/volume/1790-1820/member/shepherd-henry-john-1784-1855]
Watts, Isaac, 1809. *Logic: or, the Right Use of Reason, in the Inquiry After Truth, with a Variety of Rules to Guard Against Error, in the Affairs of Religion and Human Life, as Well as in the Sciences*. London: T. Purday and Son.
Wells, William Charles, M.D., 1818. *Two Essays: One upon Single Vision with Two Eyes; the Other on Dew*. London: Longman, Hurst, Rees, Orme, and Brown, and Hurst, Robinson, and Co.; and Edinburgh: Printed for Archibald Constable and Co. [incorporating the essay on single vision from Wells's 1792 *An Essay Upon Single Vision with Two Eyes: Together with Experiments and Observations on Several Other Subjects in Optics* (London: Printed for T. Cadell)]
Whewell, William, 1834. "On the Nature of the Truth of the Laws of Motion." *Transactions of the Cambridge Philosophical Society*, vol. 5, no. 2: 1–24. [also included as Essay 1 in an Appendix of "Philosophical Essays Previously Published" included in the 1847 second edition of Whewell 1840a]
Whewell, William, 1837. *History of the Inductive Sciences, from the Earliest to the Present Times*, 3 vols. London: J. W. Parker.
Whewell, William, 1838. *On the Foundations of Morals: Four Sermons Preached Before the University of Cambridge, November, 1837*. Cambridge: J. & J. J. Deighton; London: John W. Parker.
Whewell, William, 1840a. *Aphorisms concerning Ideas, Science, and the Language of Science*. London: Harrison and Co. [also included as a preliminary element in Whewell 1840b, vol. I]
Whewell, William, 1840b. *Philosophy of the Inductive Sciences, Founded upon their History*, 2 vols. London: J. W. Parker.
Whewell, William, 1842. "Discussion of the Question: Are Cause and Effect Successive or Simultaneous?" *Transactions of the Cambridge Philosophical Society*, vol. 7, part 3: 319–31. [also included as Essay 4 in an Appendix of "Philosophical Essays Previously Published" included in the 1847 second edition of Whewell 1840b]

Secondary Sources

Atherton, Margaret, ed., 1994. *Woman Philosophers of the Early Modern Period*. Indianapolis, IN: Hackett.
Atherton, Margaret, 1996. "Lady Mary Shepherd's Case Against George Berkeley." *British Journal for the History of Philosophy*, vol. 4, no. 2: 347–66.
Atherton, Margaret, 2005. "Reading Lady Mary Shepherd." *The Harvard Review of Philosophy*, vol. 13, no. 2: 73–85.

Bolton, Martha Brandt, 2011. "Causality and Causal Induction: The Necessitarian Theory of Lady Mary Shepherd," in *Causation and Modern Philosophy*. Edited by Keith Allen and Tom Stoneham. New York: Routledge: 242–61.

Boyle, Deborah, 2020. "A Mistaken Attribution to Lady Mary Shepherd." *Journal of Modern Philosophy*, vol. 2, no. 1: 1–4.

Boyle, Deborah, 2023. *Mary Shepherd: A Guide*. Oxford: Oxford University Press. [Oxford Guides to Philosophy]

Dubbey, J. M., 2011. *Mathematical Works of Charles Babbage*. Cambridge: Cambridge University Press.

Fantl, Jeremy, 2016. "Mary Shepherd on Causal Necessity," *Metaphysica*, vol. 17, no. 1: 87–108.

Guyer, Paul, 2015. "The Scottish Reception of Kant," in *Scottish Philosophy in the Nineteenth and Twentieth Centuries*. Edited by Gordon Graham. New York: Oxford University Press: 118–53.

LoLordo, Antonia, 2020. "Introduction," in Shepherd 2020: 1–24.

LoLordo, Antonia, 2022. *Mary Shepherd*. Cambridge: Cambridge University Press. [Cambridge Elements: Elements on Women in the History of Philosophy]

McRobert, Jennifer, 2000. "Introduction," in Shepherd 2000.

McRobert, Jennifer, 2002/2014. *Mary Shepherd and the Causal Relation*. Unpublished. https://philpapers.org/archive/MCRMSA. [revised in 2014]

McRobert, Jennifer, 2005. *Philosophical Research on Mary Shepherd (1999–2005)*. Unpublished. https://philarchive.org/archive/MCRMSA-2.

O'Neill, Eileen, 1997. "Disappearing Ink: Early Modern Women Philosophers and Their Fate in History," in *Philosophy in a Feminist Voice: Critiques and Reconstructions*. Edited by Janet A. Kourany. Princeton, NJ: Princeton University Press: 17–62.

Paoletti, Cristina, 2011. "Restoring Necessary Connections: Lady Mary Shepherd on Hume and the Early Nineteenth-Century Debate on Causality." *I Castelli di Yale*, vol. 11, no. 11: 47–59.

Index

For the benefit of digital users, indexed terms that span two pages (e.g., 52–53) may, on occasion, appear on only one of those pages.

Abernethy, John, 17–18, 19n20
abstraction, 32, 132–34
algebra, 130, 131–34, 135, 138, 139
association (mental), 37–39, 51, 58–60, 69–71, 77–78, 93, 103, 104n.20
atheism, 4–5, 7–9, 14–17, 26, 34–35, 144, 148
Atherton, Margaret, 2n.4

Babbage, Charles, 1–2, 3–4, 6, 8n.11, 29, 130–41
 calculating machine, 29, 138, 141
Bacon, Francis, 50n.18, 131–32
belief, instinctive or intuitive, 14–15, 17, 89, 91–92, 142n.3
Berkeley, George, 1–2, 24, 82n.16, 104–5, 110, 133, 148
Biot, Jean-Baptiste, 136
Blakey, Robert, 1–2, 3–4, 6, 26, 30, 148
body, human, 17, 52–55, 103–5, 107
Boyle, Deborah, 2
Boyle, Robert, 50n.18
brain, 18, 102–5, 109
Brandreth, Henry Rowland, 5–6, 139n.2, 146–47
Brandreth, Mary Elizabeth Shepherd, 1–2, 2–3n.7, 20–21, 29–30, 139
Brewster, David, 25–26, 124n.10
Brown, Thomas, 1–2, 2–3n.7, 5, 14–17, 18–21, 32, 34–35, 43, 56–57, 88, 95, 97, 98n.8, 99, 111
Browning, Elizabeth Barrett, 1n.1, 30
Butler, Joseph, 104–5

cause
 beginnings of existence must have a (Causal Principle), 9–11, 17, 22–23, 36–37, 43, 46–49, 64, 113
 definitions of, 7, 12, 14–15, 16, 19–20, 36, 39, 42, 43, 52–60, 88, 91, 95, 98–99, 112
 effect, correlative with, 44–45
 final, 24, 26, 71, 148. *See also* ends
 First, 5, 8–9, 14–16, 40, 81, 109. *See also* God
 idea of, 48, 50, 68, 69, 85–87, 92–94
 like, must have like effects (Causal Likeness Principle), 10–11, 12–14, 23, 43, 48–52, 55–57, 64–67, 76, 89–90, 96, 113
 proximate, 103, 105, 109, 110
 of vision, 120, 125, 126
 synchronous, 12, 21–22, 52–56, 71–72, 103
 whole, 12, 24, 100–2, 110
chemistry, 50–51
Clarke, Samuel, 47
Coleridge, Samuel Taylor, 1n.1, 11n.18
color ("colour"), 24, 25, 27–28, 118–19, 120–27
custom, 7, 8–17, 37–42, 43, 49, 50–52, 58–62, 65–71, 77, 78, 81, 85–87, 88–94, 112

Darwin, Erasmus, 14–15
Deity. *See* God

effects. *See* qualities and effects
elasticity, 144

ends, 26, 57–58, 71–72, 78, 81, 133. *See also* cause, final
eternity, 71–72, 109
existence, external, 22–24, 82n.16, *See also* objects, external
expectations, 10, 58–61, 73, 75, 77, 83–84, 88, 135
experiment, 50–52, 59–60, 76–77, 84, 89, 97, 102, 111–13, 120, 130, 132–33, 134, 142
experimentum crucis, 50, 70–71, 112–13
extension, 24, 27–28, 118–19

Fearn, John, 3, 27–29, 30, 118
figure
 tangible, 123
 visible, 27, 118, 124–25
Forster, Thomas, 30, 148

geology, 2–3n.7, 137, 145, 146
geometry, 133–34
God (Deity), 12–13, 14, 20, 24, 27–29, 37–39, 40, 57–58, 61–62, 65, 71–72, 81, 93, 104–5, 108, 113, 118, 144, 148

habit. *See* custom
Hartley, David, 104–5
heat, 4, 49, 71–72, 96–97, 119, 144
Holbach, Paul-Henri Thiry, Baron d', 140n.3
Humboldt, Alexander van, 136
Hume, David, 4–5, 6–17, 20–24, 33–42, 43–72, 73–87, 88–94, 97, 110, 111–12, 132, 148

imagination, 7–9, 23, 36–40, 42, 55–56, 58–59, 65–68, 85, 91–94, 104–5, 125
immortality, 17–18, 104–5
induction, 24, 30, 78, 130, 131–33, 134–35, 142
instinct, 6, 8, 23, 146. *See also* belief, instinctive
irritability, 19–20, 95, 98, 99–100, 106

Kant, Immanuel, 11, 29–30

Lawrence, William, 1–2, 6, 16, 17–21, 32, 35, 43, 95–112
laws. *See* nature, laws of

Leslie, John (Leslie Affair), 4–5, 7–8, 14–16, 19, 20–21, 26n.26, 34–35, 136
life, 17–18, 19–20, 71–72, 95, 99–100, 101–3, 105, 106–10, 111–12
Locke, John, 14, 47, 79–80, 84–85, 96n.6, 97n.7, 100n.11, 104–5, 148
LoLordo, Antonia, 2n.5, 11n.18
Lyell, Charles, 1–2, 137
Lyon, G. F., 136

Malthus, Robert, 1–2
materialism, 17–19, 35, 103–5
mathematics, 130, 131–33. *See also* algebra; geometry; numbers; reasoning, mathematical
matter, 20, 22–23, 72, 80, 91, 94, 96–97, 102–5, 108–9, 111–12, 144
Maule, William Henry, 30
McRobert, Jennifer, 2n.4, 2–3n.7, 140n.1
memory, 7, 24, 42, 49, 69–70, 73, 77, 78, 104–5
Mill, James, 1n.1, 1n.3
Milne, James, 2
mind (soul, spirit), 12, 17–20, 24, 28, 35, 72, 102–5, 110, 121–23
miracles, 12–13, 24, 64–65, 70–71, 141
morals, 144
motion, 28, 69–70, 102–5, 106, 107–9, 111–12, 118–19

names, 54–55, 60–61, 76–79, 96–100, 110, 111–12, 133
nature
 laws of, 9n.14, 21–22, 26–29, 71–72, 89, 109, 121–23, 137, 142, 146, 148
 meaning of term, 142
 regularity of, 14, 57–58, 61, 65, 79–84, 133
 uniformity of, 14–15, 38, 65, 78, 113, 137, 146
necessary connection ("necessary connexion"), 7, 8–9, 10–11, 19–20, 36–40, 42, 48–51, 56–58, 61–63, 65–71, 77, 81, 84–86, 92–93, 95–102, 112
 definition of, 12, 58
Newton, Isaac, 28–29, 50n.18, 122–23, 144, 148
nouns, 96–97, 100

nourishment (nutrition), 12, 21–22, 53, 73, 76, 81–82, 111
numbers, 73–74n.1, 135, 138

objects, 19–20, 51, 54–56, 96, 134
   external, 22–23, 88–89n.5, 118–119, 124. *See also* existence, external
   union (junction) of, 51–53, 55–56, 65–67, 71–72, 90, 96, 101–3, 107, 109, 110–11
O'Neill, Eileen, 2n.4
optics, 122–23
organization, (physiological), 17–18, 101, 105, 106–7, 111–12

Parr, Samuel, 27
particles, 73–74n.1, 80, 82, 130, 132, 144
physics, 130, 132–33, 135
physiology, 104–5
Playfair, John, 5
poles, magnetic, 136
power, 7, 14–15, 17, 19, 38, 49–52, 58–59, 61–62, 71–72, 83, 92–94
   definition of, 12, 58
powers, secret, 12–13, 14, 41–42, 56–58, 61–64, 73–75, 76–77, 79–87
Priestley, Joseph, 4
probability, 14, 54–55, 77–78, 80, 82–83, 86–87, 134–35
properties, 20, 44–45, 56–58, 74–75, 84, 96–97, 98–101, 103, 118, 119
   vital, 106, 107
   See also qualities

qualities, 11, 19–20, 47–48, 51–58. *See also* properties
   and effects, 51–56
   exhibition of, 12, 22–23, 46
   new, 12, 50, 51–53, 91, 96, 109, 110
   sensible, 14, 41–42, 52, 57–58, 61–64, 73, 79–87, 102, 118, 133

reason, 7–10, 13–15, 16–17, 38, 39–41, 43, 49–51, 57–58, 60–64, 65–70, 78, 85, 86n.21, 87, 89–92, 132

reasoning
   demonstrative, 10n.15, 14, 36–37, 38, 41, 57–58, 64, 73–74, 76, 77, 80, 82–83, 86, 92, 110, 132, 133, 135, 137
   inductive. *See* induction
   latent, 22–23, 84, 130, 133
   mathematical, 13, 64, 69–70, 73–74n.1, 90, 91n.10, 130, 131–32, 134, 135, 138
Reid, Thomas, 1–2, 7, 15, 24–25, 26, 28, 50n.18, 122–24, 142
religion, 104–5, 144
repulsion, 144
Ricardo, David, 1–2

sentiency, 95–96, 99–100, 101–3, 106, 108, 109, 111–12, 121, 126–27, 144
Shelley, Mary, 1n.1, 17–18
Shepherd, Henry John, 5–6, 130n.1, 140, 141
Shepherd, Samuel, 5–6, 8n.11, 141, 146
skepticism ("scepticism"), 7, 13, 23n.25, 34–35, 36, 39, 133
Smith, Sydney, 1–2, 30
solidity, 118, 119
Somerville, Mary, 1–2, 30, 142
soul. *See* mind
space, 11, 67, 118–19
species, 79, 109, 134
spirit. *See* mind
Stewart, Dugald, 1–2, 1n.3, 5, 15–16, 24, 25, 27, 28, 131, 142

Talfourd (Talford), Thomas Noon, 133
thought, 18, 102–5

vacuum, 144
vision, 78
   laws of, 121–23
   single and erect, 21–22, 24–26, 120–27, 146, 148
vital principle. *See* life

Watts, Isaac, 63n.33
Wells, William Charles, 25–26, 120–23
Whately, Richard, 1–2, 30
Whewell, William, 1–2, 1n.3, 3–4, 5–6, 21–22, 26, 29–30, 141n.3, 142–47

The manufacturer's authorised representative in the EU for product safety is Oxford University Press España S.A. of El Parque Empresarial San Fernando de Henares, Avenida de Castilla, 2 – 28830 Madrid (www.oup.es/en or product.safety@oup.com). OUP España S.A. also acts as importer into Spain of products made by the manufacturer.

Printed in the USA/Agawam, MA
February 21, 2025

883147.013